MATISSE

A. Liseuse sur fond noir (1939)

Paris, Musée d'Art Moderne

MATISSE

A Portrait of the Artist and the Man

by

RAYMOND ESCHOLIER

translated by

Geraldine and H. M. Colvile

with introduction and notes on the illustrations by

R. H. WILENSKI

FREDERICK A. PRAEGER, PUBLISHERS

New York

BOOKS THAT MATTER

Published in the United States of America
in 1960 by Frederick A. Praeger Inc.,
Publishers, 64 University Place,
New York 3, N.Y.

Library of Congress catalog card number 60–8715

Printed in Great Britain

To

MADAME HENRI MATISSE

in gratitude and respectful admiration

R. E.

I wish to be remembered

as a living man

HENRI MATISSE

CONTENTS

ILLUSTRATIONS

COLOUR PLATES

MONOCHROME PLATES

between pages 80 and 81

INTRODUCTION AND NOTES ON THE ILLUSTRATIONS

Henri Matisse, as intimately revealed by M. Escholier in this fascinating book, is seen to have been a typical French artist unaffectedly engrossed from first to last in aesthetic problems and deeply attached to the simple hedonisms of French bourgeois life. He produced some important mural compositions; but his main and best known output was genre painting in the form of easel pictures; and his unique achievement was the presentation of genre painting in new and compulsive decorative terms.

His easel pictures, exhibited decade after decade, were so variously arresting and intriguing by audacious design and pictorial counterpoint that we were apt to concentrate on the artist's virtuosity (the product of his brains, his aesthetic and his taste) and leave unnoticed what his paintings were about. But looking back now on his whole *œuvre* as an easel painter we find the places he worked in and the physical material with which he deliberately surrounded himself so essential a hinge of his art that we cannot think of his pictures without recalling a series of French rooms with particular furnishings and certain kinds of decorative bric-a-brac, and a series of young women (friends and models), so sharply individualized that the pictures can be dated by the order of their occurrence. The range of this material is restricted (much of it is no more than is set up every Monday morning in every art school in Europe and America); but it adds up to a small coherent local world in itself, a corner of France in the twentieth century; and the meaning of that little world, with the artist in the centre, permeates the various aesthetic systems he invented for its evocation.

It follows that some knowledge of his habitations is necessary for the understanding of his pictures which were always influenced by them; and I therefore provide here a short summary into which the paintings and drawings reproduced can be fitted.

He was born at Le Cateau (near Cambrai and S. Quentin) in 1869. He went to Paris in 1892 and had his own studio there on the Quai St. Michel from *c.* 1895 till *c.* 1908. He went to Corsica in 1898 and saw Near Eastern pottery in the Moslem Exhibition in Paris in 1903. He spent some time in the Midi (St. Tropez, Collioure, Cavalière) in 1904, 1905, 1906 and 1910, and visited

Algeria (Biskra) in 1906. He acquired a villa standing in a large garden at Issy-les-Moulineaux (near Clamart) in 1909. He saw the Moslem Exhibition in Munich in 1910, visited Spain that winter and Moscow in 1911 and worked in Morocco during the winters of 1911, 1912 and 1913. He sometimes used his old studio on the Quai St. Michel in 1914–1916. At the end of 1917 he went to Nice and worked in rooms at the Hôtel Beau-Rivage. From 1919 to 1922 he spent the summer months in a villa at Mont Alban and the winters in the Hôtel de la Mediterranée on the Promenade des Anglais; from there in these years he visited, and sometimes painted in, his villa at Issy; he also painted at Étretat; and he visited London (in connection with the Russian ballet *Le Chant du Rossignol* for which he had designed the scenery and costumes) in 1920. From 1923 he occupied two upper floors in the Place Charles-Félix overlooking the old Nice market, the beach and the sea. In 1930 he went to Tahiti and the U.S.A. and was commissioned to paint murals for the Barnes Foundation at Merion which he began in Nice the year after. In 1938 he installed himself in a new suite of rooms, with garden and two aviaries, in the Hôtel Régina at Cimiez above Nice. In the summer of 1939 he worked for a time at the Hôtel Lutétia in Paris. In 1943 he moved from the Régina-Cimiez to a villa called Le Rêve at Vence. He spent part of 1949 in Paris, and was re-installed at the Régina-Cimiez by December 31 of that year when he celebrated his 80th birthday. He made the model for the Vence *Chapelle-du-Rosaire* in his main workrooms at the Régina-Cimiez; and he died there on November 4, 1954.

The reproductions of pictures selected for this book are arranged in three groups. The first group (between pp. 80 and 81) shows examples of his early painting in Paris about 1900 (Pls. 1, 2 and 4; *cf.* p. 49), 'Fauve' works done at Collioure and in Paris between 1905 and 1910 (Colour Plate B, Pls. 5–9, Pls. 11 and 12; *cf.* pp. 66, 150, 145, 43 and 93), his decorative manner in 1907 (Colour Plate C), a 1909 version of *La danse* commissioned by Sergei Stchoukine for his Troubetskoi palace and painted at Issy (Pl. 10, *cf.* pp. 70, 79, 87, 89, 193), a Moroccan landscape (Pl. 14, *cf.* pp. 89 and 94), pictures painted at Issy in 1911 (Pl. 16), 1913 (Pl. 19, *cf.* pp. 93 and 148) and 1916 (Pl. 18); and a landscape painted near Issy in 1916 (Pl. 15). *Le peintre et son modèle* (Pl. 17, *cf.* pp. 93, 97, 146, 150) was produced during his reoccupation of his Quai St. Michel studio, in 1916. The *Tête de jeune femme* (Pl. 13), was painted from a model called Lorette (*cf.* p. 152). The nude called *Zulma* (Pl. 3), in gouache and crayon on cut paper (*cf.* p. 195), one of his last works, is inserted in this group as a contrast with Plate 2. In the same way *Les coloquintes* (Pl. 55), painted in 1916, is contrasted with a later still life in the third group of plates (between pp. 160 and 161).

Matisse's power to absorb and condition visual impressions is seen in many of these pictures: M. Escholier tells us, for example, that the movement of *La danse* (Pl. 10) was inspired by the Catalan Sardana—a round dance which can never indeed be forgotten by anyone who has seen it and heard the characteristic reed music that goes with it. His special quality as a portrait painter appears in the *Tête de jeune femme* (Pl. 13) where a subtly calculated asymmetry gives life to the curves of the hair in relation to the facial outline (*cf.* also the drawings reproduced on pp. 20 and 58). As a genre painter, concerned to create art from his immediate surroundings, his use of views actually seen from his windows is characteristic. Thus *Notre Dame* (Pl. 1) shows the view from a window of his studio on the Quai St. Michel, and another view from that apartment is in *Le peintre et son modèle* (Pl. 17). There exists a striking Fauve window piece done at Collioure (*cf.* pp. 60, 63, 64, 66) and another done in 1912 at Tangiers (*cf.* p. 94); the schematic *Fenêtre bleue* (Pl. 16) was painted in a bedroom of the Issy villa; and in *La leçon de piano* (Pl. 19) a green triangle seen through the window symbolizes the garden surrounding the Issy living rooms.

The second group of plates (between pp. 112 and 113) shows first a series of genre interiors painted in the Hôtel de la Mediterranée (Colour Plate D, Pls. 20, 22, 24, *cf.* pp. 98–102, and 167). The appointments of the rooms, typical of French hotels at the period—pink carpet, skirted dressing-table with oval mirror, lace curtains over French windows—are all recorded in these pictures. The portrait of the model Antoinette (Pl. 21) and the *Odalisque au divan rose* (Pl. 30) were also probably painted in these rooms. In 1919, when he went up to Issy, he took this model with him and painted her there en travesti in the fine composition called *La table noire* (Pl. 29). On his return to the Hôtel Mediterranée he portrayed her again in the well-known *Plumes blanches*—where she is adorned by a feathered hat of his own concoction (*cf.* pp. 152–4). On two visits to Étretat, in 1920 and 1921, he produced *Les deux raies* (Pl. 32), *Femmes au bord de la mer* (reproduced in the latest edition of my book *The Modern Movement in Art*) together with a number of still life pieces including, probably, *Les pêches* (Pl. 31); and the way he adapted his aesthetic to different environments can be seen by comparing the *Odalisque au divan rose* (Pl. 30) with the Étretat beach scene (Pl. 32) and the still life (Pl. 31). In his rooms on the Place Charles-Félix in Nice, the walls were hung with flowered papers, and here he constructed the movable screens covered with Moorish patterns made familiar to us by his odalisque and genre pictures of the middle 'twenties (Pls. 33, 34, 35, 38, Colour Plate E (p. 128) *cf.* p. 105). In these Place Charles-Félix pictures he displays superlative skill in mating discordant colours and suggesting recession without chiaroscuro or atmospheric perspective; and the decorative aspect of these works came to a climax in the famous *Figure décorative* (Pl. 38) of 1927. After this there was an evident reaction towards austerity which resulted in the Cézannesque *Le buffet* (Pl. 36) and, probably, the *Jeune Femme endormie* (Pl. 37) which I presume to be a portrait of his daughter Mme. Marguerite Duthuit.

The third group of plates (between pp. 160 and 161) shows pictures painted in the Place Charles-Félix apartments after his return from America—the *Nu rose* (Pl. 48) of 1935, the *Grande robe bleue* (Pl. 49) of 1937 and others of the same time (Pls. 50–53). The monumental simplifications evolved for the Merion murals (*cf.* pp. 113–15) distinguish the *Nu Rose* (also known as '*Grand nu couché—fond à carreaux*) for which he made a whole series of preliminary studies; and the *Grande robe bleue* an audacious colour scheme of lavender blue, lemon yellow, scarlet and black, is also conceived as two-dimensional mural decoration. Both these pictures were painted from Lydia Delectorskaya (*cf.* p. 155) who sat to him from 1935 onwards for numerous paintings and drawings (*e.g.* the drawings reproduced on pp. 137, 139, 144, 176 and 177); from 1937 onwards he also made many paintings from 'Elena' i.e. Princess Hélene Galitzin (*cf.* p. 153 and Pl. 53). The *Liseuse sur fond noir* (Colour Plate, Frontispiece) painted, with Princess Galitzin as model, in the Hôtel Lutétia in Paris in 1939 shows the rectangular severity often found in his Paris pictures (*e.g. Le peintre et son modèle* (Pl. 17)), and we must note here also that, for purposes of design, the back of the head is reflected in the mirror as a profile. At the Régina-Cimiez in 1938–43 and in the studio at Vence between 1943 and 1948 the fair-haired Lydia and the dark-haired Elena often posed to him together as in *Les deux amies* also known as *La robe jaune et la robe écossaise* (Colour Plate G, p. 172) produced in 1940 (*cf.* pp. 153, 154 and 169). The portrait known as *Le chapeau bleu* (Pl. 57 *cf.* p. 172)—a calligraphic masterpiece with pink flesh, lemon yellow chair, gold curtain and hassock, blue green fireplace, cornflower blue hat and diluted blue skirt—dates from 1944; *La robe blanche* (Colour Plate F, p. 160, *cf.* p. 172) from 1946; and in *Nature morte aux citrons et aux mimosas* (Pl. 56) he revived in 1944 an early attempt to make pictures with objects floating in sheer space (Pl. 55). Some of the equipment of his villa at Vence appears in the stupendous *Grand intérieur rouge* (Pl. 54) painted in 1948 when he was seventy nine; in the same year, with the *Intérieur au rideau égyptien* (Pl. 58) he epitomized the experience of a lifetime in a fearless challenge to Vermeer of Delft; and the story of his final achievement, the Chapelle du Rosaire at Vence is related in detail by M. Escholier (*cf.* pp. 196–213) and illustrated here on pp. 178 and 180.

Matisse made hundreds of drawings at all periods and more especially in the 'thirties and again in 1940 and 1941 (*cf.* pp. 119–33). Some were made for their own sake, others as studies for paintings and others (including etchings and lithographs) in connection with the books he illustrated (listed by M. Escholier on p. 128). Of the drawings reproduced I have already referred to some portraits (pp. 20, 58, 137, 139, 144, 176 and 177). The sketch with a fisherman (p. 54) was made at Collioure and shows Derain swimming in the distance (*cf.* p. 119); the letter with the drawing of the statue (p. 55) is referred to on pp. 160–2 and 190; the self portrait (p. 55) dates from 1900 and the nude with her knee raised from 1909. The nude on p. 53 is contemporary with the *Nu debout* (Pl. 2) of 1900. The nude with arms raised (p. 135) was a study for a figure in the large composition *Bonheur de vivre* of 1907 (referred to by M. Escholier on pp. 71 and 193 and reproduced in my *Modern French Painters*). The nudes on pp. 107, 108, 109, 120 and 136 show how outline drawings, so lifeless in the hands of the early 19th century neo-classic imitators of drawings on Greek vases, can be made a vehicle for sensibility. The lower drawing on p. 176 was etched for Matisse's illustrations to Mallarmé's poems in 1932, and the figures on p. 175 are also related to book illustrations. The landscape drawings on p. 134 were made in Tahiti (*cf.* pp. 110–12, 145, 185–6); and the landscape on p. 8, also drawn in Tahiti, served as basis for a Beauvais tapestry in 1935.

M. Escholier describes Matisse's use of cut-out coloured paper in the later years (*cf.* pp. 193–5); and these procedures are seen here in a page from the *Jazz* album (Colour Plate H, p. 192) of 1947 and in *Zulma* (Pl. 3) of 1950 already mentioned. The *Jazz* album is a series of twenty large near-abstract cut-paper compositions subtitled *Cowboy*, *Clown*, *Icarus*, *Lagoon* and so forth, reproduced by stencils; between each picture there are several pages of text in Matisse's handwriting reproduced in facsimile; this text, in lettering half-an-inch high, is an informal philosophic meditation on flowers and aeroplanes, life and happiness, and miscellaneous topics.

Matisse as a sculptor, discussed by M. Escholier in Chapter VI (pp. 138–42) is first seen here in the *Sculpture et vase persan* (Pl. 8) of 1908 and *Poissons rouges et sculpture* (Pl. 9) of 1909 where the sculptures are versions of a *Reclining nude* he modelled in 1907—related to the *Nu bleu* painting (Pl. 7) of that year; and the same theme reappears about 1929 in *Nu couché* (Pl. 47) to which the 1935 painting *Nu rose* (Pl. 48) is evidently related. *La serpentine* (Pl. 40, *cf.* p. 79) dates from 1909, the year when *La danse* (Pl. 10) was painted. The four bronze reliefs called *Nu: (vu de dos)* (Pls. 41–4) again result from long consideration of a theme, as the first in the series dates from 1909, the second and third from about 1914 and the final version from the period of austerity that produced *Le buffet* (Pl. 36) in 1929. The *Grosse tête* (Pl. 46), the most 'classical' of Matisse's sculptures, belongs to the same reaction from the uninhibited odalisque and genre paintings of the middle twenties, as it was modelled in 1927 soon after the painting of the *Figure décorative* (Pl. 38) where the nude is severely formalized.

R. H. WILENSKI

FOREWORD

No biographer wishing to express the spirit of a great man and his work should pass over the discoveries of others in that field, either before him or working at the same time.

The fairest way, it seems to me, is by quotation, so that each one can speak for himself and credit is given where it is due. This is the method I have followed before, in my works on Victor Hugo and Delacroix.

It is not surprising if the author most quoted in these pages—from numerous unpublished texts generously put at my disposal by himself and his friends, and from many others of Cartesian clarity published by this great humanist during his lifetime and shortly after his death—should be Henri Matisse himself.

Certain passages from Matisse—such as those on portrait painting—have not yet been recognized for their rich contribution to French prose, as well as to French art, comparable to the finest of Delacroix's *Journal.*

Encouraged by the great man who honoured me with his friendship, I wished to follow up the sketch I had made—far too rapidly for my taste—in 1937, with a portrait 'from the life', as it was called in the sixteenth century, in complete agreement with my model, whose letters and replies to my innumerable questions I have religiously preserved: a portrait of both the artist and the man, it being impossible to separate one from the other. (Such a quality of heroism ran through his whole life, he seems to have shared the motto of Delacroix, to whom he owes so much, 'Dimicandum'.)

I felt I had indeed succeeded, when a reporter from *Les Lettres Françaises* asked for precise details of the artist's evolution, and Henri Matisse replied,

'*All that is to be known about me is contained in M. Escholier's book. I revised it myself.*'

His answer applies even better to this deeply studied work, a long-cherished project which was held up by the bankruptcy of a publishing house. I was encouraged to persevere with it, however, in a note written by Henri Matisse on July 18th, 1948.

'*I much regret that present difficulties have prevented the publication of the second volume on my work. Perhaps someone else will take up the idea. I hope so.*
Henri Matisse'

His wish has been fulfilled by a discriminating and intelligent publisher.

E.M.L.

And while I am expressing my gratitude, I would say that I shall never forget my valuable interviews with Madame Henri Matisse and Madame Marguerite Matisse-Duthuit, with Albert Marquet, Paul Signac, Jean Puy, Charles Camoin; and finally with that remarkable man, Professor René Leriche.

There were, too, the letters I received from Matisse himself, his correspondence with Derain, unpublished, and a particularly important one given to me by Madame Derain; also his letters to Camoin, in which the secret messages of 1944 throw so much light on the tragedy Matisse went through at that time; interviews, as well, with the photographer, Marc Vaux friend of artists, and with many others.

My debt is as great to writers, living and dead, who have rendered full justice to Matisse, whom I have quoted: Marcel Sembat, Guillaume Apollinaire, André Gide, Louis Gillet, Maurice Denis, Gertrude Stein, Jules Romains, Madame Marguerite Matisse-Duthuit, Claude Roger-Marx, Pierre Courthion, Georges Besson, André Rouveyre, André Salmon, André Lhote, Francis Carco, René Huyghe, Jean Cassou, Georges Duthuit, Tériade, Aragon, André Lejard, André Verdet, Pierre Marois, Roger Fry, Gaston Diehl, Agnès Humbert, Daniel-Rops, who describes the *Chapelle du Rosaire* in Vence better than anyone (except Matisse); above all, Alfred H. Barr, whose great work, *Matisse, his art and his public* (New York, 1951) is the finest memorial we have so far to the fame of that '*prince de l'esprit*'.

And I must thank the friends who have helped me in often very difficult researches: Madame Hélène Marre, herself an artist of talent; Professor Leriche and Professor Wertheimer, who made it possible for me to see Sister Marie-Ange, one of the two Dominicans who fought for the life of Matisse; Madame Juliette Pierre Bompard, wife of a well-known painter, who, with her gentle tact, found the other nun in black and white, Sister Jacques-Marie, of whom Matisse often spoke to the man who saved his life, and so revealed that life's most significant secret.

R.E.

J'ai écrit à la + Rouge Suisse il y a déjà long-temps — aussitôt que j'ai appris la libération de la ville de Rennes — et j'ai envoyé à une dame de la + Rouge de Rennes qui écrivait de Paris par un mot bref disant que Marg. était à Rennes — j'ai envoyé un mandat — mais comme tout ceci avait lieu au milieu des combats, rien n'est certain sur la sûreté d'arrivée de mes messages.

J'espère que Paris tout est relativement calme et que toi et ta famille n'avez ~~pas~~ en a souffert en rien de ce grand événement : J'ai continué à travailler pendant toutes ces choses extraordinaires, au fond, que pouvais-je faire de mieux. J'ai fait l'illustration au ... bon copain Baudelaire

Je dépose ma lettre à la poste — elle partira par le prochain courrier. [illegible] j'ai simplement, pour le moment, contenté le désir de me retrouver un instant avec toi, vieux copain — Qu'est devenu le père [illegible], sur la Route du Beau Temps ? [illegible]

I

THE PURE ACT OF PAINTING

Le Cateau

The small town of Le Cateau, standing six miles from Cambrai, overlooking the river Selle, has many street-names derived from trade-guilds, and industries still flourish, but the chief source of revenue is sugar, from surrounding miles of beet, planted in rows in heavy clay soil and marine silt. The air smells of the sea.

In 1914, German machine-gunners, creeping stealthily over those fields, almost wiped out General French's 'contemptible little army', out-numbered as it was by twenty to one. But the British put up a defence in their finest military tradition. They fought on the banks of the Selle, and came to a final stand in the town itself, round the statue of Marshal Mortier, Duke of Trévise, who seemed by some touching irony to be in command of a last square of England's army.

Le Cateau was an Imperial town until Louis XIV, and RESIST has been the motto and pass-word of its citizens from the beginning. Burned to the ground, taken by assault, sacked five times, the ramparts crumbled, the old Nervian capital rises again from its ashes.

The character of Le Cateau, in spite of sad, rainy skies, seems to come from the violent blood of the Spaniards who ruled there for centuries. A strong, obstinate race has taken root on those marshes trampled by invaders, between the Flemish plain and the Ardennes, among the hills joining Picardy and Artois.

What really happened there between 1940 and 1945, concerned me very much, as refugees from Le Cateau were spreading the most sinister rumours, and I wrote to the Mayor. His reply makes it quite clear.

December 26th, 1950.

'Sir, this time Le Cateau has been miraculously spared the trials of 1914–18. Half-a-dozen houses were partly damaged by shells during the enemy advance in 1940.

'Except for an important factory which we fired ourselves during the Liberation, the rest of the town is intact.

'Skirmishes between our F.F.I. and the enemy on September 3rd 1944, before the Americans arrived, cost us a dozen young lives; but none of our ancient monuments and faithful witnesses of local history suffered.

'The old belfry, the splendid church of Saint-Martin, the former palace of Fénelon in its park of centuries-old limes—all are still standing and meticulously kept up.

'The ancient library, whose books were hidden during the occupation, still has its treasures, within medieval bindings, for those who seek them.

'Even the bronze statue of our fellow-citizen, Marshal Mortier, Duke of Trévise, which was looted in 1943, has been replaced on its pedestal with great pomp, on July 14th, 1945. (It was found intact in a foundry in Lille, a few days after the Liberation!)

'I thank you for the interest you show in our city, and in one of our compatriots, the great painter, Matisse, and I have the honour to remain, etc. . . .

(Signed) M. R. Haudebourg, Mayor.'

That Blue Eye

Henri Matisse was plainly the son of this warrior race. There is a suggestion of El Greco about his youthful portrait in Copenhagen Museum (1906), with its bearded face and tender gaze, oblique eyebrow, nose curving upward, alert ear set on a strong neck, hair growing low over an obstinate skull, and ardent features heavily outlined. The strange pathos of mobile planes betrays an endless, secret strife; the whole head is closely related in race and spirit to the witnesses of the *Burial of the Count d'Orgaz*, to the Apostles of *Pentecost* and the legionaries of *Saint Maurice*.

The life of Matisse, like his art, was one long resistance, based on will-power. He said as much to Francis Carco.

'*One must stand one's ground at all costs. If will-power fails, I give you the secret, use obstinacy. In great things and small, it nearly always works. For instance, I used to be always late. One evening I kept an appointment with Marquet . . . and I waited. I paced up and down for more than twenty minutes. No Marquet. When I saw him the next day, naturally, I went for him. "What!" he said, "I waited for you, too, but after fifteen minutes I gave up." You know Marquet? He is incapable of lying. That's why I said to myself, since you can always manage to be late, you can end by managing to be on time.*'

And when Carco asked if he succeeded, which any of his friends could have vouched for, Matisse replied:

'Did I? I exasperate everyone I know. I tried so hard to overcome a fault which is the privilege of pretty women, I have gone to the other extreme and arrive too early!'[1]

Vanderpyl, one of his worst detractors, remarked, 'Henri Matisse will always be remembered as a unique example of tenacity'.

'From where did Matisse get that blue eye?' asks Aragon. 'I like to think it is the Celtic eye, and that Matisse resembles his most distant ancestors, the Nervians who held the Cameracensien land against two kinds of invader: merchants and Germans. They were the best foot-soldiers of Gaul. Unconquerable people, even the Romans had to allow them the title of Freemen. Caesar speaks of their courage and spirit of independence. They passed for Barbarians; but a people who won't bow the knee is always barbarian to the invader. It all fits quite well; the name of *Fauve*, first invented by Matisse, expresses very well, in the eyes of the School, that Barbarism. Matisse is a good image of liberty. I mean French liberty, which is like no other.'[2]

The Swan of Cambrai

Henri-Emile-Benoît Matisse was born at Le Cateau, on December 31st, 1869, at eight o'clock in the evening, at the house of his maternal grandfather, Emile-Benoît-Elie Gérard, *rue du Chêne-Arnaud*, since renamed *rue de la République*.

His father, Emile-Hippolyte-Henri Matisse, after being a linen-broker for the *Cour Batave*, had taken up commerce in grain, with a druggist's shop adjoining.

His mother, Anna Héloïse Gérard, had a taste for the arts, and spent her leisure time decorating plates. (Later, Henri Matisse executed pottery designs for Vollard, as did also Rouault, Derain, Valtat and Laprade.) Before she was married, Héloïse Gérard made bonnets in Passy, like Madame Henri Matisse in the heroic days. In fact, ladies' hats were to play a very important part in the work of Matisse, with all the accessories of feminine fashion, flowers, ribbons, trifles and silks.

The Gérards were one of the oldest families in Le Cateau; a family of artisans in tannery and glove-making, going back to Philippe-Gérard Lemaire, quite possibly waiting on Fénelon, whose memory is preserved in the little artisan town. There may still be seen 'on the wall of the old fortified steeple of Fontaine-au-

[1] Francis Carco, 'L'Ami des Peintres', *N.R.F.*, 1953.

[2] *Henri Matisse, Dessins Thèmes et variations*, preceded by *Matisse-en-France* by Aragon, Martin Fabiani, ed., 1943.

Piré, a half-effaced tablet of the sixteenth century, to the name of the said Gérard family'.

That small town preserves many lovely vestiges of the past; its town-hall, with sixteenth-century out-buildings, and a delicate high belfry, where the first Henri Matisse Museum was opened in 1952, thanks to the architect Gaillard and M. Guillot; the church of Saint-Martin, once a Benedictine Abbey, with magnificent ornamental façade in Jesuit style; and the *Jardin de l'intelligence*, the old French park of the Archbishop-counts of Cambrésis.

It was in the church of Saint-Martin that little Henri was baptized. As soon as she could travel, Madame Matisse returned with the child to Bohain. And at Bohain her younger son Emile-Auguste was born, in July, 1872.

As for Henri, he did not leave Bohain until he was twelve, to attend the Lycée Henri-Martin in Saint-Quentin where, he said, he showed some ability in drawing! In fact, he was a good pupil, and became familiar with French and Latin authors.

Painting and the law

His classical studies completed, there seemed nothing to prevent Henri Matisse from carrying out his father's plans, and his father wanted him to be a solicitor. After taking his law degree in Paris early in October, 1887, he became a solicitor's clerk in Saint-Quentin.

Honoré Daumier also began as a bailiff's clerk. Law leads anywhere, if you can get out of it. And that was already the one idea of Matisse. Like many others, he owed his escape to illness—'a chronic appendicitis', Madame Matisse told me.

He was nearly twenty-one when he got his first notions of painting from Goupil, a relation of the famous art-editor. He learned about the smoothing of back-ground colour, how to lay on successive planes, and last the placing of light tones on the foreground. The young clerk had then but one ambition: to interpret what he saw, to represent, brush in hand, what awoke his sensibility, discovering in the process a satisfaction he had not suspected he could feel, for he had only been familiar until then with the sinister atmosphere of boarding school and the pettifogging study of the law, especially irritating to Henri Matisse, who all his life hated being involved in other people's affairs.

Here we must look at his first effort in painting with oils. One of them, a 'Water-mill', is signed with his anagram, Essitam; a river bank, very mediocre, showing no sign of genius.

However, in 1890 the young man who had long been drawn to the museums of Arras, Cambrai and Lille, painted an excellent still life: a pile of books on a mat almost hidden by a newspaper—*La République Française*—and to the left a candlestick with a guttering candle and an open book, drawn with a firmness and feeling rare at that age. This still life marks an advance on the preceding *Nature Morte*, a pile of books.[1]

About the same time Matisse, a born decorator, joyfully set to work with midnight blue and red ochre to paint the French-style ceiling of his uncle Emile Gérard's beautiful eighteenth-century house, where he was welcomed on holidays from Le Cateau.

From then on, painting was the only activity which helped him to find himself and grow. '*Then I was free, solitary, quiet,*' he confided one day to Maurice Raynal, '*whereas I had always been rather anxious and bored in the various things I was forced to do.*'

But if the young clerk began to paint, it was in secret. His mother made him a present of his first paint-box, but his father, excellent man that he was and a meticulous tradesman from whom Matisse no doubt inherited his taste for order and honourable dealing, set to work to discourage his artistic vocation. However, obstinacy was also inherited.

'*Don't waste time!*'

When Matisse senior had settled his eldest son in the office of M. Duconseil, solicitor in Saint-Quentin, the young man, far from being beaten, put his name down at *l'École Quentin Latour* where embroidery designers learned their trade, and where it was also possible to work from casts. The clerk went there from seven to eight in the morning, before the office opened, which was hard for him in winter. His professor, M. Croisé, was an ex-pupil of Bonnat. It is possible that a drawing of Ganymede dates from that time.

Paul-Louis Couturier, who had worked under Bouguereau's master, Picot, and become an artist of repute in Saint-Quentin, was able to soften the grain-merchant's heart. The idea that his son might work with the famous Bouguereau, who was snowed under with public and private orders, suddenly went to the honest man's head. And M. Duconseil, for all his amiability, made no attempt to retain his young clerk.

Not that the solicitor could have suspected how the departure of Henri Matisse would profit him. Many years later, the latter remembered he had been accustomed to fill page after page of the fine cream-laid paper required by the law, copying on it. . . . '*Les fables de La Fontaine. No one read those "engrossed*

[1] Thirty years later, those two still lifes painted in 1890 were exhibited at the gallery Bernheim-Jeune, entitled: 1. My First Picture; 2. My Second Picture.

conclusions", not even the judge, and their only importance was to fill up stamped paper in quantities proportionate to the length of the suit.'

Those were his first efforts at book illustration.

Assured of his father's consent, Henri prepared to set forth on the great adventure of an artist's life. Although he had faith in his star, the young man knew it would take all his strength to win. And he was quite determined to work, suffer and fight until he did. He said so in the message he read in November, 1952, at the opening of the Le Cateau museum. '*It was with the constant knowledge of my decision, although I knew I had found my true path, where I felt at home and not up against a stone wall as in my previous way of life, that I took fright, realizing that I could not turn back. So I charged, head down, into my work, with the principle I had all my life understood by the words "Don't waste time!" Like my parents, I wasted no time in my work, pushed on by I know not what, a force that I see today is quite alien to my normal life as a man.*'

Bouguereau and his Wasps' Nest

By dint of tenacity, Henri Matisse had finally gained permission to study art instead of law in Paris. At last, dazzled by the name of Bouguereau, to whom Louis Couturier had written a warm letter of introduction, Emile Matisse had given in and provided his son with money for the journey, for a subscription to the Atelier which prepared for the *Académie* Julian, and for life in the great city.

Matisse presented himself before Bouguereau early in October, 1891.[1]

From the beginning, Matisse was sickened by Bouguereau. When he arrived with his letters, the demi-god, before an admiring throng, was busily copying one of his own famous pictures, *The Wasps' Nest*.

Matisse, steeped in the lore of the schools of Chardin and Goya, saw the mechanical craftsmanship, the nymph draped like the Venus de Milo, beset by a crowd of cupids escaped from a sweet-shop, and understood that he had come straight to the High Priest of Academic Art. He wanted to turn and run.

The *Académie* Julian was not what it had been. The *massier*, Paul Sérusier, had left several months before, also Bonnard, Vuillard, K. X. Roussel, Piot and Maurice Denis. Disillusioned by the atmosphere of the place, Matisse fortunately decided, about October 10th, to attend evening classes at the *Ecole des Arts Décoratifs*. There he discovered a little man who became one of the best painters

[1] The date usually given is 1892, which agrees with the opinion of Mme. Georges Duthuit. But Matisse himself insisted it was the end of 1891. I am inclined to accept the word of Henri Matisse and of Alfred H. Barr.

of his time, Albert Marquet. A friendship sprang up between the two artists which was never broken.

This was a wise move, as it turned out. For when the entrance examination was held for the Beaux-Arts, Matisse was judged unworthy of the holy of holies, luckily for French painting. The rejected drawing is now well hung in the museum of Le Cateau, in condemnation of its judges.

What a waste of time those lessons were at Julian's! The painter of the 'Birth of Venus' would say to young Matisse: 'You rub your charcoal with your finger. That shows carelessness. Use a rag, a bit of *amadou.* Draw the casts on the wall of the atelier. Show your work to an old pupil, he will advise you. . . . You badly need to learn perspective. But you must find out first of all how to hold your pencil. You will never know how to draw.'

'*Each professor,*' said Matisse, '*corrected us for one month out of two.*' The following came from Gabriel Ferrier, in admiration of a charcoal copy from the cast, 'The Jardinier Louis XV'.

'You are a real artist, why don't you work from the living model, my friend?'

'*Cher Maître, I thought the casts were easier.*'

'You try painting figures from life. You will leave the others far behind.'

'*So I went back into the Life class, whence I had been banished by Bouguereau.*

'*After two days' work, Ferrier arrived for Tuesday's correction.*

'*Out of shyness at the Professor's approach, I had rubbed out the head, which I thought ugly, and was uncertainly fussing over the hand.*

'*Ferrier behind me, choking with indignation, said, "What, you're working on the hand and you haven't done the head! And it's bad, so bad, I dare not tell you how bad". And he passed on to the next student.*'

Gustave Moreau, what a charming master!

'*Lost in those chaotic surroundings, discouraged from the moment of my arrival at Julian's by the "perfection" of the painted figures fabricated there from Monday to Saturday, and so meaningless that their "perfection" made me dizzy, I dragged myself away to the Ecole des Beaux-Arts, to the covered court full of classical casts, where Gustave Moreau and two other professors, Bonnat and Gérôme, corrected candidates for entry to the ateliers. There, from Gustave Moreau, I got intelligent encouragement.*'

Matisse had at last found his master.

It may seem astonishing that the painter of *Hérodiades*, the tardy disciple of Mantegna, Leonardo and Sodoma, should have hatched such a brood of *Fauves* in his atelier as Matisse, Rouault, Marquet, Piot, Camoin, Charles Guérin and

Manguin, but Gustave Moreau had a far greater breadth of vision, independence and rare aesthetic quality than his two friends, Fromentin and Ricard.

'I doubt', wrote Jacques-Emile Blanche, 'whether M. Ingres ever had a like power of fascination over his pupils. It can be ascribed neither to power of speech, intelligence, theoretical conviction nor devotion to the technique of his art. One can only assume the secret lies in the atmosphere he creates: that which inspired Corot and the Impressionists, love of nature and simple feeling as conditions for a work of art, is replaced by aesthetic speculation from within.'

The art of Matisse was to keep the imprint of Moreau for a long time, despite a divergence of doctrine; the master tending to a kind of literary and symbolic idealism and the disciple to pure painting, priority of pictorial texture and eclecticism. Particularly he never forgot the precept of his master, 'In art, the simpler the means, the more apparent the sensibility.'

The relationship of Rouault to the painter of *Penelope's Suitors* is more obvious (Rouault had made stained glass before he was Moreau's pupil), but the decorative art of Matisse may be said also to owe some of its brilliance, richness and style to Gustave Moreau.

On the whole, Matisse had the happiest memories of Gustave Moreau's atelier. '*What a charming master he was! Enthusiastic in the extreme. One day he proclaimed his admiration of Raphael, another day of Veronese. One morning he arrived exclaiming that there was no greater master than Chardin. Moreau had a discerning eye for the greatest painters and made us see them, whereas Bouguereau invited us to admire Jules Romains.*'

Gustave Moreau once came into the atelier for a Saturday correction, exclaiming, 'I have just seen an acrobat by Lautrec in a newsagent's window. There's guts for you!'[1]

The master always showed great sympathy for his disciple. Matisse's father, feeling that his son was getting out of hand, unable to reach any conclusion as to his artistic vocation, decided to make the journey to Paris and ask Gustave Moreau for his real opinion.

'I am not in the least worried about him', replied Moreau. 'He is one of my best pupils.' So good a pupil, in fact, that he took over for his own use a certain outburst of his master's on the utter futility of the Beaux Arts' teaching.

Among the anecdotes which Simone Dubreuilh collected for *Actualité Intellectuelle* in 1942, Matisse describes Gustave Moreau giving way to his wrath in a cab, punctuating his indignation against most of his pupils with stabs of his

[1] From Henri Matisse to R.E.

umbrella. 'They are all half-witted, every one of them. Only one in sixty has any talent. Our best course is to discourage as many young men from painting as possible.'

If old Matisse in a better world could have heard him, he would have heartily agreed.

Matisse retained a bitter memory of his treatment by Bouguereau, Gabriel Ferrier and Gérôme. He is reported by Simone Dubreuilh as saying, '*If a young man has talent and character, nobody cares. Anything new he has to offer is repellent.*'

At the Louvre

Matisse was then a fervent disciple of the old masters as well. Between his twentieth and twenty-fifth years, strongly encouraged by Gustave Moreau, he haunted the Louvre and copied with almost as much fervour as the young Delacroix. Most of his copies still exist; *The Hunt*, by Annibale Carracci, which was bought by the State[1] and placed in the Town Hall of Grenoble; *The Dead Christ*, after Philippe de Champaigne, literally realistic, since it was an order; *Echo and Narcissus*, one of the most sensitive of Poussin's masterpieces; *Balthazar Castiglione* by Raphael, which he told me was a revelation to him in the art of portraiture; *The Tempest* by Ruysdael; *The Skate*[2] and *The Pyramid of Peaches*, free interpretation after Chardin, in which Matisse shows his preoccupation with planes and light, stressing the highest and most sonorous tones.

A still life by David de Heem, in which he interpreted the delicate values with rare fidelity, its cold, luminous greys and soft modulations, was the original inspiration for *La Desserte* of 1898 and that of 1908. Between those dates, the genius of Matisse developed with great freedom.

How many other masters have been studied by Matisse in the Louvre! Raphael, Ruysdael, the great Spaniards, and the Greek and Florentine sculptors. In those days, when the Louvre was accessible to all, anyone could enter without spending a *sou* and visit France's national Museum. The entrance fee, which a reactionary Municipality of Paris introduced into its museums in 1905, did not stop an unknown, needy little fellow—young Daumier, the bailiff's clerk—from contemplating the Louvre's treasures and sketching its antique statues. Like

[1] Henri Matisse commented on the acquisition of this copy by the State, paying tribute to the generous action of Roger-Marx: '*Roger-Marx was on the committee for purchasing copies, and he spoke for the students, mostly Moreau's pupils. Not one of our copies would have been bought otherwise, the committee preferring facsimile copies, often done by ignoramuses.*'

[2] *The Skate*, copied by Matisse in 1894, is in the Le Cateau Museum. Later, in Etretat, in 1921, he painted a masterly *Skate*.

Bonington and Delacroix, Daumier, Cézanne and Renoir, Matisse owed a great deal to his studies in the Louvre.

If all that flowering youth—Matisse, Rouault, Bussy, Baignères, Desvallières—haunted the Louvre, it was at the instigation of their master, Gustave Moreau.

The unpublished notes of my friend, Paul Baignères, one of the best painters in Paris at the opening of the century, give an interesting account of this. (A well-known canvas by Matisse shows Gustave Moreau, Paul Baignères and Georges Desvallières round a nude model.)

'At the very end of the year 1869, I first saw the light of day in Paris, hence little more light than my illustrious friend, Henri Matisse, who was born at the same time in Le Cateau. So he and I had first say in the Atelier Gustave Moreau, which in his case became the last word!

'Moreau taught us more in the Louvre than in his atelier. At the Louvre he was in full swing, so to speak. . . . Bussy made an astounding replica of Rembrandt's *Bathsheba.* Matisse found such values in Chardin's great still life, he was later able to replace them by colour. . . . In the summer months, I think the whole atelier spent its afternoons copying in the Louvre.

'To all these vanished great men, Moreau brought his high vision. He spoke for them with an eloquence and insight of which they themselves had been incapable. Many of them must have obeyed a kind of instinct and were not fully conscious of their own genius.'

We must not imagine that young Henri Matisse confined himself to the Museum and neglected life.

Far from it! During the whole of this Master's evolution, he confronted his spiritual and technical discoveries, his meditations and syntheses, with the spectacle of reality, an analysis of the model and the external world. He gave me a subtle definition of this, half a century later.

'*I spent my days in the Museum, and in my wanderings there, I rediscovered similar delights to those I had found in painting. I studied, you see, those masters who appealed to me, as a man of letters studies authors before choosing one or the other; without the least wish to learn tricks, but to cultivate the mind! I went from a Dutch master to Chardin, from an Italian to Poussin.*'

He was primarily seeking the exact relations between light and shade. What counted most to him, as it had for Corot, was the study of values. Bracquemond, in his remarkable little book on the art of drawing, gives the precise meaning of value. 'The word "value" specifies light, the intensity of brilliance, eliminating all idea of colour. It evokes the "value" of a colour, a shade, tone, tint, measured on the graded scale between white and black, extreme limits of light.'

And that explains why young Matisse went to learn first from the masters of camaïeu,[1] the painters of Holland, particularly Vermeer of Delft, whom Marcel Proust was only to discover in 1923, during the Dutch exhibition at the *Jeu de Paume*, but whom Moreau's pupil, twenty years earlier, was studying, brush in hand, from the *Lace Maker*. A small, dark lady I went to fetch every evening—my mother—was copying it at the same time.

Henri Matisse explained one day to Pierre Courthion that what he sought then '*was the gradations of tone in the silver scale, dear to the Dutch masters, the possibilities of making light sing in a muted harmony, by gradating the values as closely as possible*'. In time, Matisse carried this so far as to interpret in black and white Delacroix's brilliantly coloured '*Enlèvement de Rebecca*' for which he had come to share René Piot's enthusiasm.

Henri Matisse never forgot that he owed his deep knowledge of the Old Masters to Gustave Moreau, as is evident in the words quoted by Gaston Diehl, in May, 1932. '*In this way he saved us from the prevalent trend of the School, whose chief aim was the Salon. His attitude of guiding us to the Museum was almost revolutionary at that time, when official art, devoted to the worst pastiche, and "modern" art, attracted to out-door painting, seemed conspiring to keep us away.*'

Pearls and Precious Stones

That often cheap taste for the Orient which appeared in Moreau's work, his passion for gems, precious stones and enamels which re-appears in his pupils, Rouault, Desvallières, Piot, was bound to make a vivid impression on Henri Matisse, who loved gazing into glass cases of the Campana Museum and rooms devoted to Rhodes and Sassanide pottery.

Henri Focillon, the art historian, has rightly stressed those influences. His opinion is confirmed by Jean Puy, who had known Matisse to repeat their master's words with emotion, '*The sky seen through branches is like pearls and precious stones.*'

Derain appears

Most interesting memories of this period are André Derain's, who owed so much to Matisse and the Louvre. In *Comoedia*, Spring 1942, he explained in what spirit the future author of *Fauvism* followed Delacroix, Cézanne and Renoir in copying the masters; and he described our great national museum, in those days, when entrance was quite free.

[1] Translator's note: painting in one colour, imitating bas-relief.

'The Louvre was an obsession with me. Hardly a day passed without my going there. I had a delirious admiration for the primitives, which were to me at that time true, pure, absolute painting. . . . One day on coming into the Museum, I beheld—O, amazement!—someone working in the Primitive Room, copying "*The Battle*" of Uccello. Transposing rather, for the horses were emerald green, the banners black, the men pure vermilion, etc., etc. I drew nearer, devoured by curiosity. But what a surprise—the copier was none other than Linaret, my friend from Chaptal. . . . About the same time Matisse, before I knew him, was copying the *Christ* by Philippe de Champaigne.

'Shortly afterwards I met him at the Académie Camillo, rue de Rennes. He knew Linaret well, as they both attended the Atelier Gustave Moreau. It was the time when I undertook the copy of Ghirlandajo, which made a stir in the Museum. Visitors requested that I be forbidden to caricature the pictures. Most of them were shocked, some came to see how the copy was getting on, some were so interested they came to see the picture every day.'

The copy finished, Derain had to go to Commercy for his military service. He was back in Paris three years later and returned to the *Salle des Sept Cheminées*.

'One day in a newspaper', Derain relates, 'I saw the headline "Copyist dies at his Easel in the Louvre". I read what followed, "a copyist collapsed in front of a Primitive, seized with a heart-attack." I ran to find Matisse, for I felt it was Linaret. And it was indeed. He had died in front of *The Man with a Glass of Wine*. He had often said he would die painting, and so he did.

'We attended his funeral service at Saint-Paul and his burial in Montmartre Cemetery. *Fauvism* was then at its height. It was 1904. . . .'

There was also a picturesque glimpse—and I can vouch for its fidelity—of the Louvre as it was then, with its copiers and its indigent patrons.

'There were some strange copyists at the Louvre with Linaret, who put red and blue in all their pictures. One widow copied the Corots in all the colours of the rainbow, both light and shade. We made friends with the tramps, who stood about in the *Salon Carré*, their heads sunk between their shoulders, warming themselves between *The Marriage at Cana* and Raphael's *Archangel*, indifferent to the beauties of painting, for at that time, poor beggars could warm themselves in front of masterpieces, and no one was shocked.'

It seems clear that Matisse is only beholden to life, and to the Old Masters he chose for himself. And he knew, from his own experience, what influence the Louvre could have had on the master of the *Sainte-Victoire*.

'I can still hear old Pissarro before a still-life of Cézanne's, a Victorian cut-glass decanter, harmony in blue, at the Indépendants: "It is like an Ingres".'

'After the first feeling of surprise, I found, and continue to find, that he was right. Yet Cézanne spoke exclusively of Delacroix and Poussin.

'Certain painters of my generation were led to the Louvre by Gustave Moreau, before knowing the Impressionists. It was later they went to the rue Laffitte; and, even then, particularly to Durand-Ruel to see the famous View of Toledo *and* Ascent of Calvary *by El Greco, also some portraits by Goya, and Rembrandt's* David and Saul. *It is to be noted that Cézanne, like Gustave Moreau, spoke of the Masters of the Louvre. Cézanne spent his afternoons drawing in the Louvre at the time when he was painting Vollard's portrait. He would pass by the rue Laffitte in the evening, on his way home, and say to Vollard "I think tomorrow's sitting will be a good one, because I'm pleased with what I did this afternoon in the Louvre". Those visits to the Louvre increased the distance between himself and the morning's work, distance always necessary to an artist to be able to judge and master his work of the day before.'*

Go down into the street

But the young artist was in no danger of being stifled by museum and atelier. Gustave Moreau used to say 'Don't be satisfied with going to the Museum, go down into the street'. Excellent advice, which Henri Matisse carried out, with his fellow disciple, Albert Marquet.

How did the two great artists meet, before they found themselves together painting laurel wreaths for the *Grand Palais*? Albert Marquet told me the story in his lovely studio in the *rue Dauphine*, with its view of the *Pont Neuf*, *l'Île de la Cité* and the *Sacré Cœur:*

'The first time I saw Matisse was in the *Ecole des Arts Décoratifs*. I hadn't met him yet, when the *massier* one day announced the arrival of the "master", some professor whose name has been forgotten.

' "Hats off, gentlemen!"

' "*Oh, no!*" said a voice, "*Not in this draught. Not me!*" It was Matisse. After that, he was expelled from the school for a fortnight.

'Matisse was taking lessons in perspective there, preparing for a professorship in drawing. I believe he passed the tests quite successfully, but he decided "to do something else after all".'

One of his professors was the architect, Hector Guimard, one of the founders of Modern Style, who produced 'Castel Guimard' in the rue la Fontaine, and the Métro entrances of 1900.

'I used to meet Matisse again in the Louvre, while I was making my interpretation of the *Calvary* by Veronese.

'Matisse was engaged on admirable copies of *The Hunt* by Carracci and Chardin's *Skate*.

'We also used to meet among the classical statues of the *Ecole des Beaux Arts*, where we made many drawings from the Greeks.

'Matisse was already very interested in his elders, Van Gogh and Gauguin. We used to go and look at their pictures together, in the galleries of the rue Laffitte, especially at Vollard's.'

The lesson of the street. . . . Neither Marquet nor Matisse neglected that precious advice of Gustave Moreau's, and, after the master's death in 1898, when his place was taken by Cormon, painter of *Cain* and *Conquerors of Salamina*, Albert Marquet could not swallow the new teaching. One day as they were working from the model, he said to Camoin, 'Let's get out of here. It's more fun painting omnibuses!'

And it was Paris streets and scenes which taught Matisse and Marquet the art of simplifying their drawing, reducing it to essential lines.

Stationed under a gateway of the rue Richelieu, seizing upon the rhythmic line of a passing cyclist or carriage with its horse and coachman, they would tell each other, 'Delacroix said one should be able to draw a man while he falls from the fifth floor.'

Enter Mistinguett

They were regular attendants of the Petit Casino, which has since vanished from the Passage Jouffroy. Nothing is more synthetic than the artificial world which revolves behind the foot-lights. Daumier, Degas, Toulouse-Lautrec had been there before them, studying economy of expression from those arabesques, that strong, crude lighting. '*Times out of number, we sketched Paule Brébion, Gabrielle Lange and Mistinguett at the beginning of her career*,' Henri Matisse wrote me in February, 1937. '*Tidying up last summer, I destroyed more than two hundred of those efforts which seemed worthless to me.*'

In fact, things were not always easy for Matisse. Silence and concentration were already necessary to his work. There was nothing impromptu in his art, for which reflection, quiet work in the studio, or at least the silence of his room, were indispensable.

'*Each day I must return to yesterday's idea*,' he told Carco, '*even in the beginning I was like that, and I envied my companions who could work anywhere. Debray, the owner of the Moulin de la Galette, invited all the painters to come and work there. Van Dongen was prodigious. He used to run after the dancers and draw them at the same time. Naturally, I took advantage of the invitation too, but all I managed, was to learn the tune of the Farandole which everyone shouted with the band:*

"Et prions Dieu pour ceux qui n'en ont guère
Et prions Dieu pour ceux qui n'en ont pas!" '

He found himself whistling that same tune long afterwards, when he started his decoration *La Danse* for the Barnes Foundation at Merion, near Philadelphia.

'*I whistled it while I painted, I almost danced!*'

In the mornings Matisse and Marquet would meet outside the Atelier Gustave Moreau, and go landscape-painting in the Luxembourg Garden, far more deserted than it is now. There is a beautiful picture of the Luxembourg by Matisse. In the afternoons, they were by the Seine, with its misty skies, its quiet reflective waters, its quays and bridges spread with light. Marquet remained more faithfully attached to it than Matisse; but in those days he learned his daily lesson from the famous river, carefully and sometimes weightily analysing the quality of general tones, and trying to enhance rather heavy studies by the magic of light; and, as for Marquet, Notre Dame was then one of his favourite subjects. Until he died on July 14th, 1947, Marquet's friendship with Matisse was never broken. And Matisse paid tribute to the painter of the Seine and Algiers, an engraver of rare quality. '*When I see Hokusai . . . I think of our Marquet, and vice versa. I do not mean imitation of Hokusai, but similarity.*'

First encounter with the Orient

The admirable Exhibition of Moslem Art at the *Arts Décoratifs* Museum in 1903 awoke in Matisse not only a taste for pure tone, but also a feeling for the arabesque in colour. I should like to note in passing many mistaken references to a Moslem Exhibition of 1903 in Munich, whereas the whole world came to admire it in Paris, at the *Pavillon de Marsan.* There was one held in Munich in 1910, which Matisse visited with great interest. Then followed the discovery of Japanese prints, Hokusai and Utamaro, and with them a growing tendency to subtle simplification. Whether he realized it or not, this was a most significant, hidden side of his art.

Grisaille

Matisse was twenty-six when he first exhibited in a Salon of painting, at the *Société Nationale des Beaux-Arts* in the *Champ de Mars.* He showed two *Dessertes*, an *Intérieur d'Atelier* and a *Liseuse.* The following year, three still lifes and two *Intérieurs* in the same Salon, achieved a very flattering success for so young a man, for he was elected a member of the *Nationale*.

The die was cast. Matisse was to make an honourable career as an orthodox painter, under the wing of Carolus-Duran and Jacques-Emile Blanche . . . or so certain slanderers of Matisse would have us believe. But Roger-Marx shows more insight. 'In 1896, Henri Matisse exhibited at the *Nationale* with unusual brilliance. Without raising a finger, he was promoted to the rank of associate. . . . Fashionable success always meant less to Henri Matisse than the hard struggle to find his own truth.'

A young artist named Wéry lived on the same landing as Matisse, and practised a diluted impressionism. He was going to Brittany, and Matisse, whose colours were still rather heavy, decided to go with him.

Ever since the school of Pont-Aven, Gauguin, Van Gogh, Sérusier, Emile Bernard and Maurice Denis, that Celtic land invaded by the sea had held a strong fascination for the painters of Paris.

Wéry found only darkness and sinister shadows there, and foundered in the bitumen dear to the *bande Noire*, Cottet, Lucien Simon, etc., whereas Matisse arrived at simplification, as had Gauguin at Le Pouldu.

Wéry's drawing became infinitely more complicated, but his companion's broadened, suppressed detail and accident, and aimed at the eternal lines. In the same way, the palette of Matisse, even in the grey mists of Brittany, tended to pure colour.

'*I worked at Belle-Ile, on the wild coast, Monet's coast*,' Henri Matisse said to me about this time. And while I listened to him in his luminous rooms on the Boulevard Montparnasse strewn with light, gay colours, I had before my eyes the sea-scape full of movement, *Belle-Ile, Goulphar*, painted at that time. With its splendour of greys like Ruysdael's, in the spray of its surging waves, the silvery quality of stormy sky, cut into by reefs, there is a sort of glimmering serenity which foretells a master. The 'thing seen' is already, according to the wish of the great Florentine, 'Una cosa mentale', a thing of the spirit. It is the period when his friend Evenepoël called Matisse a 'delicate painter', master of grey tones.

Goulphar . . . Claude Monet. . . . One must remember in connection with that rich epoch, a description of Brittany by a fine Breton writer, Gustave Geffroy, friend and biographer of Claude Monet.

'Port-Coton, Port-Goulphar, Port-Domois; names attached to those capes, great blocks of stone cut into grottoes, piled up with fortifications. They are deserted coasts, jagged rocks, solitary pyramids rising under cliffs, striped with foam, shining with lichens and moss—caverns' mouths that open like mysterious crypts—yellow hillocks discoloured and devoured by autumnal vegetation, rounded and heavy as rudimentary beasts, with coarse hides—iron and rust-coloured promontories, high, square and massive as cathedrals, stretching far out to fall into the sea.'

At Belle-Ile, haunted still by his beloved Dutch painters, Matisse devoted his first efforts to intimate painting: *La Porte Ouverte* (Michael Stein coll.) and *la Servante Bretonne* (Henri Matisse coll.) in which glasses and bottles, plates and silver sparkle on a white cloth.

But one fine day, Wéry introduced his friend to a picturesque, generous character named John Russell, an Australian married to the Italian model who had posed for Rodin's *Porte d'Enfer*. He was a great friend of Monet's, whose Belle-Ile pictures he highly prized, and collected Guillaumin, Emile Bernard and Van Gogh. At that time, and particularly the following year, when Matisse came back to the 'Château de l'Anglais', Russell drew his attention to the discoveries of Claude Monet, and Impressionism.

In accordance with Duranty's theory, he set him to 'break down the solar light into its rays, its elements, and to find its unity again by the general harmony of iridescent colour'. A lesson not to be lost. Matisse brought back from Brittany 'a passion for the colours of the rainbow'.

'*Finally*,' Matisse told me, '*I worked in Finisterre at Beuzec-Cap-Sizens—separating from Wéry, for we could not agree. From Beuzec, near Pontcroix, I visited Pointe du Raz. I also spent twenty-four hours at Pont-Aven, the Bigoudens' country.*'

But Matisse seems not to have given a thought to the Symbolist group of Pont-Aven. When I questioned him about it, he replied, '*I never saw Gauguin. I instinctively avoided his already set theory, for I was a pupil of the Louvre, which made me conscious of the complexity of the problem I had to solve, in relation to myself, and I was afraid of doctrines like catch-words.*

'*I rather agreed with Rodin at that time, who said "Gauguin is an oddity".*

'*I changed my mind later, when my researches showed me where he got his theory. I have even been able to add to Gauguin's theory Seurat's on contrasts, the simultaneous reactions of colours and the relationship between their qualities of light. All of which is found full-strength in Delacroix, in Piero della Francesca, in a word all through European tradition, sometimes partially in the Orient.*'

In fact, Matisse was to realize fully Gauguin's researches into light, 'that elusive chimera of all modern Art' said Maurice Denis.

Cézanne's remarks on light, 'I have found the sun can't be reproduced, but can be represented', above all Gauguin's 'I have observed that interplay of light and shade fails to create a coloured equivalent of any light. . . . The rich harmony of effect disappears, is imprisoned in a uniform mould. What, then, is the equivalent? Pure colour . . .'—one day Matisse was to realize these observations fully and bring them to complete fruition.

Effectively, as Wéry's drawing became more and more involved, his companion's broadened, aiming at great, eternal curves, and his palette tended to the splendour of the rainbow.

After that the copyist of David de Heem and Ruysdael turned toward Impressionism. Which does not mean he ever became a real Impressionist. He had too strong a sense, innate or acquired in museums, of order and composition to consider the analysis of light except as a means. Impressionism could not be an end to Matisse, but to him, synthesis was of little value unless founded on analysis.

Hence the innumerable sketches which precede each one of his compositions. Hence his own saying that conception must have gone through '*a certain analytical phase. . . . When synthesis is immediate, it is premature, without density, and the impoverished expression comes to an insignificant conclusion, ephemeral and momentary*'.

The Sun of Signac

But Matisse did profit by the discoveries of Sisley, Pissarro, Claude Monet and Signac.

'There was a time', says his great friend, Marcel Sembat, 'when Matisse and Signac basked in the same sun. To be exact, he was never a real Impressionist. One couldn't be any more, since Cézanne. But I know the place in St Tropez where he worked near Signac's pines, and in the dining-room of Signac's adorable, welcoming house, *La Hune*, hangs the fine painting *Luxe, Calme, et Volupté*, which once delighted us in the *Salon des Indépendants*. That dazzling canvas marks the period when Matisse, serious and concentrated, was trying to find himself in the sunny ways of the *pointilliste* school.'[1]

René Huyghe was no more taken in than Marcel Sembat by Matisse's Impressionism or neo-impressionism.

'In 1896 he exhibited seven canvases at the Champ de Mars.[2] And

[1] Marcel Sembat, 'Henri Matisse', *N.R.F.* 1920.

[2] In fact, 4 in 1896 and 5 in 1897, as is proved by the National Society catalogues. Henri Matisse gave me some interesting details on this subject in 1947. Unfortunately, Roger-Marx who saved the honour of French painting in 1900 in spite of the *Institut*, was unaware of this

he painted the *Desserte* of the Freudenberg collection. He was still in a *fin de siècle* state of mind, that is, realistic. Colour found its place as an element for translating reality. It suggested those two aspects of reality which a picture cannot reproduce, light and the third dimension; pure brilliant colour to express light, thinner in the shadow to denote distance, on a chair at the back of the picture. This makes one think of Monet's *Galettes* of 1882, even more of his *Déjeuner* of '73, a realistic Monet, painter of interiors.

'In the "provisional uncertainty" of youth, obliged to imitate where there are gaps in understanding, he adopted Impressionism. He adopted even its aims as well as technique, at one time; as is shown by a screen of trees whose light foliage and shadows are reflected in the water rippling at their feet—work painted in 1898.

'Between young painters like Matisse and Impressionism, or rather *pointillisme*, there was rather coincidence than agreement; what attracted them in that technique of pure tones was the intensity of colour, whereas the *pointillistes* only used it as a trick to copy the most elusive realistic element: light.

'The *quid pro quo* held for the space of a honeymoon, then incompatibility of temperament arose. . . . "*Pure tone is to the pointillistes their most subtle weapon in an 'art of imitation'*." ' Matisse and the young *Fauves* felt it was time to demand a more direct enjoyment in painting, to make a pure translation of the magic of colour and line, and the joy of handling them; they replaced the aim of '*vérisme*' by plasticity and expression.[1]

Certainly his contact with Brittany (1896–97) had encouraged Matisse to find a stronger, more synthetic art, no longer purely dictated by the climate and quality of light. He found the freedom of pure colour. The offensive against Impressionism had been gathering for some years in Brittany, at Pont-Aven, Le Pouldu, Châteauneuf-du-Faou, under the impetus of Gauguin, Sérusier, Maurice Denis and Emile Bernard, founders of the Symbolist School.

scandalous story, another one against the '*pompiers*' of the *Beaux Arts Académie*. '*In '96, I presented seven canvases to the jury, who accepted them all and asked me to go and choose four, as hanging space was limited. It was the first year I exhibited, but I was elected associate, after a debate about me, between Jean Bérand against, and Puvis de Chavannes in my defence. Among the four pictures I chose was the* Liseuse, *bought by the State and then chosen by Mme Félix Faure for her bedroom at Rambouillet. It was from there I had to fetch it, with permission, to exhibit it in the* Exposition Universelle *of 1900. Let me tell you that the picture came before a jury which refused it! I applied to the Beaux Arts to return it. They told me to put it back where I got it from. I took it back and hung it on its hook at Rambouillet, with the help of a servant.*' Unpublished note by Henry Matisse. One must add that Mme Félix Faure seems to have been better qualified to direct the Beaux-Arts than Henri Roujon or his sad assistant, Léonce Bénédite. The *Liseuse* by the way, is still at Rambouillet.

[1] René Huyghe. 'Matisse et la Couleur', *Formes*, 1 January, 1930.

At the other end of France, a solitary painter at Aix-en-Provence, before the eternal *motif* of the Sainte-Victoire, was laying the foundations of a new art. Local tone, suppressed by Claude Monet, was being restored to a place of honour by Cézanne, who devoted his life to studying its modulations, creating what André Lhote calls 'pictorial depth'.

The time was drawing near when Matisse, like all who count in his generation, would turn to the master of Aix-en-Provence. '*Yet Matisse*' as he wrote me himself, '*never saw, or tried to see, Cézanne, believing the whole of an artist to be in his work.*'

In the meantime, the influence of Impressionism, while it made his palette freer, was a necessary source of excitement for his mind.

In Corsica

When Matisse discovered the Mediterranean in 1898, and travelled in Corsica, he was following the example of Renoir, who always, by the way, respected local tone.

'*It was in Ajaccio*' Henri Matisse confessed to me with lingering emotion, '*that the unknown wonders of the South first appeared to me.*'

And he spent a long time showing me several canvases of that period:

My room in Ajaccio, whose rich texture could be mistaken for an example of Impressionism.

The Garden Courtyard in Ajaccio, with its light, vibrant blue sky and, on the right, a stone staircase mounting to a pink house, an outside staircase not very impressionist in its solidity.

As for the *Mill Garden*, it comes nearer Renoir. Yet, in spite of its magical splendour of colour, the enamel-like brilliance of its greens, chromes, whites, crimsons, there is no divisionism of colour, no *pointillisme*. The same is true of the *Small Olive-trees*, of tender blue, orange, green and yellow.

And now we come to another master, Turner, who was discovered by Matisse that same year, 1898, at the National Gallery in London.

Honeymoon in Turner's country

A few months earlier, on January 8th, 1898, the young artist married a beautiful, tall Southern girl, Amélie-Noëlie-Alexandrine Parayre, from Toulouse and the splendid Roussillon country. Madame Henri Matisse tells me their marriage took place at the church of Saint-Honoré d'Eylau. Their honeymoon was spent in London, the land of Turner, whom the Impressionists claimed as their forerunner. Matisse was never to forget that journey, and

B. Portrait de Derain (1905)

London, Tate Gallery

happened to speak feelingly of it to my friend, Pierre Jeannerat, art critic of the *Daily Mail*: 'Matisse told me, at one of his London exhibitions, that he loved our city because he had first come here on his honeymoon.'

Turner, magician of light, was perhaps the first of the sun-worshippers. But Maurice Denis thought of Monet and Pissarro when he said, 'Turner, that brilliant romantic, was undoubtedly a forerunner, but not even he planted his easel at midday to catch a direct effect of naked sun.'

Henri Matisse does not seem to have shared this point of view entirely and his analysis is much more subtle. He told me himself that he made the journey to London in 1898 '*especially to see the Turners. I felt that Turner must be the transition between traditional painting and Impressionism. And, I did indeed find a close relationship due to form created by means of colour between Turner's water-colours and Claude Monet's work.*'

From El Greco to Cézanne, from Turner to Gustave Moreau, from Renoir and Claude Monet to Odilon Redon and Seurat and Signac: impossible to count the number of artists who influenced young Henri Matisse, who said himself:

'*I have never avoided the influence of others . . . I should have thought it a form of cowardice and a lack of sincerity towards myself. I believe the artist's personality owes its development and its strength to the struggles it undergoes . . . if he is overpowered, he deserves no better fate. . . .*'

'A copyist? Never! Impossible!' Marcel Sembat said of him. 'But he was deeply affected by the masters, and their discoveries illumined his own work.'

The die was cast. Like all painters from the North, Henri Matisse was drawn to the Latin sun, the Mediterranean and the East, which were to attract him all his life.

From the gulf of Ajaccio to the bay of Saint-Tropez, from Toulouse and Collioure to Tangiers and Nice, where he was finally to settle, Henri Matisse found his own climate, the calm which he considered all artists should strive to attain.

'*I want*' he said '*a balanced and pure art, neither disturbing nor distressing; I want people who are weary and over-wrought to find peace and rest in my painting.*'

Trois Baigneuses: blue harmony

Henri Matisse had returned to Paris after three months in Ajaccio. Contact with the Mediterranean had brought clarity and order to his vision; but when he returned to the Louvre, he felt the need to work in an atelier again, from life. For economy's sake, Matisse thought of the old Atelier Moreau, led thither by his memories. But Gustave Moreau was no more. Cormon had succeeded, without being able to replace him.

'*There*' said Matisse, '*I found the spirit of the pupils much changed. My stories of the old master were ill-received. The students said, "now we are taught our job and how to get on in life." I understood what that meant from the one and only correction by Cormon at which I was present.*

'*When my turn came, after a glance at my work and my face, he passed on.*

'*During the model's rest, when pupils ordinarily show the professor any work they have done outside, I placed on the master's easel a canvas showing a sunset seen from my window on the Quai Saint-Michel, with the Louvre as a background. Cormon looked at it and said nothing. Then he called the* massier, *and conferred with him in undertones.*

'*After the professor's departure, the* massier *came to me. "I sincerely regret having to tell you, that the director asked me your age. I told him 'Thirty'. 'Is he serious?' he asked me. 'Yes, master.' I answered. 'Then he must go.'* "

'*So I had to find somewhere else. At first I thought of returning to Julian's, without taking the corrections; but I soon had to leave; the students made fun of my work. I learned by chance that there was an atelier, I think in the courtyard of the* Vieux Colombier, rue de Rennes, *kept by a Spanish model, where Carrière gave a correction a week. Actually Carrière came only when the Spaniard was in funds. I went there, and met Jean Puy, Laprade, Biette, Derain, Chabaud: there was not a single pupil of Moreau's.*

'*At last it was possible to work in peace, for the professor corrected only his "pet" pupils, tame ones of long standing, and reserved his judgement on the more personal work of the rest. Indeed, Carrière never said a word to me. I didn't know what to think, but some years later he told me, he wished to respect my ideas, which interested him.*

'*Unfortunately, that atelier closed for lack of pupils. So we pooled together and hired a model, working at Biette's, rue Dutot.*

'*All that only lasted a year, after I left Cormon.*'

The friendships which were to create Fauvism were being formed at that time. Othon Friesz and Raoul Dufy, both from le Havre, had joined the Atelier Bonnat, and quickly learned from Matisse that 'imagination also affects colour'. Out in their own Paris suburb of Chatou, the powerful Derain of Carrière's atelier formed a firm friendship with the champion cyclist, Vlaminck. And they all had a part to play in the struggle.

What did the Fauves want? René Huyghe defines it well: 'The Fauves wanted to be concise, particularly to achieve intensity; a partnership or association can only be based on a system of mutual concession. So the Fauves were content to create a 'good-neighbours' relationship and balance between composing elements, while allowing them full individuality.

'The same applied to colour; for a time, under the influence of Gauguin, they experimented with flat tone, as they had strayed into arabesques.' Finally, for dominant harmony, Matisse and his followers substituted symphony, 'orchestrations of colour,' as Othon Friesz said of the Fauves.

'The juxtaposition of such vivid tones created those "screaming mosaics" which were to rouse the mob. They were immature, wild symphonies which were to be attenuated by the Fauves as they mellowed with age. They reverted to the principle of discontinuity, elision—that is, the white of the canvas creating indispensable transitions.

'Matisse was creating a new art, far removed from Vlaminck's violence. Charming, collected and learned, he attempted all experiments in his field. His desire for intensity already led the painter to take liberties, to isolate and exaggerate an essential element at the expense of its surroundings. The unity of the object was sacrificed to essential characteristics. Maurice Denis prophesied: "It is painting divorced from its surroundings, painting for its own sake, the pure act of painting . . . all the qualities of representation and sensitivity are excluded from such a work of art. It is, properly speaking, a quest for the absolute." '

Combining flat colours and arabesques, Matisse was in search of the absolute. Since Cézanne's *Trois Baigneuses* had reigned over his studio on the Quai Saint-Michel, the blue harmony of the masterpiece had exercised a magic power over his development. Blue, obsession of over-sensitive eyes, was to haunt him forever after. This can be seen in his *Harmony in Blue* (Museum of Western Art, Moscow) exhibited in the *Salon d'Automne* of 1908; in his *Still life with a Blue Camaïeu* (Merion, Barnes Foundation) painted during the preceding year; above all in *Blue Nude, a memory from Biskra* (Baltimore Art Museum) which, according to a letter from Hans Purrmann to Alfred H. Barr, was the result of a friendly competition in 1907, surely at Collioure, between Derain and the older painter. Which of them could best paint a figure in blue? As soon as Derain saw the *Blue Nude* of Matisse, he admitted defeat and destroyed his own picture. After having caused a scandal at the *Salon des Indépendants* in 1907, it was bought by Leo Stein, and was burned in effigy during the winter of 1913, when it was shown in New York.

Those were the days when Matisse used to declare in his rather solemn voice, '*Cézanne is the master of us all.*'

Laurels of Matisse and Marquet

1900 was drawing near. Paris had become one great building yard. The streets were seething with unrest.

Déroulède had just missed his *coup d'état*. The President of the Republic's face had been slapped at Longchamp, and Marianne insulted.

Women had never seemed prettier. They had towering masses of hair, generous behinds and bosoms (not always genuine) and no stomachs; these were unthinkable. They had Boldini hats like wide, flat flower-beds; '*robes Princesses*', rich, flowing curves, and a thousand bell-shaped skirts, a thousand saucy 'boaters'.

At the Moulin Rouge the quadrille was in full swing. Jane Avril-la Mélinite's leg twirled in a froth of petticoats, and Willette made his *mot* about all the best hams being frilled as he wandered around the city.

The roadmenders went on strike. There was a *cuirassier* charge on the *Place du Théâtre-Français*, where lovely young Henriot had been burned in her box. A hundred thousand workers downed tools. And was the strike financed by Gamelle or Guillaume?[1]

With all those tools laid down, the Exhibition could never take place. Yet the work began again. The *métro*-yards re-opened. The Pont Alexandre began to span the Seine. An international town was growing up beside the river; with the Great Wheel, so much like the penny-farthings on which pioneers of high-altitude cures climbed with such trepidation, round about the time when the Eiffel Tower was a-building. The 'moving pavement' was made, a construction doomed to many mishaps and whose failure almost brought into discredit the new technique of reinforced concrete. What matter, though, since it inspired Courteline's little masterpiece, *Article 330*?

On the ruins of the Palace of Industry, two other Palaces faced one another: the *Grand Palais* and the *Petit Palais*. Mirbeau made them a target for his jibes, but the Sunday crowd gaped in admiration.

Inside the *Grand Palais*, under the enormous glass roof just completed, a whole hive of workmen were busy: numberless confectioners for those plaster pillars, numberless decorators for that orgy of festoons and astragals.

On the slopes of the Buttes-Chaumont, in Jambon's theatrical workshops, teams of daubers were kept busy, their brushes achieving miles of laurel-leaves intended to adorn the Exhibition rooms. Squatting like stone-splitters by the roadside, two painters were working without enthusiasm; they remained silent, while the others, according to tradition, shouted fashionable ditties, '*Les amours*

[1] Translator's note: Nickname of French pretender accused, as was also Emperor William, of fomenting those strikes. Cruel enigma for a perplexed government.

sont fragiles' or '*Sobre las Olas*'. This endless unfurling of laurel wreaths was not doing much for their reputations. The small, short-legged one looked like *Monsieur Badin*, in his white linen overall. His bearded, dishevelled friend seemed tougher. He might have been a champion cyclist, in his tricolour vest. The little man consulted his watch. 'Courage, old boy,' he said mockingly, 'only seventeen quarters of an hour to go. Nine hours a day at a franc an hour. What more could we ask?'

Albert Marquet had been responsible for this. It had been his idea to look for a job, so that he and Matisse could earn their bread and butter; he had looked up the addresses of the best scene-painters; and he had taken the plunge of signing on with Jambon for them both.

The tall one turned and said sharply, '*Shut up, Albert, or I'll murder you.*'

At night, Albert Marquet and Henri Matisse, whose grave dignity had earned him the title of 'Doctor' among his friends, left the atelier quite exhausted. They found this mass-production very tiring, working with heads down and backs bent. They went home unsteadily.

'*What a life!*' Matisse exclaimed to Francis Carco in 1941, '*I have never been so completely done-in. The clever ones got themselves sacked after a fortnight, when they could draw compensation money. There were waiters, errand boys, a whole gang of toughs on whom the boss kept a watchful eye. Unfortunately, he couldn't stand me. One day when I was taking a breather, he called out, "Hey, Doctor, I see you're enjoying yourself!" I was so disgusted I answered, "A fat chance of enjoyment here!" My word, that put the lid on it. I was paid off on the spot. I had to look for a job elsewhere.*'

Albert Marquet was living in the rue Monge, awaiting a move to the quai de la Tournelle. Henri Matisse was at 19 Quai Saint Michel.[1]

A beautiful young woman was waiting at home for Matisse, and a pretty child. While their modest supper was being prepared, the young artist would lean on the window-sill smoking his pipe, letting his thoughts wander from Notre Dame to the Sainte Chapelle.

Another pipe-smoker had enjoyed the same hour, half a century earlier, on a neighbouring isle, on the Quai d'Anjou; the same repose after a long day's drudgery, the same reflections in the peaceful river. The great Daumier had also dreamed only of painting.

The Seine, dear to Julian and Napoleon, is more than a triumphal way, and more than a refuge of despair. It was a rich source of dreams, to Victor Hugo in

[1] Marquet gave me these details in 1936; the old Parcheminerie quarter where his Flemish ancestors had illuminated manuscripts and founded the École de Paris, under Charles V.

Soleils Couchants, to Baudelaire in *L'Invitation au Voyage*, and to Apollinaire: an inspiration to our best artists, from Corot to Daumier, from Claude Monet to Henri Matisse.

The frugal meal over, the painter felt his strength return. A clock struck. Matisse grabbed his hat and ran downstairs.

Below, in the Ecole communale of the *rue Etienne*, dominated by the Tour de Jean sans Peur, the City of Paris had instituted evening classes, among them a course in modelling. And there was no more industrious student than this thirty-year-old apprentice. Clay, taking shape under finger and thumb, can be a passionate joy. It was a heroic effort to rediscover the creative inspiration of Barye's wonderful group, *the Jaguar devouring a Hare*, which Matisse chose for himself, and on which he worked for two years of evening classes, '*identifying oneself with the passion of the beast* (fauve) *expressed in the rhythm of the volumes*'.[1]

That is how Jambon's *rapin* relaxed with *fauves* and genius, after a hard day's work.

Trois Baigneuses: Madame Matisse's revelations

As soon as the sun rose the next morning, behind the towers of Notre Dame, Matisse was up, moving on tip-toe so as not to wake his young wife and little Marguerite. In the clear light of the studio, he stood still in front of his secret treasures. Those were his ikons, bought from Ambroise Vollard a few months before for the round sum of fifteen hundred francs; a plaster bust of Rochefort, the only one in existence, given to Manet by Rodin; and particularly that superb painting, one of Cézanne's purest masterpieces, *Les Trois Baigneuses.*

There they were, the three bathers; the one on the right turning her back, shadowed blue and green, a dark Provençale seated firmly in the lush grass, twisting her long black hair in her left hand; another facing out, water well above her knees, her body vigorously modelled by the light; one on the left also standing back-view, a big russet woman with hair the colour of dead leaves, holding her wrap, leaning toward the bather who is making for the shady bank.

What sacrifices they had cost, those *Baigneuses*, bought when Cézanne was considered a dauber and a failure! What secret struggles they had witnessed when his friends said to Matisse, 'You're mad, old man. Return them to Vollard, and you'll be lucky if he gives the money back on your Rodin and your Cézanne.'

But proud, determined, a little scornful, he only replied,

'*If I'm not mistaken, I have chosen well.*'

[1] The master's own words. The *fauve* in Matisse is evident from 1900, as he himself underlined in the autobiographical notes he so kindly made for me, the essential basis of this work.

Little by little, as his resources dwindled and Cézanne's prices rose, it took a lion's courage to hold on to the magnificent canvas. '*No.*' Henri Matisse replied to me proudly, '*Because I loved that picture passionately.*' I told him then about the precious *Souvenirs* of Fernande Olivier, the same *belle Fernande* who considered Matisse '*le type du maître*'. He had never read those lines which tallied so well with his own feelings: 'I shall only mention Matisse, who held on tenaciously to a unique Cézanne in the days of direst poverty, encouraged by his wife, and so gave his three children the taste and love of art.' Matisse was very moved at this recollection.

However the day of defeat came. The public failed to understand, hatred and scorn greeted this new painting; the needs of his family were increasing. He entrusted his *Baigneuses* to one of his most reliable friends, Aristide Maillol, who was expecting the visit of a great dealer. But things hung fire, the great sacrifice was postponed.

Matisse took back his *Baigneuses* which were at '*the source of his art*'. Once more he could delight his eyes with the shady banks of the Arc, with its fluid tones, with the deep sky almost as blue as night, those modulated figures, like silk, mother-of-pearl, velvet, with that 'Poussin of Impressionism' as Cézanne was called by Maurice Denis.

When Doctor Barnes, the American collector, offered over a million for the picture in 1934, Matisse refused to be parted from it. But with a royal gesture, he made it a gift, from himself and his wife, a few years later to the Museum of the *Ville de Paris*, in the Petit Palais—an offering to the citizens of Paris whose trials and joys he had so long shared.

One day in Nice, on April 16th, 1955, the master's widow said to me with amusement (Madame Matisse-Duthuit was there): 'You don't know the whole of that story. Listen. My husband and I had always agreed to keep Cézanne's *Baigneuses* for our children. But for the Exhibition of 1937, the State commissioned numerous murals for the Palais de Chaillot and many other buildings, forgetting to offer even the most insignificant panel to Matisse, in spite of all he had done abroad, especially in Russia and the United States. Henri flew into a fine rage. He was beside himself with indignation.

'At the same time, you persuaded the Paris Municipality to acquire *la Danse*, the first version of his decoration for Merion. . . . And that decided me: I said to my husband, "Why not offer Cézanne's *Baigneuses*, our greatest treasure, to the *Ville de Paris* for the Modern Art Museum? . . . We couldn't give the State a better lesson."

'Henri Matisse thought it an excellent idea. He told you about it in the Boulevard Montparnasse, and you agreed. And that is how Cézanne's masterpiece went to the Petit Palais instead of the Louvre.'

These revelations of Madame Matisse reminded me of the bitter way her husband had spoken to me of the Louvre administration at that time, and how badly the works of masters were cared for in our national gallery. I was no longer puzzled.

And here are the moving terms in which that gift was made to me for the Petit Palais. These lines show the artist's generosity, so often questioned, and what a fundamental part this picture had played in his evolution.

Nice, November 10th, 1936

'*Yesterday I gave your agents the* Baigneuses *by Cézanne. I saw the picture carefully packed, and it was to go that same evening to the Petit Palais.*

'*I must tell you that this picture is of prime importance in Cézanne's work, for it is a very concentrated, complete realization for which he made many studies, on canvases which, although hung in important collections, are only leading up to this work.*

'*In the thirty-seven years I have possessed this canvas, I have come to know it pretty well, not entirely, I hope; it has been a moral support in the critical moments of my venture as an artist; I have drawn my faith from it, and my perseverance; thus, may I beg you to place it to the best advantage, in the conditions necessary to show all it has to offer. For that, there must be light and distance. It is rich in colour and technique, and distance brings out the powerful life of the lines and the exceptional sobriety of colour-relationships.*

'*I know it is unnecessary to tell you this, but still I feel it is my duty; I beg you to accept it as forgivable evidence of my admiration for this work which has grown greater and greater through the years of my possessing it.*

'*Allow me to thank you for the care you will take of it, for it is with perfect confidence that I entrust it to you.*

Henri Matisse'

All his life, Matisse spoke of Cézanne with great feeling. '*I saw two beautiful still lifes by Cézanne at Durand-Ruel's*' he wrote me in 1945, '*biscuits, milk-boxes and fruit in a bruised blue. Old Durand showed them to me when I took him some still lifes I had painted. "Look at those Cézannes" he said, "which I can't sell. You would do better to paint interiors with figures, like this and that."*

'Just as today, the way seemed completely barred to painters of the new generation. The Impressionists were all the fashion. Van Gogh and Gauguin were ignored. We had to leap over a wall to get through.'

The staircase with no banister

His first blue studies of men and women date from that period, prelude to all the symphonies in blue major of the years to come; the time of *Coin d'Atelier* and *Coiffeuse* (1901).

The artist's father was staying in the village of Villars-sur-Ollon in the Alps, and invited him for a few weeks' visit. He was glad of the chance to study a landscape of unfamiliar depth and space.

And it is interesting to know what Matisse thought of mountains as material for pictures.

'I only wanted to bring back from my very short stay, some small paintings and simple images. I don't believe mountain landscapes can be of much use to painters. The difference in scale makes any intimate contact impossible. That is why I think a few weeks in the mountains are excellent, but as a complete rest.'[1]

When he returned to Paris, life seemed very difficult materially. The pictures he was showing at the *Indépendants* (he first sent in to this *Salon* in 1901) were the last straw in his father's disillusionment. After that his purse was shut forever to such a dauber.

Those were critical days. He admitted as much to Gaston Bernheim.

'My father didn't want to send me anything more for my studies; I found myself literally with no resources. Someone told me of a job going at the Opéra-Comique which would bring in twelve hundred francs a year. I applied for it. The work consisted of this: At the back of the stage was a staircase with no banister, a sort of ladder going up into an attic where properties were kept. A man had just fallen from the stair and killed himself. It had been decided that a watchman should be posted there to prevent anyone from going up. That was the job I applied for. But I couldn't get it.'

However tempered may be the soul of an artist, there comes a time when human contingencies make him lose faith in himself. There seem to be a series of hesitations in the evolution of Matisse between 1902 and 1904. When he returned from Bohain-en-Vermandois in 1903, he was looking for local tone again, giving in to realism and going back to the muted colours of his youth. In 1904, still after colour, Matisse seemed to fall into neo-impressionism, and there is certainly divisionism in such paintings as *la Vue de Notre Dame*.

[1] Unpublished note from Henri Matisse.

It was then, that Ambroise Vollard welcomed Matisse into his gallery, in the rue Laffitte, and organized his first exhibition. In fact, there never was the slightest sympathy between Vollard and Matisse. Each time I mentioned this master, one of the greatest in French painting, Vollard, usually quite talkative, maintained a cautious silence. As for Matisse, he made no secret of his violent antipathy for Ambroise Vollard. '*You're going to lunch with that person?*' he said to me one day, '*I'm sorry for you.*'

Matisse told André Verdet what poor impressions he had received of the 'rag and bone man' of the rue Laffitte, as Forain called him:

'*Vollard was a cunning fox, a gambler with a flair . . . for business. . . . He had acquired Cézannes in considerable numbers; his walls were covered in them; they were even piled up on the floor, and stacked against the walls. He had managed to get them cheap. Cézanne, by the way, had seen through him; "Vollard is a slave-trader. . . ."*

'*Exhibitions of young artists in the rue Laffitte gallery were only a pretext to attract clients who bought well-known names. At private views, with no regard for the work on show, he soon brought out etchings by Renoir, Cézanne and others. Besides, Vollard had no regard for paintings by young artists. . . .*

'*Poor Gauguin! What a fool that Vollard made of him. . . . Gauguin sent him pictures, and received in exchange small parcels of paint, in little tubes. Yes, Vollard behaved shamefully toward Gauguin.*'

And he remembered a more recent anecdote. '*Over ten years ago, I met Vollard for the last time at Vittel. I reminded him of an old story he liked to trot out about women's logic. He said afterwards, "Matisse is a very dangerous man because he has an excellent memory."*'[1]

He certainly had an excellent memory, and with it a rare sense of justice. Thus, in 1936, he told me that some time after acquiring the *Trois Baigneuses*, he wanted to buy two Van Goghs:

'*Vollard*' he told me, '*asked two thousand francs for them. I had nothing like it. So I had to wait. A year later, having sold several pictures, I made my way back to the rue Laffitte:*

' "*Vollard, have you still got the Van Goghs I liked?*"

' "*Yes, I have. But not for long. I have a client for them.*"

' "*Good. . . . Is it still two thousand?*"

'*Vollard, leaning against the panes of the entrance door, replied:*

' "*No, now . . . it's five thousand.*"

' "*How's that?*"

[1] André Verdet, *Prestiges de Matisse*, Ed. Emile-Paul.

' "*What do you expect? Time has passed, and Van Goghs have gone up.*"

'*I only had my two big notes in my pocket.*

'*I had no more to say.*' concluded Matisse. '*It was correct. It was right.*'

But I understood that in his heart, the artist had never forgiven the dealer for being . . . so right.

I should add that much later, about 1937, Vollard said to me, 'I was quite wrong about Van Gogh. I thought there was no future for him, and let his pictures go for next to nothing.'

I knew from Maurice Denis, only too well alas, how those Van Gogh canvases got into Vollard's 'lair'.

Besides, the man's exasperating slyness could not but irritate Matisse whose nature was frank to the point of brutality. Gertrude Stein gives a witty illustration of this in the *Autobiography of Alice B. Toklas* where she describes Vollard's cautious, equivocal and year-long approach to the simple matter of buying, for a very low sum, a big Matisse painting.

1898, 1899 . . . Discovery of the Mediterranean, discovery of Cézanne . . . discoveries of life . . . 1900. Material difficulties were such that in order to provide for his family, Matisse again thought of giving up painting. But help came, and restored his confidence.

Old Druet, then a wine-seller, in the Place de l'Alma, where Rodin took his meals, was interested in young Matisse. So was Berthe Weill. She found him buyers who offered as much as twenty francs a picture, a fortune in those days.

'Were those two really useful to you?' I asked Henri Matisse. '*Yes*,' he answered '*as a dealer is useful to any beginner. But in those days the painter had to be of immediate, direct use to the dealer in order to benefit by a few sales which provided for some days, but never guaranteed security for a year. There were no contracts, and the dealers did not stock, except Vollard, who aimed at "burying" the painters.*'

After Vollard and Berthe Weill, came Félix Fénéon and Josse and Gaston Bernheim.

Félix Fénéon, whom I met every Wednesday then, in Anatole France's Villa Saïd, tall and slender, with a goatee and no moustache, had the silhouette of Uncle Sam and *Valentin-le-Désossé* rolled into one. He had been brought into the limelight by his part in the famous *Procès des Trente*. His three-line gossipy bits in *Le Matin* showed him to be a finished stylist and a dry wit and his sense of art was as sound as his literary taste. 'He is extremely subtle', said Matisse, much impressed by Fénéon. This brief description of a Matisse still life is Fénéon's: 'Allusion, in colour, to various edibles.'

Gaston Bernheim himself describes his first meeting with Matisse in *Petites histoires sur de grands artistes*. 'One day I was in my office, and our eminent director, Félix Fénéon, came to see me and said, "Gaston, there is a painter downstairs who has asked me for a job as overseer in a printing office. But I think this artist has talent. Do you want to go and see him?" I agreed, and went to Issy-les-Moulineaux, where the artist had his studio. I made a three-year contract with him at once. It has been renewed for seventeen years. He was Henri Matisse.'

By courtesy of M.M. Dauberville Bernheim-Jeune, I have that contract, dated September 18th, 1909, on my desk, and those which followed. One must admit that it worked to the advantage of both parties, and was a credit to Josse and Gaston Bernheim. A few essential points give sufficient idea of it.

'Between M. Henri Matisse, 42 rue Clamart, in Issy-les-Moulineaux, Seine, on the one hand, and M.M. Bernheim-Jeune, 15 rue Richepanse, Paris, on the other, it is agreed:

'Art. I. M.M. Bernheim-Jeune agree to buy all pictures of the following dimensions and intermediate dimensions which M. Henri Matisse shall execute before September 15th, 1912, and M. Henri Matisse to sell the same to M.M. Bernheim-Jeune, whatever the subject, at the following prices:

Format	50 fig. —	1875 frs.	15 fig. —	900 frs.
	40	1650	12	750
	30	1500	10	600
	25	1275	8	525
	20	1125	6	450

Art. II. M. Henri Matisse to receive over and above, 25 per cent of the profit realized by M.M. Bernheim-Jeune on the sales of his pictures.

Art. IX. M. Henri Matisse is entitled to accept with no claim thereon by M.M. Bernheim-Jeune, any direct commissions for portraits or decorations.

Art. X. M.M. Bernheim-Jeune will deduct 25 per cent of any orders for portraits or decorations which M. Henri Matisse may accept through their intervention.

Art. XI. Either contracting party having the right to annul this agreement at any time for the remainder of its duration, on the payment of 30,000 francs, and a simple letter addressed to the other. . . .'

From then on, as Matisse said to me jokingly, he was '*condemned to produce only masterpieces*'.

In fact, the new twentieth century was to give his genius full play.

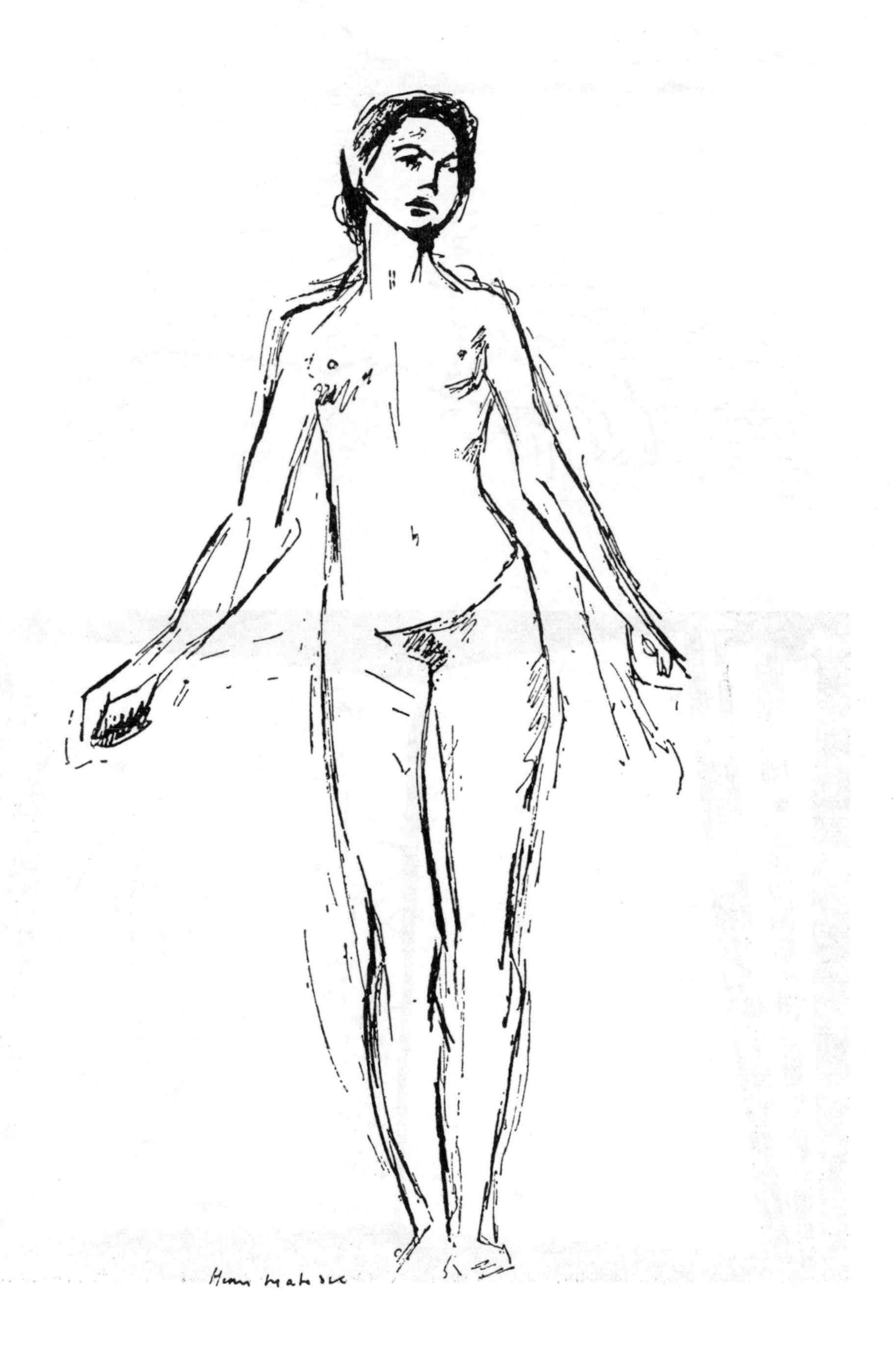
Henri Matisse

COLLIOURE
→ Angelis
ROSETTE
auberge
du PAYS
LE BONHEUR DES PEINTRES
1950

Dans le cas où on aurait à ouvrir la
caisse – un de ses côtés est vissé – après
l'avoir mise debout ou même couchée on
n'aurait simplement qu'à enlever le couvercle.
Le torse est tenu dans la caisse par deux
ceintures de bois qui l'empêchent de bouger.

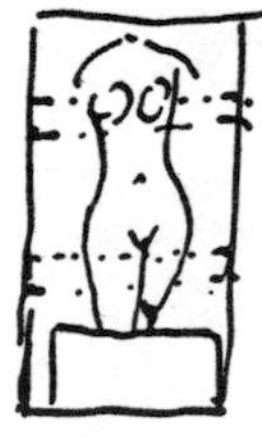

Il me reste à vous remercier
d'avoir bien voulu me prendre
cette charmante personne en
pension, en regrettant de ne pou-
voir vous envoyer ce qui lui manque.

II

FAUVES AND ODALISQUES

It is the night of October 31st, 1903. A long string of carriages is standing at the ground floor entrance to the *Petit Palais*, the entrance which would be used from 1934 to 1939 for *Artistes de ce Temps*. Under the brilliant light of the arc-lamps, scattered among arrangements of ferns, an elegant crowd is gathered; beautiful Parisian ladies in full evening-dress, protecting their bare shoulders with wraps of ermine or mink; men about town in dinner-jackets or tails.

At the late-night private view, evening dress was obligatory, decreed by Sauvage, the architect, Jansen, tapestry-maker and administrator of the new society, Frantz-Jourdain, president of the *Salon d'Automne*, and Yvanhoé Rambosson, who had obtained the basement of the *Petit Palais*.

All Paris was there, frivolous, chattering, highly entertained, moving from room to room richly lit up by Paz and Silva, among furniture by Majorelle, Dufrêne, Follot, Frantz-Jourdain, in front of pictures by Aman-Jean, Jacques-Emile Blanche, Odilon Redon, Georges Desvallières, Charles Guérin, Laprade, Marquet, Rouault, Gauguin and Matisse. Alexandre Duval rubbed elbows with comte Robert de Montesquiou; Marcel Proust and Léon Blum conversed with Anna de Noailles; Arthur Meyer was there with his very young wife on his arm, the great-niece of Turenne. An imposing couple paced the floor, Albert Besnard and Madame Besnard; and Lalique's heavy pendants glittered on women's bosoms and in the glass cases of the *Salon*.

The *Salon d'Automne* was born. A great event for Paris and for artists. The new *Salon* was unique in calling for architects and decorators as well as sculptors and painters, even writers and musicians. The following year since Henry Lapauze, then curator of the *Petit Palais*, had judged the *Salon* undesirable, it was moved to the other side of the *avenue Nicolas II*, where Henri Marcel, director of the *Beaux-Arts* and ardent defender of modern painting, offered the hospitality of the *Grand Palais* to the young society.

It was an amazing victory over academic art, and was not readily forgiven. The *Salon* of 1904, with its fine collection of Cézannes, had a good press and attracted a great number of visitors. That was enough to arouse the fury of the *Institut*. Carolus-Duran would admit no one who exhibited in the *Salon d'Automne*

to the *Société Nationale des Beaux-Arts* exhibition, of which he was president. As for the *Artistes Français*, they mobilized public administration to try and expel the vandals from the *Grand Palais*.

A town-councillor from Gascony and photographer, Lampué, gained an easy triumph at the Town Hall by reproaching the State for admitting such a band of daubers into an official building. However, Carrière threatened to resign from the *Nationale* if Carolus-Duran were not more broad-minded, and Henry Marcel kept his promise in spite of the storm, the academicians and the ministers; and his wild-boar tenacity rendered a service to independent art which proved decisive.

The Central Cage

The year 1905 came in with a bang.

And since the Salon d'Automne was giving a grand retrospective show of Manet, it was under his star that the *Fauves* made their unruly appearance.

True, the wild beasts had been heard roaring every spring for some years past in the *Cours la Reine*, where the *Indépendants* were shown. Naturally, among the jungles and virgin forests of *douanier* Rousseau.

The *Grand Palais* was another matter. . . . None who witnessed that heroic age could forget the great room splashed with brutal colour by Matisse, Derain, Vlaminck, Manguin, Rouault, Friesz, Puy, Valtat and Camoin; that 'central cage' of the *Cours la Reine*, which was invaded daily toward evening by processions of revolutionaries come down from Montmartre, rather as long lines of rioters had descended from the *faubourg Antoine*, a century before, to invade the *Convention*.

It was not Apollinaire who gave Matisse and his set their name, but Louis Vauxcelles.

Looking at the head of a child, executed in the Florentine manner by the honest sculptor Marque, Vauxcelles exclaimed, '*Donatello au milieu des fauves!*' (Donatello among the wild beasts).

The roar of the *Fauves* called forth an exasperated response.

A page of *Illustration*, November 1st, 1905, reproduced works by Rouault, Manguin, Valtat, Jean Puy, Derain (*Vue de Collioure*) and Henry Matisse, with carefully chosen, ironical praises from the rare defenders of living art: 'Monsieur Henri Matisse, gifted though he be,' wrote Gustave Geffroy, 'has strayed into coloured eccentricity, like the others, from which he will undoubtedly recover. . . .' And Louis Vauxcelles himself, in *Gil Blas*, while he sensed that Matisse had something new to say, could not resist making certain reservations of his own. 'Monsieur Matisse is one of the most assuredly gifted painters of today. He could have an easy popularity, but he would rather delve into passionate research, and lose himself in seeking greater vibration and luminosity from *pointillisme* at the expense of form.'

Which pictures by Matisse were there reproduced? First of all, a *Fenêtre ouverte*, an early one of that long series, a window opening on to the port of Collioure. One day, when Raoul Dufy and I were contemplating a rather similar subject from the painter's studio in Port-Vendres, he told me how he had watched Matisse give the final touch to that vibrant sea-scape. 'He was not satisfied with it. He could not catch the amazing brilliance of Mediterranean light. Suddenly, breaking all the rules of Impressionism, he seized a tube of black paint and strongly outlined the window-frame with it. That is how Matisse used black, one day, to make light.'

I should add that, in 1948, I received the following note on the subject. 'Matisse has no recollection of the incident, nor of a picture whose values were heightened by a black line round a window-frame.' But when I asked him again about it, Dufy insisted he had reported an exact fact.

However, in the *Salon d'Automne* of 1905, it was not the *Fenêtre Ouverte* so much as the *Femme au chapeau* which aroused angry derision among the people of Paris. They have scarcely evolved since and prefer, on the whole, the inane output of the *École*, and fashionable portrait painters. Petitions sent in to the *tribune du Conseil Municipal* against exhibiting the master of *Art Indépendant* at the *Petit Palais* in 1937, seem no less absurd thirty years afterwards, than similar pleas addressed from the same tribune, by the photographer Lampué, against holding the *Salon d'Automne* at the *Grand Palais* in 1905. Gillouin had merely succeeded Lampué.

La Femme au Chapeau

What was the *Femme au Chapeau* which caused such a stir?

This is how it was described by two onlookers of different generations, Ambroise Vollard and Francis Carco.

(In fact the artist's evolution may be said to date from this much-discussed, misunderstood portrait.) Vollard was not mistaken—after it had become evident, he rightly adds:

'If anyone has disconcerted those who expected him to continue in his accepted manner, it is, frankly, Henri Matisse. Abandoning the grey tones which delighted his admirers, he suddenly took to startling colours, as in the *Portrait de Femme* he sent to the *Salon d'Automne* of 1905, which marked a new phase in his talent. Although the artist's boldness did not exceed the bounds of pure, classical painting, his light tones seemed to ally him to the *Fauves*.'

And Vollard adds this anecdote, likely if not true,

'It was enough to offend the president of the *Salon d'Automne*, M. Frantz-Jourdain. He often appeared to understand the researches of the new painting, but like a cautious leader, he practised a certain opportunism, being careful not to break openly with academic art, which still enjoyed the greater measure of popular favour. . . . And in the constant fear that one of his "discoveries" might compromise him, he considered that Matisse, with his *Portrait de Femme*, "had gone a little too modern."

'For the painter's own sake, he urged the jury to refuse the picture, and when it was nevertheless accepted, Jourdain lamented, "Poor Matisse, and I thought all of us here were his friends!" '

Francis Carco's impressions are refreshing, for they reflect the sincere feelings of the very young man of 1905, who had written *Jésus-la-Caille*, and who was to become Louis Vauxcelles' collaborator in the art notes of *Gil Blas*, a few years later.

He too speaks of Matisse at the time of *Femme au Chapeau*.

'The painting is a portrait of Madame Matisse, and I remember what a strange effect it had on me. I had no particular opinion as yet on modern painting. Arguments about it at Max Jacob's in the *rue Ravignan*, between Guillaume Apollinaire and Picasso, or at Frédé's in the noisy night-sessions of the *Lapin Agile*, had not convinced me one way or the other. Since Picasso never, on principle, exhibited his pictures, and scarcely showed them at all except to a small circle of initiates, one had to be content with his solemn utterances, salted with a humour of just the kind to charm his hearers. The whole thing turned on palaver. And I was beginning to wonder whether, for all his wonderful powers of persuasion, Picasso was not more interested in mystifying us than in painting, when the famous *Femme au Chapeau* taught me more in one moment than all the paradoxes on the subject. I understood at last what my friends meant by a portrait. There was nothing physically human about it. The artist must have been more preoccupied with his own personality than with his sitter's. I didn't know Madame Matisse, but according to Gertrude Stein, she was "a very dark woman, with a long face and a firm loosely hung mouth like a horse". Unflattering as the description was, it suited well the impression I carried away. That strange work, of balanced lines which might have been drawn on a wall with charcoal, and colours cold as if stencilled, gave such a feeling of determination that, thirty years later I can see it still.' (Perhaps I should say here, that the cold colours (veridian greens and cobalt violets) were balanced, to say the least, by intense warm tones (madders, vermilions and carmines).)

Truly, an unforgettable painting, the body in profile, and a three-quarter face under a large, plumed hat, executed in broad, flat tones and forceful black outlines, particularly the eyes, haunting as an El Greco. He had been one of the favourite masters for study in the Louvre long before Matisse met his work again in Spain.

When I asked him one day what his impressions were of the Prado, and what he had seen there of El Greco, Velasquez and Goya, he said himself, '*Everything was confirmed which I had understood of those three masters from the Louvre, where they are well represented, in first-rate quality if not quantity.*'

As we know, he had also become familiar at Durand-Ruel's with El Greco's *View of Toledo* and *Ascent of Calvary*.

For all that, perhaps even on account of the outcry, the *Femme au Chapeau* found a buyer, and that buyer was Gertrude Stein.

Except that the purchase took place in 1905, not 1903, the picture having hung in the '*Cage aux Fauves*' at the *Grand Palais* not the *Petit Palais*, the wickedly apt comments of Gertrude Stein deserve mention here, as they are part of the history of French art. This picture which enraged the public so much that they wanted to scratch off the paint, appealed to Miss Stein, who said she wanted to buy it. Her brother had in the meantime found a white-clothed woman on a green lawn and he wanted to buy that. So as usual they decided to buy the two and they went to the office of the secretary of the Salon to find out about prices. . . . The Matisse was 500 francs, they were told, but the artist would probably be prepared to lower his price. They offered 400, and left. Matisse refused the offer, so the Steins went to look at the picture again. People were roaring with laughter at it, and scratching at the paint. Gertrude was honestly perplexed, and bought the portrait—it seemed to her perfectly natural. Leo Stein, however, was less attracted by the *Femme au Chapeau.* Matisse has since told me that the picture, today so deservedly famous, was indeed acquired by Gertrude Stein. She must have given it to her sister-in-law, Sarah, who had admired it from the first. It is now in San Francisco, in the Walter A. Haas collection.

Madame Agnès Humbert, ardent and scholarly biographer of David, has explained in one of her remarkable notes to Gaston Diehl's text, what it was that inspired such rage and sarcasm in a public addicted to the official *Salon's* beloved chromos.

'The green shadow of the hat across Madame Matisse's forehead; the shadow of the nose, again green, on a cheek stained with red and pink; vermilion hair; the violet hat and its multi-coloured feathers; the green gloves and chequered dress, all gave a shock of surprise; to say nothing of the background, patches of flat colour in arbitrary juxtaposition it seemed, ranging from golden to Naples yellow, from crude green to red, then orange, from pink to blue; all colours which reappear in *Fenêtre ouverte à Collioure*, painted at the same time; such an orgy of colour and of joy, like a song of freedom, could not fail to offend the spectator of 1905.'

An 'astonishing virility'

Gertrude Stein later learned the rest of the story from the seller's point of view; the account of how the guitar had been broken as Madame Matisse posed for *Gypsy with Guitar*; of how the Steins' offer for *Femme au Chapeau* arrived at the moment when the necessity of paying for repairs to the guitar tempted them to close with the offer; of how Mme Matisse, scenting an eager buyer, held out for the extra hundred, which would clothe 'Margot' all that winter. She describes meetings with the Matisses in their spotless little flat on the Quai St Michel, insisting on Mme Matisse's distinctive way of clapping on a hat and jabbing in its pin; and on the intense virility which was combined, in Matisse, with 'not much feeling for life'. In this seeming contradiction we may read, perhaps, her awareness of the manner which earned him the title of 'Doctor' among his fellow workers at the Grand Palais. On the other hand, 'Madame Matisse was very different, there was a profound feeling of life in her for anyone who knew her.'

Gertrude Stein became very friendly with Madame Matisse and was to learn much from her about the family and the difficulties he never mentioned, such as his natural daughter's diphtheria and its consequences, and the absence of the two young Matisse boys, being cared for by relations. She also tells the well-known story of the Matisses' desperate efforts to pay for, and then preserve, the great dishes full of fruit which the painter needed for still lifes such as *La Grande Desserte*.

On the same wall was a *Sous-bois* by Matisse, closely related to his Corsican pictures.

The sale of *La Femme au Chapeau* was important for Matisse, as it opened to him the doors of twenty-seven rue Fleurus where Gertrude and Leo lived, and of the apartment in the rue Madame belonging to their elder brother Michael, and Sarah his wife.

Sarah gave Jeffery Smith another version of the buying—she herself saw in the strange portrait a resemblance to her own mother. According to her, she and Leo resolved to buy the picture, which went first to the rue Fleurus Steins and then to Michael and Sarah in the rue Madame. Matisse agrees with this version, as is confirmed in an interview with Kimball for *Transition*, 1935.

'*Madame Michael Stein, of whom Gertrude makes no mention, was actually the most intelligent and sensitive member of the family*.' He said of Leo Stein, who had studied Italian art with Berenson in Florence, '*Leo Stein thought a lot of her because she was so sensible she aroused a sort of echo in him.*

'*It was Madame Michael Stein and her brother-in-law, Leo, who agreed to buy* La Femme au Chapeau. *Afterwards, Leo said to her, "I am going to ask you to leave the picture with me, so I can find out exactly why it appeals to me."*

'*The picture finally went back to Madame Michael Stein when Leo quarelled with Gertrude and sold his collection.*'

The Spell of Collioure

Autumn 1904, and Spring 1905, began the days of Collioure, which marked a definite phase in the development of Henri Matisse.

It is no new idea that the woman he loves can exert a happy influence in the life of an artist.

Work at the *Grand Palais* had been slavery to Matisse, and when it came to an end with 1900, perhaps at the turning point of his career, he found himself being led in a new direction. Madame Henri Matisse, with her gentle intuition, was taking him back to her native Languedoc, to the Mediterranean, this time to Roussillon, where her parents lived. The wonderful *Côte Vermeille* was little known in those days, and is still quite unspoiled in spite of all the artists who have gone there in the wake of Matisse and Maillol.

Matisse discovered Collioure. The hills and valleys seemed carved out of granite, Vauban's jutting fortifications and the castle's medieval ramparts to arise from the very rock; background to a landscape of vivid colour; light-house and belfry tipped with orange, cinnabar boats on a pale shore, white sails against blue sea, all in a semi-circle of lime-washed houses, saffron, lilac or water-melon pink.

Matisse was to find his own palette in that play of burning colour tempered by the mists of the sea. 'Possibly' said Fernande Olivier, 'the air and light in his work all came from there.'

For several years, Matisse always spent part of the summer in Collioure, returning from St Tropez, Algiers, Italy or Spain.

C. Le luxe (1907)

Paris, Musée d'Art Moderne

Even the colours and smell of the earth reminded him of his beloved Corsica, visited in the winter of 1898 before going to his wife's country, Fenouillet, Haute Garonne, (*Paysage du Midi*, Hauert coll. Paris, and *Les Maisons*, Barnes Foundation) and the following year, on his way to Toulouse where their son Jean was born.

Matisse said to Gaston Diehl, in 1943, of his work on the banks of the Garonne, '*Even the sight of soldiers splashing in the river reminded me vividly of another Cézanne, a small* Baigneuses, *in which the colour was so well graded that trees and hands were as important as the sky.*'

Maillol

In those days, at Banyuls, not far from Collioure, in a small pink house overlooking the peaceful harbour, lived a blue-eyed painter, fresh from the Beaux-Arts although well over forty, named Aristide Maillol. His first revelation of painting had come from Gauguin. And it was thanks to Maillol that Matisse was drawn away from neo-divisionism, to a closer study of Gauguin's technique and mastery of pure tones.

Maillol was fascinated by the problems of decorative art. He also designed cartoons for tapestry, executed by his wife in colours he dyed himself from herbs of his native Catalonia. Maillol directed his wife in the choice of every shade. '*In his leisure time,*' said Matisse, '*he began to carve a walnut log from his garden; he worked quite freely and found, in the end, he had made a very pretty standing figure which led him in a new direction. That is how he became undoubtedly our best sculptor.*

'*When I was taken to see him by Etienne Terrus, painter from Elne and originally his fellow-pupil at Cabanel's Atelier, he was working on the stooping figure of a woman; the bronze cast stands in the charming patio of Perpignan town-hall; the same figure, carved in marble, after many moves is now in front of the Orangerie Pavilion. I lent a hand with the casting. So I played no part in his career as a sculptor.*'[1]

[1] In her remarkable studies of Maillol (Grasset, 1937) Madame Judith Cladel recalls that this great artist attended sculpture classes at the *École des Arts Décoratifs* in 1883. He did much modelling at that time and, among other things, successfully copied the head of *Raphael's wife*, and the head of a satyr. The notes published by Judith Cladel on the subject disprove current legends of Maillol's first attempts, by showing that he was clearly gifted for sculpture at twenty-one. . . . So it was not, concludes Maillol's biographer, either Bourdelle, as has been maintained, who taught him sculpture . . . nor Henri Matisse who determined his career some twenty years later by exclaiming over some cast-away fragments in the corner of his studio, 'But that is very good! You are a born sculptor!' Henri Matisse disclosed the true facts himself, to Raymond Escholier. '*Going from Collioure, where he was staying, to see Maillol at Banyuls, he had found him busy casting a figure, the big* Nymph of Düsseldorf, *and had simply helped him.*'

Etienne Terrus, who has painted so well the rich beauty of Roussillon, was a friend of Manolo and Pierre Camo, of Derain and Marquet, Luce and Daniel de Monfreid, and he was the prime mover in the great friendship between Maillol and Matisse. The latter retained the happiest memories of Terrus and thought highly of his delicate talent, so closely allied to the soil of Catalonia, as did also the master of Banyuls.

A passage from Marc Lafargue, describes the meeting between Maillol and Matisse, when Etienne Terrus was present.

'Proud, almost misanthropic, Terrus would have liked to remain rooted in his native soil like a gnarled olive-tree. He was not, however, a *naïf* artist, nor ignorant of recent painting. He thought highly of Matisse.

'It was with Aristide Maillol that I met Terrus. An afternoon spent with Maillol and Terrus in some forgotten valley of the Albères was a great pleasure. We would sit under a laurel bush; Maillol imagining his splendid torsoes and goddesses; Terrus looking for the subject he wanted, an old farmhouse built by the Moors, its ancient walls baked in the sun. Beyond the valleys were glimpses of the sea. Terrus would be painting it.'

In the noble Roman city of Elne, famous for its marble cloister, Mlle. Terrus, sister of the painter, very kindly showed me a dual portrait of Matisse and Terrus, two solid fellows, bearded and sunburnt, painted by Derain.

Derain

Unlike Maillol, Derain was deeply indebted to Matisse, for he met with early opposition from his parents very similar to that suffered by his older friend; but the opinion of Matisse had some weight in this case. Since his vocation appeared stronger than ever when he returned from military service, Derain's parents gave in and allowed their son to rejoin Matisse in Collioure during the summer of 1905. Henri Matisse made a drawing of 'Derain fishing on the rocks of Collioure'. It was bought by Stchoukine and hung in the Moscow Museum.

Derain said himself, 'I have known moments of discouragement and Matisse bucked me up again.' Matisse painted with affectionate violence an admirable portrait of Derain at Collioure. It was bought by the Tate Gallery in November, 1954.

We know a great deal about the influence of Matisse over Derain in Collioure, thanks to the publication of his *Lettres à Vlaminck*. André Derain followed in the footsteps of the older man, free at last of the mists of Commercy—and Chatou—when he discovered the light on the Mediterranean coast: 'And so my journey was of enormous help to me in two ways:

'1st. A new conception of light which is simply: the negation of shade. Here, the colours of light are very strong, shadows very clear. Shade is a clear and luminous world in opposition to sunlight: what are called reflections. Matisse himself, true to the theory of reflections given to George Sand by Delacroix, called them "part of painting that sings".

'We had both neglected this until now, and it will enhance the expression of compositions in the future.

'2nd. To find a way, in the company of Matisse, of getting rid of the divisionist obsession. Matisse still uses divisionism sometimes, but I have completely changed my mind about it, and hardly ever use it. It is logical enough in a luminous and harmonious panel; but it is nevertheless a disturbing element, when the harmonies to be expressed are very deliberate.'

The wonderful '*petit port*' praised by Moréas, never ceased to delight Derain. 'The sea and the mountain are *très chic*. Behind, a range of colour you might not care for, but very intense. It got me. I let myself go on colour for its own sake; and I lost something in the process.'. . .

What matter? Contact with Matisse and the Mediterranean light gave Derain something new. And what admiration for the future head of the *Fauves*! 'I have been swotting with Matisse and I don't think he suspected me of having a science of colour, like the one in the manuscript I read you.'

Matisse was secretly on the verge of giving up divisionism for single colour spaces that would convey his own sensation, and this could not escape Derain's keen observation. His culture was wide. It enabled him to foresee the genius of his companion. 'At the moment he is going through a crisis in painting. But I had no idea he was such an extraordinary bloke in other ways, in logic and psychological speculation.'

We know what that crisis was from Matisse himself, and its development and happy outcome were most likely affected by the dual, apparently contradictory, influences of Maillol and Derain. The latter's project for a treatise on 'Oil Painting' interested Matisse.

Madame Matisse was attracted by Madame Maillol's loom and learned the art of tapestry from her, so well that she wove a screen, from a cartoon by Derain, destined for exhibition in the *Indépendants*. (Marquet painted *Madame Matisse weaving a tapestry*.) At that time, Maillol, deeply impressed by the work of Gauguin, insisted on taking Matisse and Terrus to Daniel de Monfreid's house, where the Tahiti canvases were stored. And sometimes they went on to the Abbey of Fontfroide, to see Gauguin's other collector, Gustave Fayet, who later bought works by Matisse.

Matisse had first discovered Gauguin through Vollard, who sold him a small canvas in 1899. The very fine paintings by Gauguin exhibited in the *Salon d'Automne* in 1903, just after his death, had been to Matisse, as to most art lovers, a great revelation. But it was not until he was in Collioure that Matisse fully realized what a powerful lesson he was learning from Gauguin, precisely at a revolutionary phase in the final break with divisionism, when he was sacrificing colour transitions for pure colour. It was then, in a stormy atmosphere, that the rich quality of his particular talent became evident. This does not mean that the king of the *fauves* ceased to use his plumb-line, or despised formula, such as the one mentioned by Jean Puy: '*A very luminous tone inevitably calls for a very dark one next to it.*'

The palette Matisse brought back from his long stay in Roussillon, at Toulouse and Fenouillet in the Haute Garonne, Cassis and Saint-Tropez, comprised a magical range of colour. And in spite of the resistance to a highly revolutionary art, it was, in the end, accepted with joy.

As Marcel Sembat wrote, Matisse was on the verge of 'a period of beautiful, high-quality work'. Druet had the great luck to get all of those 'hundred or so sketches the size of a man's hand' which the artist brought back from Roussillon and Provence. 'The small studies of the Midi were true to nature for all their violence. No sign of dots. But the new harsh contrasts of which we spoke. Among others, *Souvenir de la Côte provençale*, a cove near Cassis—in which a green horizon gives quality to dark blues and frothy whites of the sea, confined between cliffs, seeming to move in glittering waves caught by the sunlight. The Steins bought several of those small studies from Druet. Where are they now? Scattered abroad, as were almost all the Matisses of that period. Few Frenchmen had the courage to admire them. Numbers of his best canvases were no sooner finished than they were sent to other countries.'

It was the time of *l'Italienne*, Stchoukine Coll., *Carmelina*, *l'Idole*, so magically luminous; *la Coiffure*, fine, pyramidal composition; *Portrait de Marguerite*, bent over her home-work, the time of *Tapis bleus*, peacock, cineraria, midnight blues, in the Stein collection; *Tapis rouges*, bought by Marcel Sembat with the *Portrait de Marguerite*.

'Period of beautiful, high-quality work', as Marcel Sembat had said, 'Sometimes his friends call it the Collioure days, because he worked there a lot.'[1]

[1] I am told that Matisse stayed not far from the station, opposite 'the doctor's house' (today Hotel des Templiers) *Les Tapis rouges* was left by Marcel Sembat and his wife, G. Agutte, to the Grenoble Museum.

In all the paintings of that period, the joy of colour is triumphant. Entrancing blues, as in the Stein's *Tapis*, powerful reds heightened by yellows and black. And in the *Portrait de Marguerite*, the light of Velasquez. A daring green on the back of her hand! 'What force and simplicity in the features.'

Marcel Sembat, who had an observing eye behind his eyeglass, gives an excellent picture of the Matisse of Collioure. 'At that time, Matisse was known as the chief of the *Fauves*. The public considered him to be Disorder Incarnate, a furious breaker with all tradition, a mad-hat, half anarchist, half charlatan! It was a shock to meet him. What! That serious schoolmaster in gold-rimmed spectacles? He might have escaped from a German university, with his precise, opinionated way of speaking, his obstinacy and will to convince!'

Negro Art

It has been claimed that Picasso introduced Matisse to Negro art. In fact, it was just the contrary, for which we have the testimony of Gertrude Stein, whose admirable portrait left to the Metropolitan Museum in New York, was being painted by Picasso in 1906. 'It was Matisse who drew Picasso's attention to it. . . . She was not at any time interested in African sculpture . . . it lacks naiveté . . . it is very ancient, very narrow, very sophisticated but lacks the elegance of the Egyptian sculpture from which it is derived. To Matisse it was exotic and naive; to the Spaniard, Picasso, natural, direct and civilized.'

Hence, the *Demoiselles d'Avignon*, which at the time so grieved the great Russian admirer of Matisse . . . and of Picasso. 'I remember' says Gertrude Stein again, 'Stchoukine, who had so loved Picasso's work, came to see me one day and, with tears in his eyes, said "What a loss for French art!" '

It was Gertrude Stein who introduced the painter of her portrait to Matisse. The two painters became, according to her, 'friends and enemies', and when they exchanged pictures (an artists' custom then) each chose a dull and uninspired work of the other. This is not quite true. For the *Portrait de Marguerite*, still in Picasso's possession, is a very remarkable painting, and much influenced by Far Eastern art.

Matisse, with his wife, regularly frequented the Steins' evening parties in the *rue Fleurus*, and was annoyed to see the growing affection between Picasso and Gertrude, which was to last until the latter's death. '*Mlle Gertrude*' Matisse explained, '*likes local colour and theatrical effects. It would be impossible for anyone of her quality to have a serious friendship with anyone like Picasso.*'

Gertrude Stein, to whom 'Picasso was like a little bull-fighter followed by his squadron of four' or 'like Napoleon, followed by his four enormous grenadiers,

Derain and Braque were great big men, so was Guillaume Apollinaire a heavy-set man, and Salmon was "not small",' Gertrude Stein never forgave Matisse for that remark.

However he still went to the *rue de Fleurus*, but the heart had gone out of their meetings. 'It was about this time that Gertrude Stein and her brother gave a lunch for all the painters whose pictures were on the wall. It was at this lunch that Gertrude Stein made them all happy and made the lunch a success by seating each painter facing his own picture. No one of them noticed it, but they were naturally pleased, until just as they were all leaving Matisse, standing up with his back to the door and looking into the room, suddenly realized what had been done.

'That day they nearly quarrelled for good. Matisse intimated that Gertrude Stein had lost interest in his work. She answered him "There is nothing within you that fights itself[1] and hitherto you have had the instinct to produce antagonism in others which stimulated you to attack. But now they follow".'

Such was the end of the conversation, if not of their friendship.

Le Bonheur de Vivre

How is one to make people understand that Matisse was at heart deeply attached to order, discipline and tradition?

It was the time of *Bonheur de vivre* (Barnes Foundation), a great decorative, lyrical composition which created a scandal in the *Salon des Indépendants* of 1906.

Bonheur de Vivre was a paean of the *Fauves*, a triumphal hymn; but it was also a swan-song, for after that Henri Matisse found other subjects, to him more stimulating, of rarer and deeper quality.

But the Mediterranean composition and stress of that great canvas already foretold the Bacchanalian mood of *La Danse* and *La Musique*. Long, voluptuous pink forms, groups of lovers, the mad whirl which ever after haunted the pictures of Matisse; the tawny beach, blue forest and cerulean sea, all vibrate to a powerful and victorious rhythm. The arabesque certainly plays its part, but so does the magic of clear, bright, pure painting; and an outburst of primitive nature and instinct. Apollinaire exclaimed, 'Instinct has been found again!'

'Most significant' wrote Maurice Denis a few months later, 'are certainly Matisse's paintings, on show this year in the *Salon d'Automne* between the black Courbets and the truly Venetian room devoted to Gauguin. Matisse's

[1] In which Gertrude Stein was strangely mistaken. From beginning to end the life of Henri Matisse was an unceasing fight against himself.

paintings'—(of course Matisse himself and some of his followers like Friesz are gifted with extraordinary sensibility)—'compete with one another in brilliance and in their determination to create light. They give an effect of sun that is a discomfort to the eye, an optic shudder, a painful sensation of being dazzled, like the shock of a white wall or esplanade in full Southern summer. It is quite in accord with their aesthetic code to try and blind the spectator, and no light effect is too crude, nor effective colour too cruel, to achieve this end. Brush-strokes of many colours on the white canvas ground, a mark, a line, a streak of pure colour are enough to suggest all the violence of solar light. We have come a long way from Seurat's *Plage du Nord* or *Bords de la Seine*! How restrained were Monet's *Meules* ("Haystacks")! But most remarkable is the newness of optical vision—echnique is too obvious a word—Apart from extreme simplicity in execution, nothing whatever remains of the Impressionist theory. It is the chromatic scale with all its gradations, tones, dissonance, opposition of pure colour and neutral grey, substituted for Chevreul's old diatonic scale.'

It is not surprising if someone 'not in the profession', Gertrude Stein, showed greater insight on that occasion than did Maurice Denis, although he was one the best writers on art among our painters. In any case, there is no more pertinent comment on the famous composition:

'Matisse at that time was at work at his first big decoration, *Bonheur de Vivre*. He was making small and larger and very large studies for it. It was in this picture that Matisse first clearly realized his intention of deforming the drawing of the human body in order to harmonize and intensify the colour values of all the simple colours mixed only with white. He used his distorted drawing as a dissonance is used in music or as vinegar or lemons are used in cooking, or eggshells in coffee, to clarify. Cézanne had come to his unfinishedness and distortion of necessity, Matisse did it by intention.'

Apollinaire

Guillaume Apollinaire pointed out, to his credit, in *Phalange*, December 15th, 1907, the classical element in the genius of Matisse, as in that of Delacroix, and to what extent also his art is fundamentally French, in direct descent from Jean Fouquet, Georges de la Tour and Chardin:

'This is a tentative essay on an artist whose work combines, I believe, the most sensitive qualities of France: the force of her simplicity and the softness of her light.

'When I approached Matisse, the crowd had stared at him, and when it laughed, he had smiled.

'They saw a monster where a marvel stood.

'I questioned him, and his replies showed the poise of his reasoned art:

' "*I have worked*" he told me "*to enrich my mind, following what aroused my curiosity, making myself familiar with the different ideas of the masters of plastic arts, ancient and modern. And it was material work as well, because I tried at the same time to understand their technique. Afterwards, I discovered myself, first by considering my early works. They rarely lie. I found in them something constant which at first I took for a repetition making for monotony in my pictures. It was the manifestation of my personality, appearing to be the same no matter what divers moods I had been through. I did my best to develop that personality, counting first of all on my instinct, always going back to principles, saying to myself when difficulties held up my work: I have colours and a canvas, and I must express myself with purity even if I do it briefly, with a few touches of colour, or with four or five lines which give plastic expression.*"

'Matisse went on to say he had never avoided being influenced, and made no secret of his sources. "*All kinds of plastic records—the hieratic art of the Egyptians, the Greeks with their refinement, the voluptuous Cambodians, the works of the ancient Peruvians, the statuettes of African negroes, proportioned according to the passions which inspired them—all can be of interest to an artist and help to develop his personality.*"

'This is not an extremist venture', adds Apollinaire. 'Matisse is nothing if not reasonable. And here is an idea which was fundamental throughout his life!

' "*When we speak of nature, we should not forget that we are part of it, and we should observe ourselves with as much curiosity and sincerity as when we study a tree, a sky or an idea, for there is a correspondence between ourselves and the rest of the Universe. We can discover that correspondence and then give up trying to go beyond it.*" '

The Convent of the Sacred Heart

In 1906, Henri Matisse became the head of a school. He tells us about it himself, and many things fall into place. '*Hans Purrmann and Bruce having asked me through Madame Michael Stein to give them advice, I suggested that they work together so I need only pay one visit. Others, such as the Norwegians, Revolt, Sorensen, Grünwald and Dardel having joined them, they had to rent premises in the former Couvent des Oiseaux, rue de Sèvres. That is how my Academy came about. I refused any fee for my corrections, not wishing to be tied by such considerations when I might have reason to give it up. Then as the*

Atelier grew, Purrmann and Bruce had to move it to the one-time convent of the Sacred Heart, boulevard des Invalides.'[1]

André Salmon, a contemporary of early *Fauvism*, has written of that Academy: 'It was the most prosperous of free institutions, where pupils from all over the world came under the sway of Henri Matisse. The teaching was so well received that in many places of Central Europe, and particularly in Czechoslovakia where a very interesting school of painting was growing up, the most rigid Cubists used colour in the manner of the Matisse Academy. This Academy, the principal Fauve school, was in fact, the cradle of the cosmopolitan *Ecole de Paris*'.[2]

Every morning about fifty students came to the Sacred Heart Convent, mostly Scandinavian, German and American. They worked in the old white-washed, spotless refectory, overlooked by a cast of the Apollo of Piombino; some drawing, some painting either from plaster casts or from a female model of great beauty. (Matisse only used very beautiful models.) Sometimes old Beli-vacque, Rodin's 'Saint John the Baptist', came to pose.

A select few, Pierre Dubreuil who became a painter of rare frankness and a fine engraver, Greta Moll, Dardel, Revolt, Heiberg, were allowed to come in the afternoons and work near the master in the sculpture studio—for Matisse never neglected this art, which gave him an outlet for surplus energy.

At the Saturday corrections, they all took full advantage of each other's lesson, which was given with an open mind, respect for the pupil's individuality and insight into his tendencies; for in this Matisse resembled his old master, Moreau. I myself have only found these qualities as a teacher in André Lhote, who also urges study in the Louvre, while respecting the most recent discoveries.

Dubreuil never forgot this liberal teaching, and he has reported some of its principles in a letter to Gaston Diehl dated June 23rd, 1952:

'*The human body is an architectural structure of forms which fit into one another and support one another, like a building in which every part is necessary to the whole: if one part is out of place, the whole collapses. . . . If you are not sure, take measurements, they are crutches to lean on before you can walk. Construct your figures so that they stand, always use your plumb-line. Think of the hard lines of the stretcher or the frame, they affect the lines of your subject. . . . All human shapes are convex, there are no concave lines. . . . Paint on the white canvas. If you place a tone on a surface already coloured, without reference to*

[1] From Henri Matisse to Raymond Escholier.

[2] '*Histoire de l'Art Contemporain*' published under the direction of René Huyghe, *Naissance du Fauvisme*, André Salmon, p. 103.

your subject, you sound a discord from the start which will hinder you all the way. One tone is just a colour; two tones are a chord, which is life. A colour exists only in relation to its neighbour. . . . Determine your impression from the beginning, and hold to that impression. Feeling counts above everything.'

And from the first days of the 'Académie Matisse', Sarah Stein (Mrs Michael Stein) one of the master's most faithful pupils, was making careful, daily notes of what he said while teaching. Professor John Dodds of Stanford University gave these wonderfully precious notes to Alfred H. Barr Jr., who published them in his fine work, *Matisse, his art and his public.*

When it came to drawing, he insisted primarily on the study of Greek and Roman sculpture.

'Antique art will help you more than anything to achieve fullness of form. In those works, each part of the body was given equal importance. Which gave unity and peace of mind.

'In the moderns, one often finds a passionate expression and some part treated very fully at the expense of others less carefully worked; which gives lack of unity . . . and disturbs the mind.'

And they were to study the model. *'Remember, a foot is a bridge. When the model has slender legs, they must have a construction powerful enough to bear the weight of the body. You are not surprised, are you, that a sparrow's tiny feet can carry his body. . . .*

'Arms are like rolls of clay, but forearms are like ropes, since they can be knotted or twisted.

'The pelvis, fitted in to the thighs, gives the feeling of an amphora. Adjust the different parts of the body to each other, and build up your figure as a carpenter builds a house. Each part should be constructed; made up of dissimilar elements, it is for you to make a unity. A tree is like a human body, a human body is like a cathedral.

'To be successful at this work, it is first of all important to know what you are doing. One has to contemplate the model, or any other subject of inspiration, for a long time.

'Above all, enrich what your eyes see with your imagination! If it is a model, try taking the pose yourself. If you feel a strain, be glad, it is the key to the movement.

'If the model is young, take care to render her youth. Notice carefully the model's essential characteristics. They should reappear in the finished work. If not, you have lost your thread on the way. Everything has its peculiar physical character. Example: a square, a triangle. Only an undecided and confused form

expresses nothing. For that reason, don't be afraid to exaggerate character for the sake of expression.

'*Look, you may consider this black model as a cathedral, composed of elements which make a strong, lofty and noble building—or equally, as a lobster* (at the same time, Anatole France used to compare Notre Dame's apse to a cray-fish) *because of what one might call her carapace, by the tension of the muscles fitting into one another so well, with joints just large enough to take the bones.*

'*However it is essential that you remember from time to time that the model is also a negro, don't lose sight of him, or forget yourself, in building up your drawing.*

'*Remember that no line exists alone. Only its relation to another one can create a volume. So you should draw those two lines "at one go".*'

And this, perhaps involuntary, reminder of Gauguin and Maillol:

'*Translate the curves of the body as in sculpture. Look for their volume and fullness. The outlines should be enough* (as in *Bonheur de Vivre*). *Speaking of a melon, one uses both hands to express in one gesture its spherical shape. In the same way, two lines are sufficient to express one form. Drawing is like that expressive gesture, but it has the advantage of permanence. A drawing is sculpture; but it can be examined closely, so that suggestions are grasped; these would have to be expressed far more definitely by a sculptor, whose work must be looked at from a greater distance. . . .*'

And this surprising reminder of Ingres, who advised his pupils to start drawing a face from the ear.

'*Ingres said, in drawing a head, never leave out the ear. If I don't insist on this point, I must remind you, that an ear adds enormously to the character of a head, and it is important to express it carefully and fully, and not to indicate it by a more or less careless sign.*'

In Sarah Stein's note, the passage dealing with Still life—in France stupidly called *nature morte*—deserves attention.

'*As for still life, it is painting that consists of colouring objects chosen by the artist for his composition, allowing for the divers qualities of tone and their relationships.*

'*When your eyes are tired, when the relationships seem all wrong, then look at one object. "But that brass is yellow!" Then put in a clear yellow ochre, and start from there to harmonize the divers tones.*

'*It is nothing to copy the objects which compose a still life. What matters is to express the sensation with which it inspired you, the emotion aroused by the whole thing, the relationship between the objects represented, the specific character of each of them, modified by relationship with the others, the whole intertwined like a rope or like a serpent. . . .*

'*A still life is as difficult to render as antique sculpture. The proportions of the various elements composing it: lines, volumes and colours, are as important as the proportions of head or hands, for instance, in a Greek or Roman statue. . . .*'

Stories told about his Academy by Henri Matisse in those days to the disrespectful ear of Gertrude Stein, are very amusing.

'The applicants were of all nationalities and Matisse was at first appalled at the number and variety of them. He told with much amusement as well as surprise that when he asked a very little woman in the front row, what in particular she had in mind in her painting, what she was seeking, she replied, *Monsieur, je cherche le neuf.* He used to wonder how they all managed to learn French when he knew none of their languages. . . . Someone got hold of these facts and made fun of the school in one of the French weeklies. This hurt Matisses's feelings frightfully. The article said; "where did these people come from," and gave its own answer: "From Massachusetts." Matisse was very unhappy.

'But in spite of all this, and also in spite of many dissensions, the school flourished. There were difficulties. One of the Hungarians wanted to earn his living posing for the class and in the intervals when someone else posed go on with his painting. There were a number of young women who protested; a nude model on a model-stand was one thing but to have it turn into a fellow-student was another. A Hungarian was found eating the bread for rubbing out crayon drawings that the various students left on their painting boards, and this evidence of extreme poverty and lack of hygiene horrified the Americans. There were quite a number of Americans. . . . And then every once in a while someone said something to Matisse in such bad French that it sounded like something different from what it was, and Matisse grew very angry and the unfortunate had to be taught how to apologize properly. All the students were working in such a state of tension that explosions were frequent.'

Gertrude Stein enjoyed all these complications immensely, Matisse was a good gossip and so was she, and at this time they delighted in telling tales to each other.

She began at that time always calling Matisse the C.M. or *cher maître.* She told him the famous Western story, 'Pray, gentlemen, let there be no bloodshed.' Matisse came not unfrequently to the *rue de Fleurus.*

If, like Delacroix, Matisse had kept a journal, he also would have included many a delicious recipe. He was an epicure, as was Gertrude Stein herself. And like many Southerners Madame Matisse could prepare excellent savoury dishes, not only *cargolade* and *perdreau à la Catalane*. Sometimes a relative sent Matisse a hare. 'Jugged hare prepared by Madame Matisse in the fashion of Perpignan, was something quite apart. They also had extremely good wine, a little heavy but excellent, a sort of Madeira, called Rancio,[1] which was very good indeed.'

At the beginning of the summer of 1907 (in 1906 he had been to Biskra) Matisse set out with no enthusiasm on his voyage to Italy. He preferred France, Spain or Morocco to that too-academic land, 'but Madame Matisse' wrote Gertrude Stein 'was very keen to go. It was a girlish dream fulfilled. She said: I say to myself all the time, I am in Italy. And I say it to Henri all the time and he is very sweet about it, but he says, what of it?'

On their way to Italy, the couple stopped at Cavalière. 'I saw Matisse for the second time,' wrote Derain to Vlaminck, 'He passed here with his wife on the way to Italy. He showed me photographs of his pictures, they're marvellous. I believe he is entering the seventh garden, the garden of happiness.'

We shall see that Matisse was deeply moved by the frescoes of Giotto in Padua, by the Duccios of Sienna, and Piero della Francesca in Arezzo. Matisse and his wife also stopped in Venice. At Florence they were guests of the Steins, in their villa in Fiesole.

Matisse really only acquired in Italy a love for the Trecento and Quattrocento. As he wrote me a few years ago, '*In front of the primitives of Sienna, I thought "Here I am in Italy, the Italy of the primitives which I loved. When, in Venice, I came to the great Titian, Veronese, those wrongly termed Renaissance masters, I saw in them superb fabrics created for the rich, by those great sensuous artists of more physical than spiritual value.*" '[2]

Although Matisse has been closely studied by the greatest critics, such as Gertrude Stein, Maurice Denis, André Salmon, Roger-Marx, Apollinaire, André Gide, Jules Romains, Georges Duthuit, Marcel Sembat, George Besson, Tériade, André Rouveyre, Jacques-Emile Blanche, Roger Fry, André Lhote, Gillet, René Huyghe, Jean Cassou, Claude Roger-Marx, Waldemar George, Gaston Diehl, Celia Bertin, Catherine Valogne and the first-rate Alfred H. Barr, one always comes back to Aragon, and his excellent book, *Matisse-en-France*. He observed a rather negative attitude in the master of *Joie de Vivre* toward the so-called 'Golden age' of Italian art: 'Michelangelo is certainly not his type of

[1] Name of delicious wine from Rivesaltes, country of Joffre, and from Banyuls, birthplace of Maillol.

[2] Unpublished note of Henri Matisse.

artist. I mean that Matisse is suspicious of the Renaissance men, Michelangelo, Leonardo. . . . Those men who dissected in secret. Those demonstrators of anatomy. Who were not looking to surprise the movement of a hand, but to find out how the smaller bones fitted into their sockets and how tendons worked. He came near to thinking, indeed he said as much to me, that Renaissance art was decadent, terribly decadent.'

First Laurels

On their return from Italy in the autumn of 1907, they went to live at Issy, near Clamart. They knew the government would shortly take back the Convent of the Sacré-Cœur, and the days of the Matisse Academy were numbered.

In 1909, thanks to a contract with the Bernheims, and the patronage of Stchoukine, the artist knew his present and future were assured. 'He now had an established position' says Gertrude Stein, 'He bought a house and some land in Clamart and he started to move out there. Let me describe the house as I saw it. This house in Clamart was very comfortable, to be sure the bathroom which the family much appreciated from long contact with Americans, although it must be said that the Matisses always had been and always were scrupulously neat and clean, was on the ground floor adjoining the dining-room. The grounds at Clamart were large and the garden was what Matisse between pride and chagrin called *un petit Luxembourg*. There was also a glass forcing-house for flowers. Later they had begonias in them that grew smaller and smaller. Beyond were lilacs and still beyond a big demountable studio. They liked it enormously. Madame Matisse, with simple recklessness, went out every day to look at it and pick flowers, keeping a cab waiting for her. In those days only millionaires kept cabs waiting and then only very occasionally.'

For Matisse the great decorative phase was beginning, the works being produced then, being now in the U.S. and the U.S.S.R.

'Soon the enormous studio was filled with enormous statues and enormous pictures. It was that period of Matisse. These were the beginning of very prosperous days for the Matisses. They went to Algeria and they went to Tangiers and their devoted German pupils gave them Rhine wines and a very fine black police dog, the first of the breed that any of us had seen.

'And then Matisse had a great show of his pictures in Berlin. I remember so well one spring day, it was a lovely day and we were to lunch at the Matisses. When we got there they were all standing around an enormous packing-case with its top off. We went up and joined them and there in the packing-case was the largest laurel-wreath that had ever been made, tied with a beautiful red ribbon. Matisse showed Gertrude Stein a card that it had in it. It said on it, to Henri Matisse, Triumphant on the Battle Field of Berlin, and it was signed Thomas Whittlemore. Thomas Whittlemore was a Bostonian archaeologist and professor at Tuft's college, a great admirer of Matisse, and this was his tribute. Said Matisse, still more rueful, I am not dead yet. Madame Matisse, the shock once over, said, but Henri look, and leaning down she plucked a leaf and tasted it, think how good it will be in the soup. And, said she still further brightening, the ribbon will do wonderfully for a long time as hair-ribbon for Margot.'

Ever since his first visit to Collioure, Matisse had certainly rejected Impressionism and Pointillism. And with his first great success (*Salon des Indépendants*, 1906) material conditions improved for him daily. The collection of his works bought by the Steins—Gertrude and Leo, Michael and Sarah—and shown by their owners with pride, in the big studio of the *rue de Fleurus*, brought him new admirers, mostly from America: Miss Harriet Levy, Dr Claribel Cone, her sister Miss Etta Cone, of whom the artist made a fine portrait, thanks to Sarah Stein who had taken works by Matisse to the U.S. In 1906, the New York painter, George Of, bought the first picture Matisse sold in America, *Nu dans les bois*, a remarkable picture.

Except for Marcel Sembat who kept a few masterpieces of that period in France, the chief buyer was the Russian, Stchoukine, importer of Oriental fabrics, who not only bought some forty pictures, but in 1909 commissioned Matisse to decorate the old Troubetskoi palace with *La Danse* and *La Musique*. The latter was a failure because it was entirely 'imagined', the artist having received no impression from nature as he had when he first saw the 'Sardana' dance which inspired the marvellous *La Danse*.

In April, 1909, Matisse showed Charles Estienne, to whom I had sent *Les Nouvelles*[1] the decorative ideas he had imagined for Stchoukine's commission:

'*I have to decorate a studio. There are three floors. I imagine the visitor coming in. The first floor appears to him. It must be stimulating, give a feeling of lightness. My first panel represents* la Danse, *a round dance, whirling above the hills. On the second floor, one is inside the house, in the silent heart of it. I see a musical scene, with attentive listeners; finally, on the third floor, all is at peace, I paint a scene of repose, people lying on the grass, talking or dreaming. I shall get it by the simplest, by the minimum of means, which are the most apt for the painter to express his inner vision.*'

The great *Fauve*, who had been playing with the baroque in his recent sculpture, *Nu couché* 1907, *Serpentine* 1909, now seemed to aspire only to great

[1] *Les Nouvelles*, 12 April 1909.

peace. '*We are moving toward serenity by simplification of ideas and means*' he said to Estienne again. '*The whole is our only objective. We must learn, perhaps relearn, to express ourselves by means of line. Plastic art will inspire the most direct emotion possible by the simplest means. . . . Three colours for a large panel of* la Danse; *blue for the sky, pink for the bodies, green for the hill. . . .*'

Doesn't this already foretell the great later decoration *La Danse* for the Barnes Foundation?

Expression

At this decisive period, on the request of Georges Desvallières, staunch prophet of independent art, and his senior under Gustave Moreau, Matisse published the essentials of his doctrine. (*La Grande Revue* December, 1908.) Before it became part of the history of art, this manifesto was translated into several languages and spread across two continents. In fact, in Central Europe, Scandinavia and America, it was received at once as a gospel of modern painting.

What, according to Matisse, is the artist's primary aim?

'*It is expression I am after, more than anything. It has sometimes been admitted that I have a certain knowledge, while my ambition is said to be limited and goes no further than purely visual satisfaction produced by the sight of a picture. But the painter's idea should not be considered apart from his means, because it is only of value in so far as it is served by those means, which should be complete (and by complete I do not mean complicated) according to the depth of his idea. I cannot distinguish between my feeling for life and the way I interpret it.*

' "*Expression*" *does not to me reside in the passion which will light up a face or will be translated into violent gesture. It is in the whole arrangement of my picture: the place taken up by the bodies, the spaces round them, the proportions, all play their part. Composition is the art of arranging, in a decorative way, the various elements the painter has at his disposal to express his sentiments. Each element in a picture should be visible, and play its allotted part, of first or secondary importance. Whatever is useless in a picture is for that reason harmful. A work demands harmony of the whole; any unnecessary detail, in the eye of the spectator, will usurp the place of another, essential one.*

'*Composition, which should aim at expression, is modified according to the surface to be covered. If I take a sheet of paper of given dimensions, I shall make a drawing necessarily related to its proportions. I should not repeat the same drawing on a sheet of paper differently proportioned, which was rectangular, for instance, instead of being square. And I should not be content to enlarge it if I had to reproduce it on a similar sheet, but ten times bigger. The drawing should have*

1. Notre Dame

London, Tate Gallery

2. Nu debout

London, Tate Gallery

3. Zulma

Copenhagen, Statens Museum for Kunst

4. La Coiffeuse

Philadelphia, Museum of Art (Chester Dale)

5. Roses, gueules-de-loup et iris

Private Collection

6. Portrait de l'artiste

Copenhagen, Statens Museum for Kunst

7. Le nu bleu (Souvenir de Biskra)

Baltimore, Museum of Art (Cone)

8. Sculpture et vase persan
Oslo, National Gallery

9. Poissons rouges et sculpture
Copenhagen, Statens Museum for Kunst

10. La Danse

Philadelphia, Museum of Art (Chrysler)

11. La femme aux yeux verts

San Francisco, Museum of Art

12. Le chasseur de papillons

Minneapolis, Institute of Art

13. Tête de jeune femme

Private Collection

14. Paysage Marocain: Tanger

Stockholm, National Museum

15. L'arbre près de l'étang de Trivaux

London, Tate Gallery

16. La fenêtre bleue

New York, Museum of Modern Art

17. Le peintre et son modèle

Paris, Musée d'Art Moderne

18. La fenêtre

Detroit, Institute of Arts

19. La leçon de piano

New York, Museum of Modern Art

an expanding force which gives life to its surroundings. The artist who wants to transfer a composition from a small canvas to a larger one should, to keep the expression of it, conceive it afresh, modify its appearance, not simply square it up.'

After the manner of classic art, unlike the impressionists, Henri Matisse avoids the accidental in search of the eternal.

'One can obtain most delightful effects with colours by stressing their relationship or their contrast. Often I start on a picture by noting fresh and superficial sensations. A few years ago, the result often satisfied me. If I left it at that today, now that I think I can see further, it would remain a vague picture. I should have recorded the fugitive sensations of the moment which did not entirely define what I felt, and which I should scarcely recognize the next day. I wish to reach that state of condensation of impressions which makes a picture. Were I to be content with a spontaneous painting of a picture, I should be bored with it later, and I would rather continue working on it so as to recognize something in it afterwards which represents my mind. At one time I never hung my pictures on the wall, because they reminded me of a state of over-excitement, and I didn't care to see them again when I was calm. Today I try to put calmness into them, and I work on them until I succeed.

'I have to paint the body of a woman; first I give it grace, charm, and then I must give something more. I must condense the meaning of the body in finding its essential lines. The charm will be less evident at first glance, but it should be finally manifest in the new image I have obtained, which has greater, and more fully human meaning. The charm will be less obvious, not being the only characteristic, but it will be there none the less, in the general conception of my figure.'

Those familiar with the thought and work of Eugenè Delacroix, will recognize an echo of his musical inspiration when Henri Matisse speaks of composition.

'Each relationship of tone, I have found, should produce a chord of living colours, a harmony like that of a musical composition.

'To my mind composition is everything. So it is essential to have a clear vision of the whole from the outset. Look at a picture by Cézanne; everything is so well combined that, from no matter what distance, and however many the figures, you can distinguish them clearly, and understand to which among them every limb belongs. If there is great order and light in a picture, it is because that order and light existed from the beginning in the painter's mind, or that the painter realized their necessity. Limbs may be intertwined, mingled, but each one will remain, for the spectator, attached to the one body and expressing the idea of that body: all confusion has gone.'

Harmony in dissonance

Above all, colour should be expressive, and in spite of what has been said, Matisse had little use for the theory of complementaries. Just as did Debussy and Ravel, this painter sought harmony in dissonance.

'The dominant tendency of colour, should be to serve expression. I put down my tones without preconceived ideas. If at first, and without perhaps my knowing it, a tone has delighted or struck me, I usually find when I have finished my picture that I have respected that tone, whereas I have gradually modified and transformed all the others. The expressive qualities of colours impress me purely instinctively. To paint an autumn landscape, I should not try to remember what colours were proper to that season, I should only be inspired by the sensation they gave me: the icy purity of the sky, which is an acid blue, would express the season just as well as the colours of the leaves. My sensation itself can vary: autumn can be sweet and warm like a prolonging of summer, or conversely cool with a cold sky and lemon-yellow trees, which give an impression of cold and already foretell the winter.

'The choice of colours does not rest for me on any scientific theory. It is based on observation, on sentiment, on what my sensibility has felt. An artist like Signac, inspired by certain pages of Delacroix, is preoccupied with complementaries, and theoretical knowledge of them leads him to employ such a tone in such a place. But I simply try to use the colours which express my sensation. An essential proportion of tones can induce me to modify the form of a figure or to transform my composition. Until I have obtained it, everywhere, I look for it and go on working. Then arrives the moment when all parts have found their final relationships, and after that I could not touch my picture again without repainting it entirely.

'Indeed, I do not believe that even the theory of complementaries is absolute. Studying the pictures of painters whose knowledge of colour rests on instinct and feeling, on a constant analogy with their sensations, it would be possible to define the laws of colour to some extent, and enlarge the bounds of the theory of colour as it is now understood.'

Priority of the figure

Those who deny a hierarchy to different forms of painting, who maintain that three apples on a plate interest them as much as Giotto's *Crucifixion*, could well consider the page where Matisse expresses his '*religious feeling for life*', a feeling so deeply rooted in him that it blossomed and transfigured his last years.

'What interests me most, is neither still life nor landscape, it is the figure. It is by the figure I can best express the almost religious feeling I have for life. I do

not attempt to portray all the details of a face, to render them one by one in exact anatomy. If I have an Italian model who suggests to me at first sight a purely animal existence, I discover in him, none the less, essential features, I go into the lines of his face, and discover those which express the character of profound gravity persistant in all human beings. A work should carry its whole meaning in itself and impress it on the spectator even before he has understood the subject. When I see Giotto's frescoes in Padua, I do not trouble to find out which scene in the life of Christ is before me, but I understand at once the feeling of it, for it is in the lines, the composition, the colour, and the title would only confirm my impression.'

What Matisse has to say besides on working from nature, is comparable to many pages written on that subject by Delacroix.

'People like to distinguish between painters who work directly from nature, and those who work purely from imagination. I do not think, myself, one should praise one of the two methods of work to the exclusion of the other. It happens that both are used in turn by the same person, either because he needs actual objects from which to receive impressions and thereby stimulate his creative faculty, or because his impressions are already classified, and in either case he can arrive at a whole which makes a picture. . . . However, I believe one can judge of an artist's vitality and power when, once directly impressed by the spectacle of nature, he is capable of organizing his sensations and even returning to them, on several occasions and different days, continuing them in the same state of mind. Such a power implies a man sufficiently master of himself to obey his own discipline.

'The simplest means are those which best allow an artist self-expression. If he is afraid of being commonplace, he will not avoid it by a strange exterior expression, in seeking bizarre drawing and eccentric colour. His means should derive almost essentially from his temperament. He should have the simplicity of mind which leads him to suppose he has only painted what he has seen.

'I like what Chardin said, "I put on colour until it looks like the thing." And Cézanne, "I want to paint an image." And also Rodin, "Copy nature." Leonardo said, "He who can copy can create." Those who use a deliberate style and depart from nature on purpose, are beside the truth. An artist should realize, when he reasons, that his picture is artificial, but while painting he should have the impression that he is copying nature. And even when he gets away from it, he should still feel convinced that he does so in order to render it more completely.'

ON COPY

That Henri Matisse never varied, in feeling the contact between artist and nature indispensable, is shown in the answer to my questions on non-figurative art, which he sent me in 1947.

I said, 'The background of El Greco, who has visibly influenced you, is Byzantine. Have you not been deeply impressed by the lineal side of Byzantine and Moslem art? Severini thought so and talked to me a long time about it.'

Matisse answered, *'Yes.'*

'You who have written, "what interests me most is neither still life nor landscape, it is the figure," what do you think of the non-figurative tendencies of the young school? Do not such tendencies lead to a dead end? How can the ideas of liberation and freedom be reconciled with the dictatorship of non-figurative art?'

Without hesitation, Henri Matisse replied:

'Starting from direct contact with nature as I do, I have never wanted to be confined inside a doctrine whose laws would prevent me from getting health and strength by contact with the earth, like Antaeus. It is always when I am in direct accord with my sensations of nature, that I feel I have the right to depart from them, the better to render what I feel. Experience has always proved me right.[1]

'What interests me most is neither still life, nor landscape, it is the figure. . . .'

It is difficult to reconcile those words of Henri Matisse, also borne out by the artist's whole evolution, with declarations which Aragon attributes to him in his fine essay, *Matisse-en-France*.[2]

'Henri Matisse states that his attitude toward one of those most voluptuous of models is in no way different (and one believes it most of the time) from his attitude toward a plant, vase or any object. . . .' What the artist must have meant was that all was voluptuous to him; and indeed he has expressed already his feeling of hierarchy and above all his love of the human figure.

Only during his last twenty years do his feminine nudes take on a sensual character, not unlike a similar development in the work of Ingres, at the same age of mastery and maturity—the Ingres of the *Bain Turc*.

And there is an anthropomorphic touch of antique fable, in a note connecting the woman and the tree. *'An acacia of Vesubia, its movement and slender grace, perhaps led me to visualize the figure of a woman dancing.'*[3]

This shows a healthy doctrine, one which is not far removed at heart from the essential virtues of our race, from the Cartesian philosophy which is found in all Frenchmen.

[1] Unpublished note of Henry Matisse.
[2] *Henri Matisse, Dessins, Thèmes et Variations* preceded by *Matisse-en-France*, Aragon, Martin Fabiani, 1943.
[3] Conversation of Henri Matisse with Tériade, *Minotaure*, 1934.

That everlasting classicism

'*There are no new truths*' proclaimed our great revolutionary (actually a great classicist at heart) to whom we nevertheless owe the discoveries which determine the trend of modern painting—the organization of sensation through coloured volume. 

It was with a desire to illustrate those theories that Matisse repeated the theme of his *Desserte* of 1898. *Desserte harmonie bleue*, and *Desserte harmonie rouge* (Stchoukine coll.), show the artist freed from detail, freed of all objective preoccupation, simply in search of fine polychrome arabesque.

Fernande Olivier, in her witty book *Souvenirs sur Picasso et ses amis*, describes Matisse at that time as 'Solemn, deeply serious, saying gravely "Yes" or "No", and embarking on endless discussions.'

We have seen that Picasso and Matisse met at the Steins' (Leo, Michael, Sarah and Gertrude), those American art-lovers who did so much for modern art in their homes of the *rue Fleurus* and the *rue Madame*. 'What a shame' said her servant to Gertrude Stein, looking at a nude by Matisse, 'to have done that to a pretty woman!' On which Gertrude Stein remarked subtly, 'So she saw that it was a pretty woman!'

Matisse, much older, serious, circumspect, never had the same ideas as Picasso. '*We are the North and South poles.*' he said of Picasso and himself.

According to Gertrude Stein, if Matisse introduced Picasso to Negro art and *Fauvisme*, the man from Malaga opened new horizons to Matisse on abstract art.[1]

It is no less true that twenty years later, Francis Carco still hesitated to speak of Picasso to Matisse. 'How was I to speak to him of Picasso? The old enmity, which had steadily been increasing between them since Cubism, might have spoiled the end of our conversation. It was likely that time and success had softened any old bitterness toward his former rival, but I couldn't be sure.'

Carco could very well have spoken of Picasso to Matisse by that time, for he had long since reached the age of serenity. But there was no need, for Matisse replied as follows, on August 30th, 1945, to all who might wonder about the judgements of the future:

'*About different modern trends, I remember Ingres and Delacroix, who seemed to differ in everything in their own day, so much so that their disciples were ready to fight it out for them had they so desired. Yet, today, their similarities are very apparent. Both expressed themselves by "arabesque" and "colour". Ingres, for*

[1] I had this from Gertrude Stein herself.

Matisse & Picasso

his full colour almost in compartments, was called "a Chinese lost in Paris".[1] *They forged the same links in the chain. Only the slightest of variations make it possible to tell them from one another.'*

Writing about *La Musique* twenty years later, Henri Matisse defined the development of his ideas on Divisionism and Fauvism, although he disliked, as he wrote me, '*words ending in -ism.*'

'*Neo-impressionism, or rather that part called divisionism, was the first attempt to take stock of the means of Impressionism; but the result was purely material, often mechanical, only corresponding to a physical emotion. The breaking up of colour led to the breaking up of form, of contour. Result: a jumpy surface. There is only a visual sensation, but it destroys tranquility of surface and outline. Objects are differentiated only by the luminosity given them. Everything is treated in the same way. Ultimately, there is only a sensory vibration, comparable to "vibrato" of voice or violin. As Seurat's pictures become greyer with time, they lose the theoretical side of his use of colour, and retain only their true values. Those human values in painting, which are today more intense than ever.*

'*Fauvism shook off the yoke of divisionism. One can't live in a house too well kept, a house kept by maiden aunts.*[2] *One has to go off into the jungle to find simpler ways for oneself which won't stifle the spirit. The influence of Gauguin and Van Gogh were felt then, too. The ideas of that time. Construction by coloured surfaces. Search for intensity of colour, without regard to texture. Reaction against the diffusion of local tone in light. Light is not suppressed, but it is achieved by a harmony of highly coloured surfaces. My picture,* la Musique, *was composed of a fine blue for the sky, the bluest of blues. The surface was coloured to saturation, to the point where the blue, the idea of absolute blue, was entirely evident, the green of the trees and the violent vermilion of the bodies. With those three colours I had my luminous harmony, and also purity of tone. Note, the colour was proportioned to form. Form was modified, according to the reaction of neighbouring colour. For the expression came from the coloured surface, which struck the spectator as a whole.'*[3]

After a brief stay in Algiers and Biskra in 1906, after the exhibition of Moslem art in Munich in 1910 where the painter of *Luxe* was able to see again a great collection of Islamic pottery, and after his voyage to Andalusia, Matisse had but one wish, to go to North Africa. Every winter from 1910 to 1913, he was drawn

[1] It is little known that Victor Hugo, aged 17, was undoubtedly the first to connect Chinese art with Ingres, in the *Conversation Littéraire*, 1819, 'That *Odalisque* by M. Ingres, painted in the Chinese manner, without shadow or relief.'

[2] Amusing memory of the interiors of his relatives of Bohain and Cateau.

[3] Interview with Tériade (*l'Intransigeant*, 14.1. '29).

to Algiers and Morocco, where he found Marquet and Camoin as guides. He became assured of his decorative feeling for the external world, his taste for sober line and pure, essential colour.

Those journeys had a decisive and permanent influence on his work. The light of the Moghreb induced him to simplify his composition even further, to suppress all unnecessary details and superfluous tones; the light and the ceramics, the glazed tiles of the mosques were to affect his painting from then on.

Hence, those large compositions for Stchoukine, in three colours, *La Danse* and *La Musique*, expressing joy and sunlight, as the master had wished, like a symphony.

'We have seen an amazing picture at the *Salon d'Automne*, *La Danse*' wrote Marcel Sembat, 'A ring of pink figures madly whirling on a blue ground. On the left, the tallest leads the dance. What intoxication! What a bacchante! Superb arabesque, alluring curve from the averted head to thrust of the hip and long, tense leg. The very incarnation, to me, of Nietzsche's orgiastic dithyramb, the passion of young Greece.'

Matisse had hardly finished it before he decided it was too materially passionate, dionysiac, agitated. He drew for himself the true *Danse*, which he saw after painting the other, as if born of the first. It is a charcoal drawing of an ample dance, solemn and calm.

Here, calm means classicism, that which Baudelaire saw in the master of *la Sybille au Rameau d'or*, and Jules Romains in the painter of *Joie de Vivre*. What he had to say with such delicacy yesterday, remains as true today, and will tomorrow.

'Classicism' as he said ten years ago, 'is neither a quality nor a technique, it is a structure.' And understanding it in that sense, sooner or later one must see, I think, how the different arts of our country, since the twentieth century began, have happily attempted to regain classical dignity.

'Of course the most vulgar processes have remained in favour, and the public shows no sign of tiring of them. On the other hand we have seen many a desperate attempt to break the old spell of tradition; with such tense gestures and strident cries of despair, no amount of complacence could find any promise in them of joy and serenity! But statistics do not show the truth about an epoch in art. . . . And among thousands of contradictory daubs, it is enough that a few great works agree, for one human phase to find face and voice.

'If our age in the future wins the praise which I venture to give it here, it seems to me it will be owing to a few painters, and notably to Henri Matisse.

'His work is no desperate effort, nor the incoherent rage of a prisoner cursing too-solid walls. The most striking aspect of his painting is its daring, the most applauded or deplored, its open lack of conformity. But neither admirers nor detractors of Matisse have the right to stop there. It is important not to confuse anarchy and autonomy, although the appearance of autonomy sometimes seems disordered.

'With each work, Matisse showed more clearly the balance at which he was aiming, the peak of self-mastery to which he was climbing. And now his maturity gives real contentment of mind.

'He has not reached "an age of reason", depressing term which usually denotes the decline of artistic creation, renunciation of youth, surrender to mediocrity. Quite the reverse, he is further than ever from recognized formulae. He is self-possessed and controlled, with a wonderful economy of means.

'That is how he will, in his own time, join with eternal classicism, which is a "structure", not a collection of subjects or an arsenal of procedures. It is the other name for style, which gives nobility to an Ode by Horace, a Japanese drawing, a prelude by Bach, a poem by Goethe, Baudelaire or Mallarmé.'[1]

It was in the land of Islam, so loved by young Delacroix, the chief of romantics, that Henri Matisse, the first of the *Fauves*, discovered classical calm and style. He found there, like his illustrious forerunner, substance for his art until the end of his days; he too will have his *Femmes d'Alger*, his obsessing and fascinating *Odalisques*.

[1] *Henri Matisse* by Jules Romains.

III
MUSIC IN COLOUR

Camoin

It will be a long time before lovers of modern art forget the exhibition at Bernheims, *rue Richepanse*, of Henri Matisse's Moroccan pictures of 1913. 'There was a Moorish café there, with long bodies reclining round a bowl of goldfish, which seemed a symbol of his longing for calm; and the immense green warrior so proudly planted there, is one of the most significant figures ever produced by his brush.[1] But the gardens were particularly revealing. I know one, repeated three times, and each time more decorative, calm and simple in its abstraction. The first time I saw it, the trees and grasses on the ground struck me by their original life; then the ground melted into a uniform tone, the grasses became a garland of lianas, the trees changed into trees of an earthly Paradise, and today the whole painting breathes a sense of idyllic repose.'[2]

Several stages mark the progress of Matisse: the Louvre, Corsica, Collioure, Nice, the West Indies, the United States, Vence and Cimiez.

We must not forget Tangiers, which exercised as strong an influence as Collioure on his technique, his ideas, and the evolution of his art.

Two good companions and true friends went with him to Morocco: Albert Marquet, in the winter of 1911–12; and the next year, Camoin and the Canadian painter, James W. Morrice.

There, confronted by that antique world, a light which destroys detail and only brings out essentials, Matisse was at last free of Paris. He could 'come down to earth' again, forgetting doctrines and doctrinaires, reaching that absolute simplicity, a kind of pictorial nirvana, without which, according to the painter of *la Danse*, no art endures.

Three months spent in Marrakesh and Fez had decided the trend of Delacroix's whole life as a painter; and Matisse never tired of telling those round him how much he owed to Morocco. Tériade heard him say, '*Those visits to Morocco helped me to make a necessary transition, and to gain a closer contact*

[1] *Standing Riffian*, Moscow Museum Stchoukine coll. *Seated Riffian*, green and yellow harmony, Merion.

[2] Marcel Sembat op. cit.

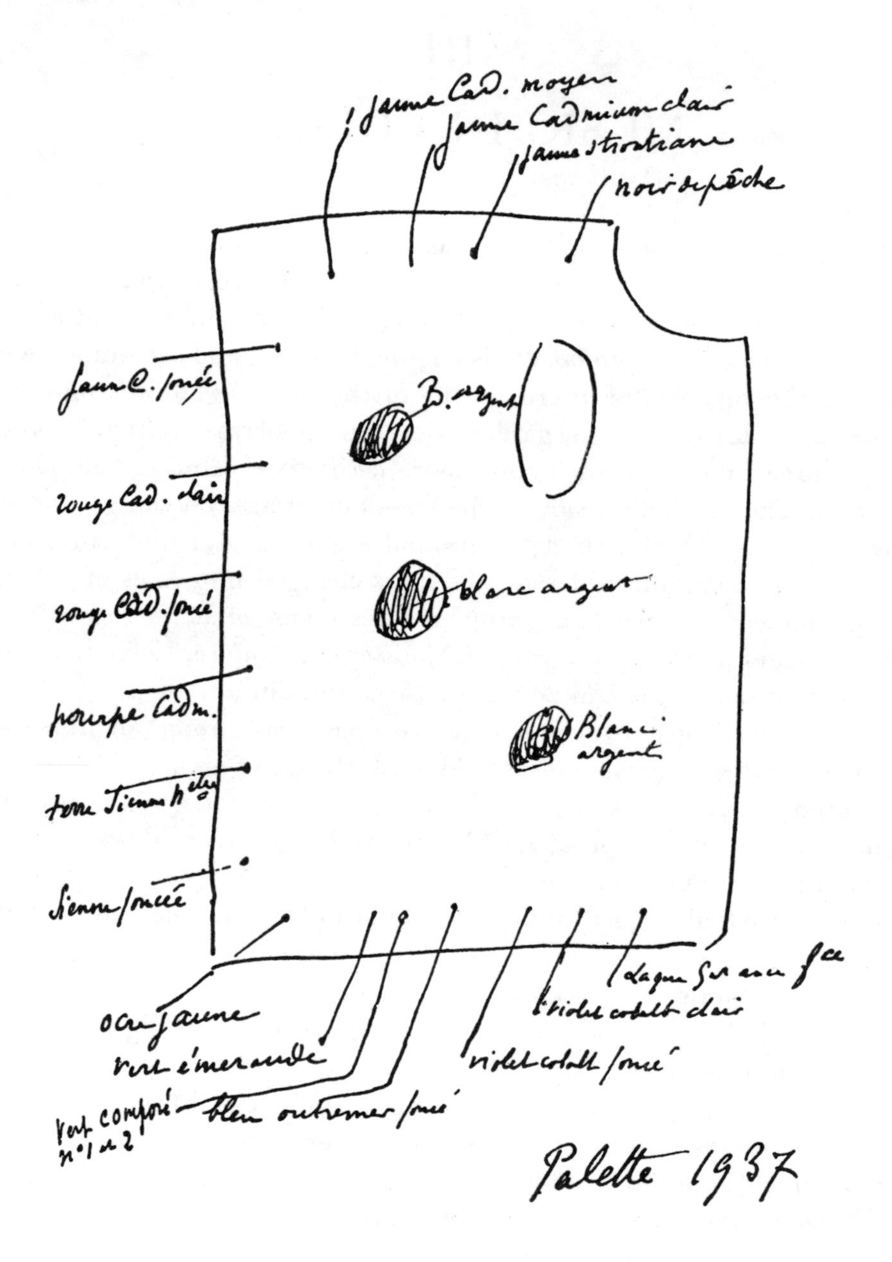

Jaune Cad. moyen
Jaune Cadmium clair
Jaune strontiane
noir de pêche
Jaune C. foncée
rouge Cad. clair
rouge Cad. foncé
pourpre Cadm.
Sienne foncée
B. argent
Blanc argent
Blanc argent
ocre jaune
vert émeraude
vert composé n° 1 et 2
bleu outremer foncé
violet cobalt foncé
violet cobalt clair
Palette 1937

with nature than would the practice of any theory such as Fauvism had become, alive but somewhat limited.'

I asked Charles Camoin what he remembered of the journey to Morocco, in the early spring of 1913—with Henri Matisse, his friend since the visit to Corsica in 1899. That fine artist, whose painting was full of *joie de vivre*, accompanied Madame Henri Matisse to Tangiers, and in spite of the extreme modesty of that great-hearted woman, I feel I must repeat what Charles Camoin said of her: 'His marriage was a happy one for him—Madame Amélie Matisse, exceptionally devoted, working to leave him free to paint! Charming, courageous, and full of faith in her husband's talent.

'It was in her company that I went to join Matisse in Tangiers, where we spent the three Spring months of 1913.

'In those days, Matisse was a very devoted friend, not as solemn as he became later, given to reasoning and explaining everything by A + B, but with a generous spirit and heart, too.'

In spite of what he said himself, Matisse was then an excellent horseman. (Madame Alexina Matisse has a good photograph of the painter on horseback, taken then, which Alfred Barr reproduced in his book.) Camoin confirms this, 'Matisse, a very good rider, initiated me into that noble sport, which his wife did not quite appreciate. We led a happy life together. Henri Matisse always felt this too. On July 23rd, 1944, at Vence, he recalled to "*his very dear Camoin, those beautiful hours in Morocco*" and strangely, "*Madame Matisse, petulant and gentle partner at dominoes in Tangiers*"! And in cruelly trying times, the master asked, "*do you remember those days, those happy days?*"[1]

'Then the 1914–18 war kept me in the trenches, and toward the end, working on camouflage. Matisse wrote asking me to let him know everything I needed. . . .'[2]

Moscow and Stchoukine

Before going to Tangiers, Matisse had been summoned to Moscow by Stchoukine, and there he had discovered those Byzantine ikons, to which the art of El Greco owes so much. Coming after the revelation of Moslem art at the Paris and Munich exhibitions, this definitely attracted Matisse to the East. We know that Persian pottery was his special guide in the difficult path he had chosen. And even the abstractions in the technique of Islam served as encouragement when it came to the audacious decoration of the *Chapelle du Rosaire*.

[1] Unpublished letter from Henri Matisse to Charles Camoin.
[2] Letter from Charles Camoin to R.E. January 14th, 1955.

When I asked him, in 1948, about the impressions gathered in Russia, Matisse said to me,

'In Russia I saw ikons to equal the French primitives. In comparison with the Mediterranean, I found myself in Asia. What a future that country has, so rich in every way!

'Revelation had always come to me from the East,' he said to Gaston Diehl, *'At Munich, I found many of my theories confirmed. The Persian miniatures, for instance, showed me the full possibilities of my sensations. That art, by its accessories suggests a greater space, a really plastic space. It helped me to get away from intimate painting. So it was quite late when that art affected me, and I understood Byzantine painting by contemplation of the ikons of Moscow.'*

And at the same interview, the master explained how the Orient had inspired him to the utmost daring. *'One goes forward with greater confidence when one's efforts are confirmed by a tradition, however ancient. It helps one to jump the ditch.'*[1]

Encounter with Cubism

Matisse returned from his two visits to Morocco and contemplation of those long, blue-shadowed walls, with a new sense of construction which made him sympathetic to the discoveries of the cubists; these also recognized him as a master. . . . Following his lead, they studied the radiant quality in the colour of objects. Like Matisse, they dissociated the structural elements of external reality to pursue the separate study of each one. Perhaps an article by Gino Severini best explains the common ground of Matisse's researches and those of the cubists. 'Matisse one day showed me a study he had made from nature, in a Tangiers street. In the foreground, a wall painted blue. That blue influenced all the rest, and Matisse had given it the greatest importance possible in keeping the objective structure of the landscape. Nevertheless, he had to admit he had not expressed the hundredth part of the "sensuous intensity" produced on him by that blue. He had attained that degree of intensity in another picture (*Les Marocains*), but here the real architecture of the landscape had gone to make way for an intentional yet sensuous one.'

'This makes clear' said André Lhote, 'how the mechanism by which M. Matisse subordinates absolutely his plastic sense to that of colour, is parallel to the Cubist mechanism "to reconstruct" reality plastically by colour as the essential means. This comparison enables us to fix the mental process of the two

[1] Gaston Diehl, op. cit.

opposed schools; in which M. Matisse proceeds from the sensation to the idea, the cubists from the idea to the sensation.'[1]

There indeed lies the disagreement which increased with the years. As opposed to the cubists, Henri Matisse, who valued the shock to his senses above everything, never thought or could think of writing without consulting his 'dictionary', as Delacroix called nature,[2] the external world, and the successive states of his most recent pictures show him always anxious to study the objective truth before looking for a stylization.[3]

Nevertheless, at that same stage, while he affirms his preoccupation with form by underlining it with a firm stroke, as in the *Nu au bracelet*, Matisse does seem influenced by the cubists. One feels a geometric bias, as a will to synthetic structure in his important works from 1915 to 1917. (*Les Poissons rouges avec personnages, la Leçon de Piano; Le Peintre dans son atelier; les Jeunes filles au bain.*) In the last, Matisse carried simplification to the extreme, which allowed Jacques-Emile Blanche to say, with some slyness, the technique of Matisse 'consists of suppression'.

Morocco

As early as 1907, the impact of Islam on the work of Matisse is evident in the *Nu bleu* (*Souvenir de Biskra*) (Baltimore Art Museum) which was formerly owned by Leo Stein. The nude is lying in flowered green grass, against a background of palms, streaked with cadmium, madder and emerald green. Still belonging to the Fauve period, it shows a powerful deformation of right hip and feet: It was painted at Collioure on the return from Biskra, and could as well have taken its decorative palms from the Côte Vermeille, where they abound between Perpignan and Banyuls, especially at Collioure.

L'Algérienne of 1909 (*Musée National d'art Moderne* in Paris) is also *Fauve.* Except for the intense black of the hair, it might pass for a portrait of Colette at that time, with its feline gaze, nose like the curve of a dagger, avid gash of a mouth, and powerful jaws giving weight to a triangular chin. Black leonine mane, black underlining vehement curves, heightening the pink and green striped haïck, a vermilion and Prussian blue background. Decidedly after Cézanne, and contrary to the Impressionist and divisionist theories, this was a return to black.

Black appears triumphant in many of his most famous pictures of that period, notably in *Grande Nature morte aux aubergines* (1911–12) which was on show

[1] André Lhote, *La Peinture*, pp. 36–8.
[2] '*There is no dictionary for painters, poor things*' Matisse, noted by Aragon.
[3] Tériade, *Constance du Fauvisme, Henri Matisse, De la Couleur* (*Verve*, Vol. IV, no. 13, 1945.)

at the *Exposition d'Art Indépendant* at the Petit Palais in 1937, to the marvel of visitors, and was later given by Madame Matisse-Duthuit to André Farcy, for the Grenoble Museum.

There are fine, nocturnal blacks in the vast composition designed for Stchoukine, representing a corner of the studio at Collioure, over which play like a precious Chinese silk, pure tones of turquoise blue and flax blue, jade greens and viridian, cinnabar and bright pink. Two figs and three egg-plants are lying on a table near a terracotta statuette. And this, after the discoveries of Munich, Moscow and Morocco, is as far from Fauvism as from neo-Impressionism. Indeed, this work already foretells the cut-outs to which Matisse devoted himself at the end of his life. It is done in distemper, which shows the relationship between the two techniques.

Most of the pictures painted in Morocco at this time, are more subdued and austere, with an increasing trend to simplification. Occasionally, in Tangiers, the artist wandered in the gardens, with Camoin and Marquet. He was perhaps influenced by them, when he painted *Paysage vu d'une fenêtre* (Moscow Museum of Western art) and the *Jardin Marocain* (Chicago, Samuel A. Marx coll.) which Marcel Sembat describes so well. The truth is that here Matisse simply gave way to delight in seeing and in painting.

The pictures inspired at that time by Zorah, a young Moroccan girl, are of quite another quality. They bear witness to the artist's constant quest for greatness through submission to the eternal laws of the mind. These pictures show the full value of renunciation and sacrifice; which are, as we know today, the very characteristics of genius, often heroic; for whom art, just as love, can only be proved by sacrifice. In *Zorah debout* (1912, Moscow Mus. of Mod. Art) or *Zorah en jaune, accroupie, Zorah sur la terrasse* (1913, Moscow Mus. of Mod. Art) we see the same wild young girl with long, almond eyes, sensitive nose and mouth like a cherry, with her many-coloured dress, or in a simple one caught up with woollen braid. In these important pictures (two are well over three feet high) everything shows the artist's resolve to discard for the time his joyful coloured symphonies of Oriental silks and pottery.

There is another kind of energy, an epic virility in *The Riffian* (Barnes Foundation, Merion) painted in 1913, which Sembat, remembering our first illumined books, compared to the Saracens in the *Chanson de Roland*. That great canvas (79″ × 63″), with its yellow, green and red ochre harmonies, does indeed attain an epic power. It is clearly related to our most famous medieval tapestries. It is magnificently barbaric.

Later, in 1916, having gone through Cubism, Futurism and Orphism, Matisse resumed all he owed to Tangiers in a composition nearly abstract yet perfectly intelligible—*Les Marocains* (New York Museum of Modern Art). On a black ground, Moroccans at prayer stand in the left foreground, turbans orange and clothes green—the colours of the Prophet: in the background, a stylized mosque. On the right, a Moroccan in yellow turban and robe, under a blue burnous, turns his back and seems to contemplate the pink walls of a house. Agnès Humbert appreciated the hidden character, 'This unreal composition, nearly abstract, suggests above all a notion of intense, physical heat and the moral certainty of an immutable, as it were, eternal order.'

The Closed Shutters

Since 1914, we have seen that works of a decorative nature began to make way for an expression of greater weight, built upon depth by planes, an intimate painting which lasted more than twenty years. The painter who copied Chardin and David de Heem, must have returned to the humble objects of our daily lives with a kind of secret, voluptuous joy. No one else, particularly from the time he lived in Nice, has painted with such brilliant grace the magnificence of a shot or embroidered material, the splendour of a bunch of flowers glowing in a still interior, in cool shade, behind closed shutters. Many, since Matisse, have closed the shutters against the glare of the sun, many have opened windows on the sea; but where can one find such delicate blue, dove grey, tender green, such rare colour in the shadow, or such, rich, flaming colour where the Southern sun floods the room with its light?

Perhaps André Rouveyre has most delicately expressed the effect of shutters on the genius of Matisse. 'Shutters always play a fine part in the settings of Matisse. They appear in his pictures as the mobile frontier between his boundless country and his private world. It is there that the pointed arrows of sunlight break for him, or filter through, or frankly enter in. There begins the field of his spiritual and visual sensuality, his pensive emotions, his concertos of colour, where often women play a part, dressed or nude, but always subject to something latent and imperious which is the sovereignty of the artist. The rooms in his pictures are haunted by variations on the delight of discovery and the anguish of search. Shutters to Matisse, intimate painter of interiors, are like a parasol in a vast landscape. With them, more even than Joshua with his trumpet, he is master of the sun.'[1]

[1] André Rouveyre, 'Henri Matisse', *Verve*, Vol. IV, 13.

That is precisely with what Maurice Denis reproached him in 1906, to be 'master of the sun', what infernal pride!

'. . . multi-coloured brush-strokes on a white canvas, a mark, a line, a suggestion of colour, suffices to suggest all the brutality of solar light.'[1]

Vain research, according to Denis. But the Denis of 1906 and Matisse of 1918–1920 should agree on one golden rule: '*What matters, is that a picture should constitute a harmony of colour.*'

Volunteer for Verdun

Then came the 1914–18 war. We can't do better than turn back to the lucid Gertrude Stein: 'The Matisses stayed in Clamart more or less until the war. They were lonesome and troubled, Matisse's family in Saint-Quentin, in the north, were within the German lines and his brother was a hostage. It was Madame Matisse who taught me how to knit woollen gloves. She made them wonderfully neatly and rapidly and I learned to do so too. . . .'

The life of Matisse became increasingly sad. He suffered not only anxiety for his family but also as a true Frenchman, for France.

'One can't forget in all this,' wrote Aragon in 1943 'that Matisse is French. A Frenchman from the North, one of those fittest to unite all the diversity of France. . . . Also nearly forty years of Matisse's life were spent in Nice. . . . So there was in him a synthesis of France. . . . The North and the South. Reason and unreason. Imitation and invention. Mist and sun. Inspiration and reality. But the contrasts are in the man, in his attitude, and what he says: his work is indeed a balance of contraries, France.'

As good patriots, Henri Matisse and Albert Marquet were burning to defend France otherwise than brush in hand; and in spite of their age beyond the service limit, the two friends longed to take part in the battle of Verdun. (Both Matisse and Marquet had been rejected for constitutional weakness.) The two artists agreed to ask the advice of their faithful friend, Marcel Sembat, whom the war had made a minister. They did not agree with a certain *Fauve*, of ferocious appearance but very anxious to be out of harm's way. '*Derain, Braque, Camoin, Puy, are at the front risking their lives. . . . We are sick of staying at home. . . . How can we serve the country?*'

Sembat answered briefly,

'By continuing to paint as well as you do.'

Matisse and Marquet went away, but little satisfied, especially as the former had personal reasons to dislike the Germans, who had acclaimed him a few

[1] Maurice Denis, *Théories* (*Le Soleil*).

D. La liseuse distraite (1919)

London, Tate Gallery

years earlier in Munich and Berlin. His exhibition, organized in 1914, had been frozen and finally, in spite of Purrmann's efforts, scattered to the four winds.

He said himself, '*All who could go on working like me, found it immeasurably difficult to do so.*'

Remembering the anxiety Matisse felt at being unable 'to take part in the struggle of Verdun', Agnès Humbert says of *Demoiselles de la Rivière* (1916–17, H. Pearlman Coll., New York) 'that picture gives one a strange impression of uneasiness and disquiet, no doubt cruelly felt by the artist at that time in his life.'

And we have the best evidence of the feelings of Matisse during those trying years, a letter given to me by Derain's widow, written to that fine artist when he was at the front, in 1916. Matisse is preoccupied with the disintegration of matter in these pages, just as Delacroix foretold the coming of tanks, in the second Empire. The painter of *Bonheur de Vivre* was again living at 19 *Quai Saint-Michel.*

'*Monday*

My dear Derain,

We were pleased to have your letter, although I have been very long in replying. The month of January has been a nasty one for us! We have all had 'flu badly, except Marguerite, and I mean badly! Three of us were in bed at the same time. Personally I had it in the nose, with otitis, and just escaped sinus trouble. I only suffered in the head, but that made up for all the rest! Otitis gave me unpleasant turns of giddiness. Marguerite was also very ill. In short, we can produce a tale of woe: You see, it is not all roses behind the lines. In addition, we painters see our beautiful work moving further and further away from us—beautiful only in our dreams. The absence of family news, and continual anguish from the uncertainty in which we live, the little we know, and all that is concealed from us, you can imagine the life of a civilian in wartime.

'. . . *I have seen Camoin lately. He has just entered the Camouflage Corps. After two weeks of his pictorial performances, he writes me it is an appallingly trying job. He is working in Champagne—all morning he unloads bales of canvas, and all night, and the next night, he sets up his efforts between the French and Boche lines, where he is more exposed than he was in the trenches. . . . That is not the case with everyone. Some have not left the Paris studios. Laprade, for instance. Camoin saw him as a sergeant. In the midst of the daubers, he looked like a generalissimo in command.*

'*I must tell you that Camoin is commanded by Guirand de Scevola and Abel Truchet, to whom Camoin is enemy no 1. It's bad to have fallen into their hands.*

'Galanis is luckier. He is still at Montargis, as librarian. He fiddles about with books most of the time. He has just read La Science et l'Hypothèse *by Henri Poincaré, in which he found the origin of cubism! ! !*

'Have you read it? There are such daring hypotheses, one feels quite dizzy. The last one, for instance, on the destruction of matter. Movement exists only by means of the destruction and reconstruction of matter.

'Poincaré admits that the proof is not yet complete (the hypothesis is Langevin's) I'll send it to you if you don't know it.

'My wife is at Collioure, just now, moving from our house which we are giving up altogether.

'I sold my picture after David de Heem, to Rosenberg. Madame Derain came to see us the day I delivered it, and I couldn't even tell her the buyer's name, for he begged me not to speak of it.

'At his place I saw a Picasso in a new manner, a Harlequin, with nothing pasted on, only painting. Perhaps you know it?

'In a few days the Triennale opens. I am sorry not to have the prospectus. You would have relished it.

'Forgive this higgledy-piggledy letter, I let myself go. . . .

'A warm handshake,

H. Matisse'[1]

Fascination of the south

George Besson gives a lively, faithful account of how Matisse came to live in Nice, in 1917.

For nearly twenty years, Matisse was under the spell of the South, like so many Flemish, Norman and Lorrain painters, Van Eyck, Poussin and Claude.

As we know, it began in the beautiful island of Corsica, where the artist lived for over a year, in a paradise of light. '*At Ajaccio,*' he wrote me in 1948, '*I discovered the wonders of the South for the first time.*'

Later, he had been to Collioure, St.-Tropez, Spain, Algiers, Morocco, and briefly to Italy.

In the cruel winter of 1917, when his native town was destroyed by the enemy, and there was no more art life in Paris, Matisse decided to follow his inclination and settle in the South. He had found a new form of beauty there fourteen years before, a new poetry in colour. Although Vanderpyl could see no poetry in Matisse, another Norman-Mediterranean, Raoul Dufy, saw it very well:

[1] Unpublished.

'After the realism of Impressionist colour, in the picture called *Luxe, Calme et Volupté*, exhibited at the *Indépendants* about 1905, Matisse introduced an imaginative quality, poetry, or better, the music of colour. It was my great revelation, a new reason for painting.'[1]

In December, 1917, Matisse broke his journey first at Marseilles, and such a painter could find no better port of call.

There his dear Marquet was installed on the *Quai de Rive Neuve*, in a room sublet from Eugène Montfort. Matisse put up at the hotel Beauveau, which has once again become one of the best hotels in Marseilles, overlooking the great Phocæan port. Anyone who has lodged there *en route* for Corsica, the Moghreb or the East, will not easily forget the sight.

After making a few studies from a wharf of the *Vieux Port*, and toying with a fancy to pitch his tent in Estaque, where Cézanne painted, Matisse decided on Nice. 'It was about December 20th, 1917' says George Besson, 'that Matisse took up his residence at the hotel *Beau Rivage* in Nice, later at the hotel *de la Méditerranée* on the *Promenade des Anglais*, then for two summer months with one of his sons, in the small '*Villa des Alliés*' standing in the luscious *Parc Harris* under *Mont-Boron*, in the midst of eucalyptus, olive trees, cypress, rose hedges and wild anemones: finally in the *place Charles-Félix*, in the quarter of old trading streets, the church of Sainte-Répérate, the steps leading to the castle, and markets steeped in the rough smell of the sea, *pissaladières*, and carnations.

'From these successive lodgings, Matisse found the serenity in Nice which he needed for his work. There he painted portraits, landscapes, and the first three-coloured interiors of his hotel bedroom: red in the carpet, white in the long, muslin curtains, blue in the sea, or a half-open violin-case.'[2]

Renoir at Colettes

Above all there was Renoir near Nice, at Cagnes. The first interview Renoir-Matisse, is described by George Besson: 'Matisse first went to Cagnes to pay his respects on December 31st, 1917; and Renoir was evidently astonished by the apparition of such an impeccable, sumptuous person, whose pale felt hat harmonized with his ample Shetland wool overcoat of a rare colour—chosen by a painter's eye. Perhaps he had imagined Matisse as some of the legendary figures of Montparnasse at the time (Soutine, Modigliani). . . . Matisse confronting

[1] 'Hommages à Matisse' (*Les Lettres Françaises*, December 2nd, 1952.).
[2] George Besson, 'Matisse et Renoir, il y a trente-cinq ans (*Les Lettres Françaises*, December 1952).

Renoir, crippled and shrunken in his armchair, his eyes sharp and piercing under his grey cap, might have been the ambassador Rubens presenting his credentials to some ancient pope Pius, Gregory or Leo.'

Afterwards Matisse took his first pictures painted in Nice to Renoir, at the beginning of 1918: *La Baie des Anges* (*vue du Château à travers les pins*) his *Portrait* just finished, and that first of the series which so many have imitated, *Fenêtre Ouverte* which charmed Renoir. 'How well you have caught the atmosphere of a hotel bedroom in Nice. Why, I wonder, does that blue of the sea not jump forward? How does that black bar above the curtains remain in its proper place? Everything is right. And it was a challenge, right enough! It makes me furious!'

And when Matisse had left, Renoir, laughing and making random movements with a paint-brush, said 'I thought the fellow worked like that! Quite wrong! He certainly takes a good deal of trouble!'

The theorist of pure tone was able to explain his doctrine to the old master. 'The two painters were soon on friendly terms' says George Besson. 'Renoir loved to talk. He told about the hard years of his apprenticeship. And the *gavroche* old painter told Matisse how Vollard had come to him for material for a serious book, and received a lot of absurd, invented stories. And he listened good-humouredly to Matisse, methodical in his work as in everything, who took the liberty of warning the old painter against certain dubious colour-mixtures.'

Renoir had many anxieties at that time, beside his own sad state of health, so lamentably obvious in a snapshot taken by Vollard. His son Jean was a constant worry. After the battle of Bapaume he was threatened with peritonitis; he was seriously wounded as a subaltern in the 6th Alpine Battalion in 1915; then when he was invalided out of the army in 1917, he joined the aviation as pilot in a reconnaissance squadron. Indeed, he was such an anxiety to his parents, that Madame Renoir died of sorrow. As we know, the war hero became a brilliant film producer.

After the offensive of April 17th had failed, trench warfare began again.

'They ought to kill off the old and infirm in those holes, not all these young men.' said the great Renoir, 'We're the ones who ought to be there.'

Life in Cagnes and his own work, however, consoled him for all his sufferings.

'Never' said his old friend, Georges Rivière, 'was he more prodigal of brilliant fresh colour than in the many nudes of that period, never did he express more joy in all he painted.'

'Doctor' Matisse nurses Carco

From Nice, when he wasn't visiting Renoir at Cagnes, Matisse sometimes went to see different friends on the coast, Simon Bussy at Cabbé-Roquebrune, Rouveyre at Vence, Bonnard at Antibes. . . . Sometimes he even spent an evening at the cinema. 'And what about love, Matisse?' asked George Besson one day.

Imprudent question. Like Delacroix, the master of *Joie de Vivre* was a man of great reserve. '*Love*' he replied to his indiscreet questioner. . . . '*Not very compatible with hard work . . . one can't express oneself fully in all ways. . . .*'

About this time, in Nice, at the *Hôtel de la Méditerranée*, Matisse made the acquaintance of Francis Carco, author of *Jésus-la-Caille*. He gives a touching account of how he was nursed by Henri Matisse during an attack of influenza.

'We had adjoining rooms. One morning, Matisse came into mine.

' "*Well, well!*" he said to me in his furry voice, coming to the bed, "*What's the matter? Ill?*"

'I had 'flu. Matisse felt my pulse, and by his grave manner, I knew why his comrades, at *père* Jambon's, had nicknamed him "the Doctor".

' "*What a bore,*" he said, "*I started a canvas yesterday at Cimiez and the car is waiting for me. Never mind. Wait a minute!*"

'He left the room, and came back with several pictures, a hammer and nails. In an instant, the nails were planted in the walls, the pictures hung. Matisse pulled his cape about his shoulders.

' "*There!*" he said, "*Until tonight. I'll come and see how you are. Stay in bed, take care of yourself! My painting will keep you company.*" '

Strangely enough, Madame Albert Marquet told me he did the same for her husband when he was ill.

Carco reminded Matisse of this in 1941, and it brought back to the master all the colours of the Nice caravanserai, and the windows of the *Hôtel de le Méditerranée*, giving on the blue sea.

'*An excellent old hotel, indeed! And what pretty Italian ceilings! What tiles! It was a great mistake to tear it down. I stayed there four years for the pleasure of painting. Do you remember the light that came through the shutters? It came from below, like stage lighting. Everything was fake, absurd, surprising, delicious. . . .*'

The violin and the false notes

Life in Nice was strictly organized by Matisse from the beginning. When he wasn't painting he was sculpting, says George Besson. 'The day after his arrival at the hotel *Beau-Rivage*, Matisse had already arranged his austere, laborious life. Between the morning and the afternoon's work (when he modelled for some time at the *École des Arts décoratifs de Nice* from Michaelangelo's *Night*) he would eat a frugal lunch in a dairy, spend an hour under a parasol at the *café Pommel*, *place Masséna*, and another hour playing the violin in a distant bathroom of the hotel '*so as not to plague the neighbours*'.

Ingres had first earned his living as a violinist. And later, contrary to legend, had charmed young Gounod, his accompanist at the Villa Medicis. Delacroix interpreted Mozart brilliantly on the violin. He had almost chosen music as a career. And Matisse practised this art for a long time.

It is not surprising that those three masters wanted to transpose the musical arabesque on to canvas.

If one is to believe Gaston Bernheim, however, Matisse hardly attained the skill of Ingres or Delacroix. It is an amusing anecdote.

'Matisse was taking lessons from Parent and, for the sum of his fees, sent him a magnificent drawing, with the inscription, "*For all my wrong notes.*"

'As the lessons went on, one day Parent said to him, "What's the matter, Matisse? Are your ears plugged? It's all off the key."

' "*I understand,*" said Matisse, "*You want another drawing for my wrong notes.*" '

The secret of the artist's mania for music at that time, was explained to me after his death, by Madame Henri Matisse. I was speaking of the complaint which threatened his eyesight in his last years, which was looked after by Dr Madeleine Schiff, head doctor at Quinze-Vingts, sister of Professor Wertheimer. His widow gave this surprising answer. 'The trouble, really, must have come from his early days, for I have always known my husband worried for fear of losing his sight. To such an extent, that when we came to live in Nice in 1918, obsessed by this idea, he began seriously studying the violin, and when I asked him why, Henri told me quite simply, "*It's a fact that I'm afraid I shall lose my sight, and not be able to paint any more. So I thought of something. A blind man must give up painting, but not music. . . . So I could always play the violin in the streets. I should still be able to earn our living, yours and Margot's and mine.*" '

For close on forty years, in spite of the 1940 cataclysm, Matisse loved and longed for Nice, as a haven of grace.

'Landscapes, interiors, odalisques, all show this delight in that country, the light, scent, and carefree feeling of its long, sweet days.'

Prophecies of André Gide

In his *Promenade au Salon d'Automne* in 1905, the year of the *cage aux Fauves*, André Gide demonstrated how those colour constructions were premeditated, mind always controlling matter.

'For convenience sake, I will admit that M. Henri Matisse has a beautiful native gift. In fact, he has given us, in the past, works full of imagination, reverie and happy vigour. . . . The pictures he shows today look like the exposition of theorems . . . I stayed a long time in that room. I listened to the people passing through, and when I heard them exclaim about Matisse's work: "Its mad!", I wanted to reply, "Oh, no, Monsieur, quite the reverse. It is the product of theory." Everything there can be deduced and explained; intuition has no part in it. No doubt, when M. Matisse paints a woman's face apple-green, and a tree trunk bright red, he can explain, "It's because. . . ."

'Yes, that painting is reasonable, one might even say, reasoned.

'What a long way from the lyric fury of a painter like Van Gogh! And behind the scenes I hear, "All tones should be excessive. . . ." The enemy of all painting is grey.[1] Let no artist be afraid of going too far.'

'I understand also, from watching "the others" pretend to style by use of connectives and clichés, holding on to transitions as cover for their timidity and support for would-be boldness, never daring to let go a line, a contour, a colour, reinforcing it and darkening it in the shadows; I understand how you drove yourself to extremes. . . . "To write well" said Montaigne, "skip intermediate ideas."'

'But,' went on André Gide—and in Matisse of 1905 he foresaw Matisse of 1940–50—'but art does not consist of doing away with "syntax". Honour to him, rather, who can enlarge the least of terms, reveal the value of the smallest conjunction!'

And this penetrating definition of the art of Matisse: 'Art does not exist in extremes; it is a "tempered" thing. Tempered by what?—By reason, by Jove! But by reasoning reason.'

And just about the same time, the very opposite could be read on the walls of Montparnasse: 'Matisse makes you mad, Matisse is more dangerous than absinthe. . . .'

What André Gide so well named 'reasoning reason', was to prevent Nice from playing the same part in the great adventure of Matisse, as Capua after

[1] Impressionist tenet, refuted by the works of the great masters of painting, Vermeer de Delft, Velasquez, Courbet, Corot, Daumier . . . and Matisse.

Hannibal's victories. The painter of *Bonheur de vivre* was not at all submerged by all that beauty, he used it as an unfailing source of inspiration.

It was undoubtedly in Nice that Matisse 'renounced his elementary force of 1905–10, compromise between abstraction and sensuality, for a tendency toward more objective truth and confirmation of his life-long aim (which was also Debussy's): "*I am engaged in creating an art intelligible to any spectator, whatever his culture.*"'

By an apparently indirect road, an increasingly subtle orchestration of colour, Matisse found a new arrangement of his sensations. For his insolent, happy vitality, he will remain as a great virtuoso of 'the pure act of painting', reconciling 'the exquisite and the barbaric'.

Odalisques by Ingres, Odalisques by Matisse

From this happy and calm epoch, dates *l'Attente*, in which two young girls are held as by enchantment at a window opened on the sea.

How could it be said that the women of Matisse are always impersonal, inexpressive? Look at the girl on the right, so pensive, so absorbed, and at so many other faces with their pathetic expressions. Look also at those drawings, flowering arabesques, to which he was inspired by a model of exceptional quality, Lydia.

Indeed, that wonderful peace which Matisse always sought, is found especially in his feminine nudes. Like Delacroix, he brought back from Morocco an enduring love for the odalisque, voluptuous product of the harem, like a flower in full bloom.

Whether he dresses her in a light haïk of figured silk or velvet stamped with silver and gold, loads her arms with heavy bracelets, her throat with the necklace of a favourite slave, or undresses her entirely, his model is always a passive creature, a lovely pearly object among many other desirable objects.

Great unwavering eyes, high, firm breasts, wide hips and rounded thighs, she is truly the perfect flower of *luxe, calme et volupté*.

In 1919 and 1923, during extensive exhibitions at Bernheim's, it was she who overcame the last opposition of the general public and disarmed certain critics. Among them, André Lhote: 'Matisse is a magician. . . . Scarcely has one glanced at those slight canvases, seemingly brushed over by a vague and rapid hand, than one forgets all objections, and gives in, vanquished. If colour often flatters in us some inferior instinct, it can also, when distributed with sensibility, subject to a certain vaporization by a high frequency of tonal interchange, arouse a delicious reverie, akin to poetic ecstasy.'

The enchantment never came to an end. With the years, his touch was lightened by spirit; the large surfaces slowly became a tracery of broken tones which remind one of the 'flecking' of Delacroix's ripe years.

It was the period of *Odalisque à la culotte rouge* (1921); *Odalisque dans la pose de Bouddha* (1923); *Odalisque au magnolia* (1924); of *Odalisque au tambourin* (1927); of *Repos des modèles* (1928); *Odalisque au feuillage vert* (1929); *Odalisque au turban blanc*, and finally of that *Odalisque* in the *Petit Palais*, typical example of what inspiration Henri Matisse owed to Moorish decoration and, strangely, to the pottery of the Moghreb, whose daring arabesques and strong, subtle colours impressed as vividly the painter of figures, still lifes and interiors.

Claude Roger-Marx has shown the difference—in spirit and sensuality—between an Ingres *Odalisque* and one by Matisse.

'The painter's plastic imagination is aroused by the sound of that chamber music composed of one or two figures in an interior. He loves to load them with ornament—scarves and mantillas, strange head-dresses, linen harmonized with flesh—there is something Oriental in this Northerner. These young women, adapted to surroundings invented to receive them, decked in ornaments they have not chosen, are but a pretext for self-expression.

'Consider one of the masters of French painting (I am thinking of Ingres). One feels that in the presence of those same Odalisques, his very deformations are voluptuous. Whereas Matisse, so anxious as far as technique is concerned, faced with the model preserves an absolute sentimental and sensual serenity. His people breathe a somewhat abstract air; they are asked to decorate a space, adorned with eyes and lips of less account than flowers on curtains or carpets, they are docile instruments on which he composes a delicate song.'[1]

Matisse seems to confirm the idea, in a letter he wrote to me in 1947:

'For me, nature is always present. As in love, all depends on what the artist unconsciously projects on everything he sees. It is rather the quality of that projection which gives life, in the eyes of an artist, than the presence of a living person.'

[1] Claude Roger-Marx, *Les Dessins d'Henri Matisse.*

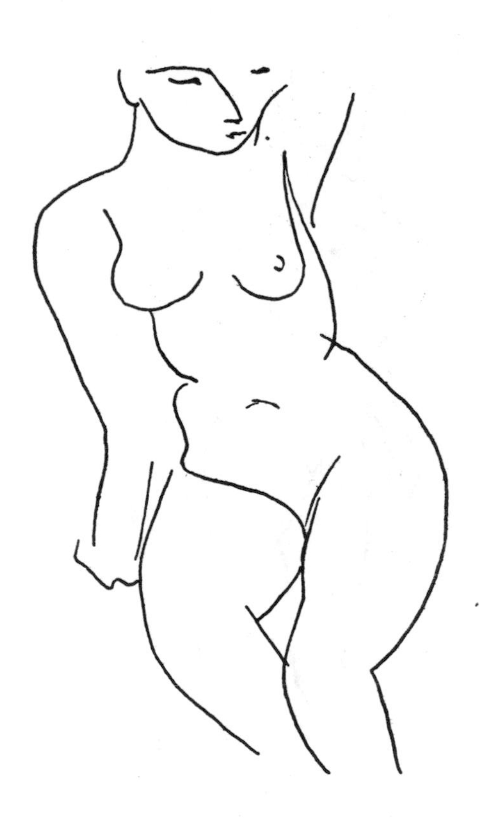

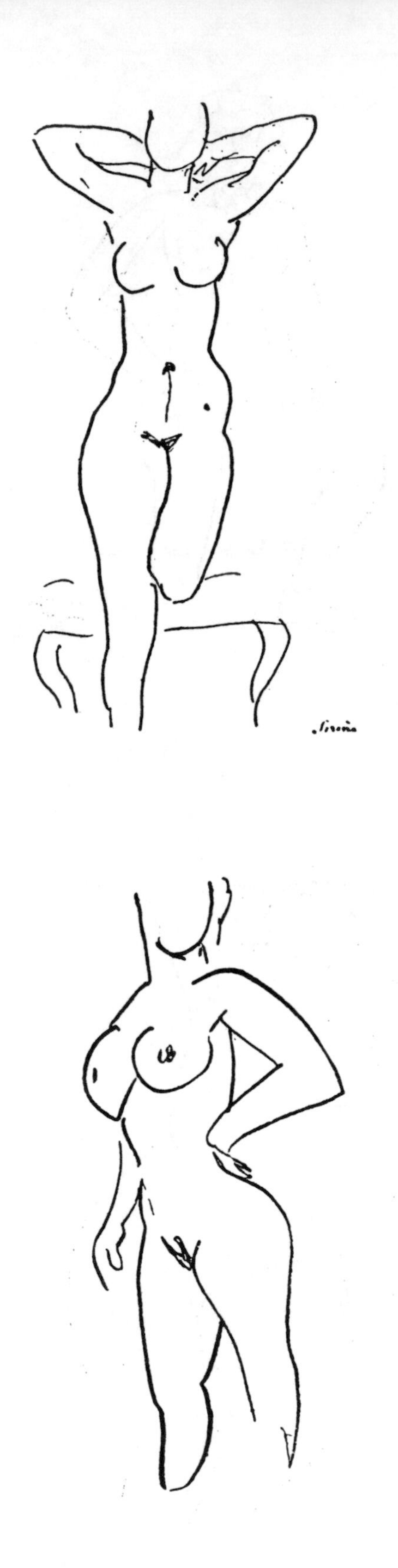

IV

CRYSTAL LIGHT

Oceania

In 1927, Henri Matisse received first prize at the Pittsburgh International Exhibition.

As a result of his numerous exhibitions abroad—at the *Toison d'Or*, Moscow 1908; at the *Internationale Ausstellung des Sonderbundes* in Cologne; at the Berlin *Sécession* in 1913; at the *Sécession Romana*, 1913; at the Exhibition of Scandinavian Museums, Copenhagen, 1924; at the *Kronprinzin Palast*, Berlin, and the Tate Gallery, London, 1926; in 1927 at the Carnegie Institute and in 1929, the Exhibition at the *Palais des Beaux-Arts* in Brussels—almost all the important works of Matisse of that period are owned abroad.

A great number of his youthful pictures had been bought by Gertrude, Leo, Sarah and Michael Stein; and when Leo left the rue Fleurus to go back to California they had to be divided up. Following the dictates of her heart, which had always a softer spot for Pablo than for Matisse, Gertrude had kept for herself the works of Picasso; whereas the Frenchman's pictures followed Leo to California. Which meant that after 1929, a number of Matisse's pictures had crossed the Atlantic.

And many were in Russia, in the possession of Morosoff and Stchoukine, whose 'nationalized' collections are now on view at Moscow's Museum of Occidental Art.

Henri Matisse was much impressed by his three visits to the United States, and particularly by the quality of the light, strangely 'crystalline' it seemed to him, which gave the painter new problems of atmosphere.

But his journey to Oceania impressed him more than any. He had dreamed of going there ever since he was twenty, and was at last able to do so.

'*I have always been enthralled*' he said, '*by the sort of light surrounding the subjects of my contemplation, and I have often wondered in my mind, what peculiar quality it would have on the other side of the world. I lived there three months, absorbed in my surroundings, with no other ideas than the newness of all I saw, annihilated, unconsciously storing up many things.*'[1]

[1] Note by Henri Matisse, 1936.

H. Matisse mai 43

It was all there, the vast spaces, the splendid tumult of the forest, the virgin soil and the untrammelled humanity painted by Gauguin. His famous phrase was surely murmured by Matisse, 'Barbarism makes me young again.'

Ten years later, Matisse told me his voyage to Oceania was still an inspiration and enchantment to him. *'I have always been in love with light and the poetry of light, I longed to see how it would be at the equator. It is all of gold, whereas ours is silver. . . .'*

And when I asked him if he had found any trace of Gauguin, he replied, *'I have found, in the suburbs of Papeete, a small* rue Gauguin, *which had houses only on one side.'*

In André Verdet's essay, *Prestiges de Matisse*, he has more to say.

'I gained a great deal from my stay in Tahiti. I had a strong desire to see what light there was on the other side of the Equator, to know the trees growing there, to be familiar with those things. Each light has its peculiar harmony. In the light of the Pacific, of the islands, one seems to be looking into a deep goblet of gold.

'I remember at first, when I arrived, it was disappointing, and then, little by little, it was beautiful. . . . It is beautiful. The leaves of the high coco-palms, turned back by the trade-winds, made a noise like silk. The sound of the leaves was imposed on a rumbling orchestral background of the waves of the sea, waves which rolled in and broke on the reefs surrounding the island.

'I used to bathe in the lagoon. I swam among coral colours, accentuated by the sharp black of different sea-cucumbers. I put my head under the water, transparent over the absinthe bottom of the lagoon, with my eyes wide open. . . . Then, abruptly, I raised my head above water and gazed at the spectacle of luminous contrasts. . . .

'Tahiti . . . the Islands. . . . But the quiet desert island does not exist. We Europeans bring our worries with us. For, in that island, there were no worries. The Europeans were bored there. They waited comfortably to retire, in a suffocating torpor, and they did nothing to get out of their torpor, to fill their time, or forget their boredom; they no longer even thought. Above them, and all around them, was that wonderful light of the first day, that magnificence, but they no longer noticed it.

'The factories had been closed, and the natives were idling with animal joy. A beautiful country sleeping in the brilliant sun.

'No, the quiet desert island, the lovely paradise does not exist. One would soon be bored there, with no cause for worry.

'Even the memory of Mozart seemed strange and out of place.'[1]

[1] Unpublished.

20. Intérieur: L'étui à violon

New York, Museum of Modern Art

21. La ceinture verte

Chicago, Art Institute

22. Nice: Intérieur: Jeune femme à la fenêtre (Le boudoir)

Private Collection

23. La dame à l'ombrelle

Private Collection

24. Nice: la femme au canapé

Private Collection

25. Nice: Fête des fleurs
Cleveland, Museum of Art

26. Le pare-brise
Cleveland, Private Collection

27. L’été—Jeune femme dans un fauteuil

New York, Private Collection

28. Nu couché

Private Collection

29. La table noire

Winterthur, Private Collection

30. Odalisque au divan rose

Chicago, Art Institute

31. Les pêches

Private Collection

32. Étretat: Les deux raies

Norton Gallery and School of Art, West Palm Beach, Florida

33. Odalisque aux bras levés

Chicago, Art Institute (Chester Dale)

34. Le concert au paravent mauresque
Private Collection

35. Autour du piano
Private Collection

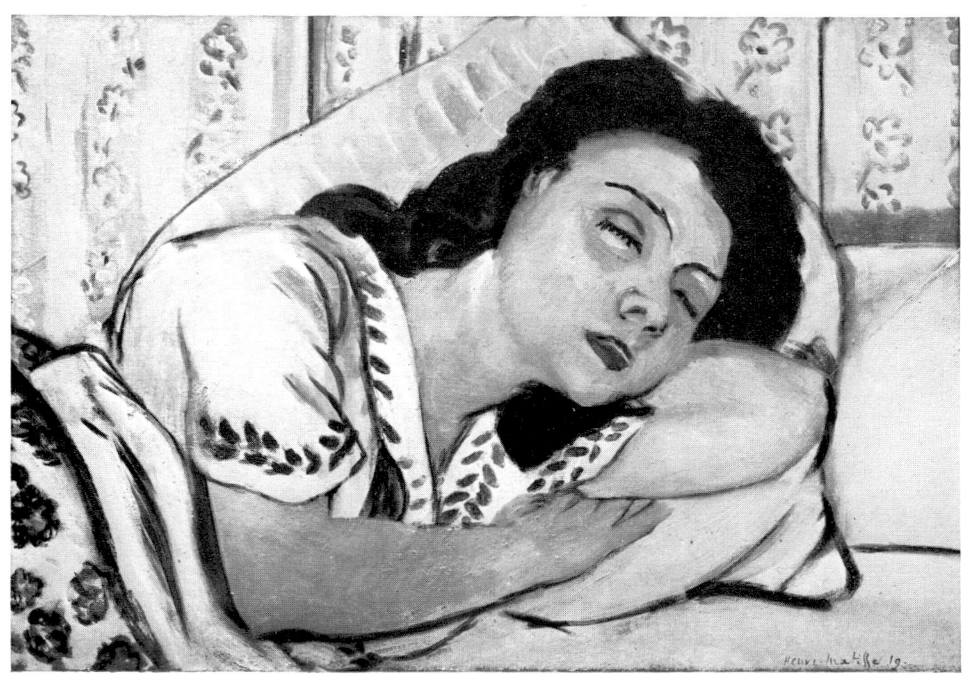

36. Le buffet
Paris, Musée d'Art Moderne

37. Jeune femme endormie
Private Collection

38. Figure décorative

Paris, Musée d'Art Moderne

39. Jeune fille en jaune

Baltimore, Museum of Art (Cone)

U.S.A.

Returning from the South Seas, Matisse stopped in the United States, to sit on the Carnegie Jury. During a visit to the Barnes Foundation, the Doctor invited him to decorate part of the ceiling in his museum's largest room.

For twenty years, symphony had been giving way to melody, but it was time for the painter of *Joie de vivre* to measure his strength against high walls, with a sublime structure of gigantic reds and blues, and to set in motion the frenzied Bacchanalia of *La Danse* (1933). The figures are about twelve feet high.

For this, Henri Matisse employed quite a new method of which he was good enough to give me the secret. It was a deliberate denial of the squared-up sketch, foreseen by the manifesto of 1908.

'*Perhaps it would be important to indicate that the composition of the panel arose from a struggle between the artist and the fifty-two square metres of surface, of which the spirit of the artist had to take possession, and not the modern procedure of the composition's projection on the surface, multiplied to the size "required" and traced.*

'*A man looking for a plane with a searchlight, does not explore the vastness of the sky in the same way as the aviator.*

'*If I have made myself clear, I think you will grasp the essential difference of the two conceptions.*'[1]

Louis Gillet wrote an admirable commentary on that great work of Henri Matisse, to which the *Ville de Paris*, at my urgent request, made an unhoped-for response.

'The work was executed in Nice, and took two years: the author, as a result of an error in scale, having to do it twice from beginning to end, his heart was so set on a work which gave him opportunity to show his strength and at last say something important. . . . At Merion, for the first time the artist had a precise ground, a space to fill, of vast proportions, demanding of him forms and subject.

'It was three half-moons, three archways determined on the wall's surface by the sections of the arches of a hall with three naves. The base came a little below the springing of the arches. This disposition dictated the curves, a series of arcs which would render the architectural design in living line: *precisely, visible music*. The whole composition is conceived in counterpoint, a fugue of scrolls blending, duplicating, contradicting or repeating each other. That in itself lends the idea of a dance or a ballet: three cuts, two figures to each half-moon, with their attitudes convex or concave, opposing, reflecting, diversifying,

[1] Note from Henri Matisse to R.E.

repeating in human silhouettes the shapes of the building. Two additional reclining figures link the three panels, forming pendants or abutments below the pendatives. Those recumbent forms serve as intermediary between the architecture and the decoration, between the immobile and the movement, making the point, the pivot, where static energy is liberated into dynamic values and unbridled figures.

'Impossible to imagine a more rigorous and yet inspired composition, filled at the same time with mathematical order and the breath of orgy. Never have power of rhythm, spring of arabesque, been carried so far, geometric and demoniac, as in this amazing frieze. Eight feminine bodies, by their curves, leaps, falls, graces, by an electricity both animal and divine, translate into movement the captive forces of the wall. The delighted eye feels structure, stress and strain, the marriages, the secret music of the edifice. In short, all the abstract harmonies of a building resolve themselves into a living garland of girls.

'It seems as though Matisse had been allowed to restore a painting of which the secret has been lost since the potters of Corinth and Athens: a linear painting, without shadow or *trompe-l'œil*, in which the modelling is expressed by contour and quality of line. It is what Ingres meant when he said, "I shall put a notice on my door: 'School of drawing,' and I shall make painters." The figures are painted in pearl-grey; all the colour and fire, all the daylight and shadow in the conception of light, is concentrated in the background of alternating pinks and blacks (the colours of Attic pottery), but divided into sections, cones and triangles, which form a tapestry or stained-glass behind the figures, and are reminiscent also of spotlight effects in music-hall.

'One can imagine how such an appearance of flashing light multiplies the force and frenzy of the mime.

'The figures are three metres high. To complete the impression of their Orphic character on a higher, Bacchic level, these figures have no faces; the heads are ovals without features, impersonal. What could be the thoughts of such creatures, twice the size of our women? Who could hope for a glance or a word from them? Who could watch the expression of a god-inhabited bacchante, whose whole genius is to be a whirlwind? Some will surely reproach the artist for this. But think! Among the many reasons Matisse could give (the mask of greek drama for instance), he might have found precedents in the primitive sculpture of the Cyclades and from impersonal idols, from old Aegean fetishes with heads shaped like a palette or cactus leaf, such as the ones in the archaic Greek rooms in the Louvre. And why should the expression be concentrated in the features instead of being felt in all the limbs? Why not leave the way open to dreams, and allow each, according to his desire, his own image of beauty?

'One last word in conclusion: it is a great pity that such a work should go to the United States, and that France should make no single attempt to retain it.'[1]

In deference to Louis Gillet's wish, the City of Paris did take the necessary steps to keep that masterpiece of French art on the banks of the Seine.

Since 1933, Merion possesses the second version of *La Danse*, but the *Musée d'Art Moderne*, of the City of Paris, acquired the original decoration in 1937, first conception of the admirable Bacchanalia.

Return to Fauvism

'Barbarism makes me young again.' In December, 1936 Matisse made Gauguin's famous phrase his own. In an interview with Tériade, he proclaimed his return to Fauvism, as his following work shows.

'When the means of expression have become so refined, so attenuated that their power of expression wears thin, it is time to return to the essential principles which made human language. They are principles which "return to the source", take new life, give life. . . . Pictures which have become refinements, subtle degradations, dissolutions without force, call for beautiful blues, reds, yellows, matter to stir the sensual depths in men. It is the starting point of Fauvism: the courage to return to purity of means.

'Our senses have an age of development which does not come from immediate surroundings, but from the time of civilization. We are born with the sensibility of an era of civilization. And that counts far more than all we can learn about an era. The arts have a development, which comes not only from the individual, but also from a whole acquired force, the civilization which precedes us. One can't do just anything. A talented artist can't just do as he likes. If he only used his gifts, he would not exist. We are not the masters of what we produce. It is imposed on us.

'In the last paintings, I have united the acquisitions of the last twenty years to my essential basis, to my very essence.'

With Matisse, work, application, reinforce at every moment his innate gifts, the discoveries of that miraculous eye, unsuspected tones and subtle relationships.

'The brain of M. Matisse can be compared to a snare' wrote André Lhote, 'Not trusting to his imagination, the artist leaves his studio, which no ghosts inhabit. He goes out into the street, the garden, the country, wary of the unexpected impression, which he captures on the wing with unequalled skill. At the moment

[1] Louis Gillet, 'La Danse d'Henri Matisse, Merion, near Philadelphia'.

when the bird-sensation has been caressed, and fed to its full size, the painter uses all his ingenuity to give the greatest lustre to his captive's plumage. One has to admit that it is a method of working which gives discoveries of great rarity in colour, of which no painter before M. Matisse had dreamed.'

More simply put, for a biographer, Matisse noted, '*Extremely regular work, daily, from morning to night.*'

'The only time Matisse talked to me about his habits and customs,' writes Jacques-Emile Blanche, 'he told me that he goes out with his materials after breakfast, when he is in the South. He looks for his subject, sets up his easel. By midday, he has either succeeded with his study, and signs it; or he considers it a failure, and will begin it again tomorrow. As a dandy flings a white tie he has crumpled in the clothes basket, and another, and will go on trying fresh ones until his skill has won.'

Those were the necessary preparations for the various stages which his pictures underwent, stages of which the superficial observer has no idea, which long created a state of total incomprehension between the artist and the general public.

'Matisse' says Claude Roger-Marx, 'exhibited his manifesto pictures as soon as they were painted. That is to say, although they looked like spontaneous works or rough drafts, in the mind of their creator they appeared to be final. Rapidly executed, they had been slowly conceived. In order to understand them, one must have heard the painter explain his intentions with grave sincerity. Then all that seemed the effect of chance, appeared as carefully concerted. Where the public only saw provocation and incoherence, there was purely a research for style, and sacrifice. Not one of the incorrections but could be explained. That absolute lack of expression—in the literary sense of the word—was—plastically—expression itself, and the phrase was to have great success in Germany. . . .'

It all depends on the feeling you're after

Yet, those improvisations were hard work, with their successive eliminations to reach the essential form. They were various halting places before the top of the climb. Henri Matisse himself said:

'*My reaction at each stage is as important as the subject. Because the reaction comes from me and not from the subject. It is a continuous process until the moment when my work is in harmony with myself. Like someone writing a phrase, rewriting, and making new discoveries. At each stage, I reach a balance, a conclusion. The next time I return to the work, if I find a weakness in the whole, I find my way back into the picture by means of the weakness—I return through the breach—and I conceive the whole afresh. So that the whole thing comes alive again. And as each element is only one of the component forces (as in an orchestration), the whole can be changed in appearance, and the feeling sought remain the same. A black could very well replace a blue, since the expression really derives from the relationship between colours. One is not tied to a blue, green or red if their tones can be interchanged or replaced, as the feeling demands. You can also change the relationships by modifying the quantity of the elements without changing their nature. That is, the painting will still be composed of a blue, a yellow and a green, in modified quantities. "A pound of green is greener than half-a-pound," as Gauguin would have Cézanne say in a visitor's book at Pont Aven. Either you can fix the relationships which make up the expression of a picture, or you can replace a blue by a black, as a trumpet may be replaced by an oboe in an orchestra. It all depends on the feeling you're after.*'[1]

As Gino Severini has said of Matisse, 'his constant effort to maintain spiritual and technical union with an ancient tradition (perhaps of Byzantium), and his intensely French quality, make him probably the greatest painter of our time, undoubtedly the richest in sane teaching.'[2]

Relationship to Delacroix

His influence on the evolution of modern art is very broad, and André Lhote, exponent of Cubism, acknowledged as much. 'After the empiricism of the Impressionists (which Renoir got away from, escaped, being as disciplined as Cézanne, although outwardly not so stern), it was necessary, in order to see clearly again, that we should put our colour-sensations in order, and reconsider the architectural laws of painting and drawing. Matisse helped us to solve several primary problems, and we mustn't forget it. He stands in the garden of French painting as a brilliant flower, sometimes too precious, but entirely significant of the most troubled period in the history of art. But an artist, were he even more specialized than M. Matisse, is never isolated. His researches, however particular they may be, are none the less attached to several recent schools: Orphism and Futurism owe him much. At one time, his influence even affected painters saddled with the most thankless task of Cubism.'

It seems today that Matisse has won over, not only the artists, collectors and critics, but also the general public.

[1] E. Tériade, op. cit., unpublished note by Matisse.
[2] *Severini Ragionamenti sulle arti figurative* (Hœpli, Milano, 1936, p. 213).

People are no longer disposed to mock or get indignant, they are ready to contemplate and admire. What they have been shown between 1919 and 1945, undoubtedly seems a long way from the great deformations of the *Fauve* period: olive groves, full of serenity, gardens of Provence, flowers in some precious Oriental pottery, lovely nudes with eyes like gazelles, reclining on many-coloured silk veils, an atmosphere full of pollen, peculiar to the coast near Nice, an irresistible enchantment.

Even such a detractor as Jacques-Emile Blanche (who also decried Delacroix) had to admit his defeat in analysing its cause: 'There is such an enchantment of magical, rare colour, that without noticing what goes on above, below and around, and reasoning no more than before an underground poster, one marvels. . . . To use no varnish, requires the self-confidence of Henri Matisse, but what research in execution, colour-mixing, are required, what subtle expedients in order to spread layers of the same colours over vast surfaces, to break them up, adapt them to the requirements of effect, of light—of a light and shade sustained by the shrillest notes of the palette.'

In fact, the conquests of Matisse have a higher origin. Colour here is the agent of the mind. In his substantial study on *Matisse et la Couleur*, René Huyghe was the first to discover clearly the general principles expressed in a very French art. The art of this 'revolutionary' appears to be a fundamentally balanced one, a balance sometimes disturbed in earlier attempts the better to succeed today. Nothing in his career can be disowned: everything came in its own time, just as everything in his pictures keeps its right place and importance. The painter submits his faculties to spiritual harmony; and the disposition of his talents is typical of French art: a fine sensibility, attentive to sensations enriched by the external world, and inventive but always lucid, so that mind controls emotion and gives to it, not a fugitive character but a sureness and certainty equivalent to the productions of method. Matisse echoed Delacroix when he described genius as '*following an essential direction, prescribed by higher laws*', and when he defined the artist: '*a man with sufficient self-mastery to follow his own discipline . . . able to organize his sensations.*'

It would be impossible to give a better summing up of the art and thought of Henri Matisse.

V

BLACK AND WHITE

Swarming bees

In many ways besides his sense of colour, Henri Matisse resembled Eugène Delacroix, particularly in his deportment, the dignity of his life, his aspiration to a classical style, Oriental serenity, combined with a passionate love of risk, a tireless search for the new and for renewal.

No one now has anything to say against Matisse. Art has so evolved in the last half-century that educated people, and even a section of the public at last weaned from the *Salon* chromos, can hardly fail to consider the master of *La Danse* as the greatest colourist of our time.

Impossible, since the exhibitions at Bernheim's, in 1920, to be unaware of the enchantment of colour offered to the discerning by that wonderful painter's eye.

His drawings, like Delacroix', are another matter. Either they are not known, or little appreciated at their true value.

Yet, as with all the great masters, it would be childish to neglect the drawing for the painting, or to prefer the one to the other.

Both are parts of a whole. His early drawings can be studied at the Petit Palais, in Moscow and above all in America: youthful drawings of nudes, powerful, sharp, chiselled with a kind of fierce cruelty. . . . But a change came after the influence of Van Gogh who so powerfully affected the *Fauves* at the beginning—witness the drawing of a *Fisherman* (Moscow) with Derain swimming in the distance in the bay of Collioure. Pierre Courthion found an exact, charming phrase to describe the pen-drawings of nudes, worked in commas, between 1905 and 1910: 'They are like bees swarming round the form.'

Waldemar-George felt this also: 'Matisse's line is mobile. Is his dynamism just an effect of handwriting? Not at all. The line is not an ideal limit of form. The form it contains, or rather resumes, seems at times to be extensible. Its outline is so simple that it seems to give, under pressure of spontaneous life. Matisse knows how to make his spaces eloquent. His line is often fragmentary. But even his spaces seem to speak, his touch is so sure. They indicate the area of volume better than scholastic modelling.'[1]

[1] Waldemar-George, *Henri Matisse, Dessins, Editions des Quatre Chemins*, 1925.

How different are the gracious charcoal or pencil drawings of 1912–18, which blossomed a few years later in those harem flowers, the odalisques!

Between 1935 and 1939, in Paris, Nice, Cimiez, among his gorgeous multi-coloured textiles, pottery, flowers and birds, Matisse, returned from the West Indies and America, sought to reduce his drawing to the essential, working from a model of flowing, magnificent grace, in an infinite number of pen-drawings which are like the plumage of a bird of paradise.

It has been normally the human form which inspired his drawings, but often in the South, he took pleasure in tracing the curve of a palm-tree, or working under the cypresses in Renoir's garden, or from a sturdy nude in an olive-grove. . . . In those swift, but carefully studied sketches, all is flame, spirit, light, as in certain feminine faces caught with one elliptic line, in perfect character.

In studying the different phases of his graphic art, one must call to mind his paintings of the same period, and the stages of the colourist, chiefly built upon those pencil or ink drawings. And no one has examined the drawings with greater discernment than Claude Roger-Marx who remarks that his drawing, even more than his painting, is characterized by sacrifice and renouncement: 'It may seem paradoxical that such an inventor of harmonies should put aside his greatest gift, colour. But analysis of his drawing helps, precisely, to better understand what discipline Matisse imposed on himself even in the composition of his pictures. It is to be noted that exceptionally his most instinctive qualities come out in his painting; on the other hand, the drawings and engravings show far less spontaneous reaction of temperament than obedience to the dictates of will.'

And to those who belittle and misunderstand, 'When the line grates, be sure it is intended to do so; an apparently impossible fore-shortening is the expression of a sure logic. Whatever may appear to the uninitiated as incorrect, is on the contrary a deliberate correction, an intentional deformation. Nothing is so thought-out as those seemingly hasty arrangements; I would even say that the artist has anticipated the exasperation aroused by his studied negligence, his pseudo-nonchalance, and all the liberties he takes with anatomy and perspective. It is impossible to deny the heroism in such an attitude, or the quality of a pride that comes from a multitude of vanquished fears.'[1]

'Nature is always with me. . . .'

All his graphic studies are in essence figurative.

[1] Claude Roger-Marx, *Les Dessins d'Henri Matisse.*

In that respect, the drawings called '*Thèmes et Variations*' introduced by Aragon's important essay, *Matisse-en-France*, have the value of a manifesto. These drawings of 1941 and '42, illustrate perfectly this saying of the artist: '*To work from the model until I have absorbed enough to improvise.*' For a model in fact is indispensable for him. As Pierre Marois observed: 'The strange part of it is, that Matisse can't do without nature altogether.'

But Marois forgets that for his art, Matisse needs a shock, the shock given him by the sight of a woman—or an object. For the model can as well be a palm-tree as a young woman, an apple, a spray of ivy, a Chinese vase, a Louis-Philippe tea-cup or a Second Empire chair.

'*What can you expect?*' he asked Aragon. '*I belong to an age when we were in the habit of always referring to nature, when we always painted from nature. . . .*' He has also said, '*Nature is always with me, and excites me. . . .*'

And he tried to explain, that at such times the contradiction between contemplation and action was resolved in him: '*It is contemplative action, or active contemplation . . . so to speak.*'

After having attained full mastery and reached the heights of fame, Henri Matisse went back to work with simplicity.

As he well knew that there has never been a more beautiful or intricate subject for drawing than a tree, he drew acacias and palm-trees, and explained this to Aragon, with a precise definition of what he sought and obtained from nature and how he made use of it.

'*I have shown you the drawings I am doing now, haven't I? to learn how to express a tree, trees? As if I had never seen or drawn a tree. . . .*[1] *I can see one from my window. I have to take in patiently how the mass of the tree is made, then the tree itself, the trunk, the branches, the leaves. First the branches symetrically placed on one plane. Then, how the branches twist, passing in front of the trunk. . . . Don't misunderstand me. I don't mean that, looking at the tree from my window, I try to copy it. The tree is also a whole series of effects it has on me. It is not a matter of drawing a tree I see. I have an object in front of me which produces an effect on my mind, not only as a tree, but in relation to all sorts of other feelings. I shan't get rid of my emotion by exactly copying the tree, in drawing its leaves one by one, as we say. . . . But after identifying myself with it, I must create an object which resembles the tree. The sign of the tree. And not the sign of the tree as it appeared to other artists, to those painters who learned to make leaves by drawing 33, 33, 33, as you have to say 99 for a doctor with a*

[1] '*Until then I'd been concentrating on the trunk and main branches. The rest existed, no doubt . . . the leaves . . . but only in relation to the other, mass and colour.*' Words of Matisse noted by Aragon.

stethoscope. . . . That is only other people's left-overs. . . . The others have invented their own sign. To repeat it is to repeat a dead thing; the outcome of emotions that belonged to them.'[1]

And Aragon recorded this precious truth of Matisse, his own truth.

'*The importance of an artist is increased according to the quantity of new signs he has introduced into the plastic language.*'

Devoting his attention from the beginning to vast surfaces, no one was better qualified than the painter of *Bonheur de vivre* to understand the drawing of the great decorator of the *Palais Bourbon*, the *Luxembourg* and the *Chapelle des Saints-Anges*, and plead a cause which was also his own:

'*Why do they say that Delacroix never drew a hand . . . ? That he always made a claw . . . like that? Because Delacroix composed on a large scale. Here and there it was necessary to end the movement, line, curve, arabesque, which completed the picture. He brought it to the extremity of an arm, a figure, and there he turned it, completed it by a sign, a sign, you understand. Always the same, not a particular hand, but his hand, the claw.*'[2]

Matisse in fact was never tired of defending Delacroix's drawing which meant so much to him. '*There are two kinds of artist . . . those who paint each time the portrait of a hand, a different hand every time, Corot for instance . . . and those who make the sign of a hand, like Delacroix. With signs one can compose freely and ornamentally. . . .*'

He also explained his own drawing and the art of drawing in general, better than anyone in *le Point* (July, 1939):

'*My line drawing is the purest and most direct translation of my emotion. Simplification of means allows that. But those drawings are more complete than they appear to some people who confuse them with a sketch. They generate light; looked at in a poor, or indirect light, they contain not only quality and sensibility, but also light and difference in values corresponding obviously to colour. Those qualities are also evident to many in full light. They derive from the fact that the drawings are always preceded by studies made in a less rigorous medium than line, charcoal or stump drawing, which enables one to consider simultaneously the character of the model, the human expression, the quality of surrounding light, atmosphere, and all that can only be expressed by drawing. And it is not until I feel exhausted by that work, which may go on for several sessions, that I can with a clear mind give rein to my pen without hesitation. Then I feel clearly that my emotion is expressed in plastic writing. Once I have put my emotion into line*

[1] Aragon, op. cit.

[2] How many magnificent nudes, for which Lydia posed, in which the hands are in fact 'just claws'!

and modelled the light of my white paper, without destroying its endearing whiteness, I can add or take away nothing further. The page is written: no correction is possible. If it is not sufficient, there is no other possibility than to begin again, as if it were an acrobatic feat. . . .[1]

'I have always considered drawing not as an exercise of particular dexterity but as, above all, a means of expressing intimate feelings and moods, means simplified to give greater simplicity and spontaneity to expression, which should speak without heaviness directly to the mind of the spectator.

'My models,[2] *human figures, are never just "dummies" in an interior. They are the principal theme in my work. I depend entirely on my model whom I observe at liberty, and then I decide on the pose which best suits her nature. When I take a new model, I guess the pose that will suit from the abandoned attitudes of repose, and then I become the slave of that pose. I often keep those girls several years, until interest is exhausted. My plastic signs probably express their souls (a word I dislike) which interests me subconsciously, or what else? Their forms are not always perfect, but they are always expressive. The emotional interest aroused in me by them does not necessarily appear particularly in the representation of their bodies, it is often, rather, in the lines by special values distributed over the whole canvas or paper, forming the orchestration or architecture. But not everyone sees this. It may be sublimated voluptuousness, and that may not be yet visible to everyone.'*

And on the same theme, we have this reply to Gertrude Stein, speaking of Matisse's feminine models with her servant-girl.

'I replied to someone who said I didn't see women as I represented them: "If I met such women in life, I should run away in horror." First of all. I do not create a woman, I make a picture. . . .

'In spite of the absence of shadows or half-tones expressed by hatching, I do not renounce the play of values or modulations. I modulate with a more or less heavy line, and above all with the surfaces it bounds on the white paper, without touching them but by their relationships. This is clearly seen in the drawings of Rembrandt, Turner, and of colourists in general.

'To sum up, I work without theory. *I am simply conscious of the forces I am using and I am driven on by an idea which I really only grasp as it grows with the picture. As Chardin used to say, "I add (or I take away, because I scrape out a lot) until it looks right."*

[1] Matisse was compared to the famous juggler, Rastelli, about 1930. He replied, '*No, rather I am an acrobat.*'

[2] Matisse always chose very beautiful ones.

'Making a picture would seem as logical as building a house if one worked on sound principles. One should not bother about the human *side. Either one has it or one hasn't. If one has, it colours the work in any case.'*

Engraving and lithograph

In his engravings, and particularly in his lithographs, one can feel the full weight of Matisse's drawing.

The engraved work of Henri Matisse is very important. In the catalogue compiled by his daughter, Madame Duthuit, in 1932, there were listed already four hundred pieces (dry-points, etchings, lithographs). Today we could count more than eight hundred.

In 1933, Claude Roger-Marx contributed an essay of great insight to *Print Collector's Quarterly* on the engraved work of Henri Matisse. One can't speak of Matisse as engraver without continual reference to it.

His first attempts in this line date from 1903, and are generally dry-points. At first his models are angular, aggressive; at the time, he avoided grace and only sought expression and he would attack the plate with violence. . . . Like his drawings, his dry-points and etchings have always been drawn from nature, and never from his own paintings, which they often preceded. A first sketch is done with the brush on the copper or on the varnish; then the etching point, always in the presence of the model, extracts from these indications the essential, that is to say, a few lines confining generally a nude body, sometimes a face. No crossed lines, no shading, nothing but contours. One is astonished, at first, to see such a colourist deny himself those orchestrations of values, those modulations, which are one of the most striking charms of etching and among the things which justify its existence.

But just as in his pictures he expresses himself preferably by means of flat tints, so he simplifies his technique as an engraver by reducing his plates, which are generally of quite small dimensions, to relations of volumes suggested by a mobile and quivering tone.

We have only two or three woodcuts by Matisse, of about 1906. But from 1905 on, he drew a great deal on stone, and also on lino. Senefelder's process gives a richness and, finally volume to his drawing. These are certainly not cursory notes, studies, researches, sketches, variations, but completed works wherein the play of values has been patiently observed, and very refined form appears in powerful outline. Although treated in black and white, at times the Odalisques of the lithographs have a colour to equal their sisters in paint.

As Claude Roger-Marx judiciously remarks, a number of those lithographs show the artist eager to render the most diverse textures, as if he wished to show from time to time that nothing would be easier for him than to 'finish' (in the sense habitually given to the word by the general public), and to please.

The album of the *Danseuses*, published in 1927, is very revealing in this respect, as are also certain portraits of women 'carried very far', in which Matisse delighted in differences of texture between varied materials: hair, fur, a pearl necklace; and that with an astonishing perseverance. This is surprising indeed in work usually so elliptic.

Rembrandt

Perhaps we can put that down to the magic of black and white. . . . At the turn of the century, after a long eclipse, original work in lithography reappeared with technicians like Lunois, painters like Lautrec, Bonnard, Vuillard and Maurice Denis, with colour as its outstanding feature. Some day those delightful plates will be treasured. Their colours have the ephemeral quality of powder left on the fingers by a butterfly wing.

But in fact Matisse demanded of the lithographic stone something quite other than brilliant and subtle colour. He was seeking to record the very essence of his graphic researches in the full range of black and white; to arrest the sinuous line of his arabesque, and to resume, in the harmony of the print, the successive variations aroused in him by contemplation of a beautiful woman, adorned with Oriental jewels and fabrics, and surrounded by the brilliant luxury of rich pottery and dazzlingly bright flowers.

A century before Matisse, even before the *Femmes d'Alger*, a great French painter who had never touched on the shores of Islam, M. Ingres, also contemplated the mysterious life of the Odalisques, seeking inspiration from them, not only for his oil-paintings, but also for his lithographs, in which the technique is not unlike the Odalisques in Henri Matisse's lithographs.

It is curious that those two painters, so preoccupied with arabesque in drawing and painting, show themselves equally concerned with volume when it comes to lithograph. As if no one, whatever his personal bent, could escape the imposition of the medium. As if the engraver, who has not used the verb *sculpsit* throughout the ages for nothing, were finally obliged to obey the fundamental laws of the sculptor, and work with 'the masses like the antique sculptors and like Daumier'.

There, as in painting, Matisse was haunted by his great predecessors, and primarily by Rembrandt, who was for a long time, as Aragon noted, his great preoccupation: '*I noticed that Rembrandt himself had no need to touch his paper to give it quality; the first states of Rembrandt's etchings are very interesting in this respect, for their indication of the quantities of paper he encompasses and defines. . . .'*

It is well known how meticulous was Rembrandt when it came to paper (the famous first state on Chinese paper of the etching called the *Hundred Florins*, for instance). Matisse was no less careful, and as Claude Roger-Marx notes, each proof was printed with the greatest care, under the supervision of the artist himself, or his daughter, on very fine Indian paper.

There, at least, Matisse could freely indulge his great love of white, which Aragon described so delightfully, showing us the white ceiling in Matisse's house in Cimiez.

'It is a white sky. A paper sky. A white paper sky. The sky of Matisse.'

Henri Matisse's daughter, 'Margot', Madame Georges Duthuit, has not only written some remarkable pages on her father's lithographs, but as she often took part in their creation and printing, what she has to say on the subject is of great value.

'Nothing distinguishes the lithographs of Henri Matisse from his other works in black and white. He had no taste for tricks of the trade, finely cooked-up results; no interest in producing an effect, the flattering possibilities of stone and lithographic pencil. He simply drew with the new tools. Exactly the same writing as with an ordinary pencil and paper: he presents us with slowly elaborated plates, which have sometimes required many sessions to reach their final state, over several years. In such proofs, the black has been enriched by a slow process, or has submitted to sharp attacks, in which acid and pumice took the place of india rubber.

'Thus, by a closely followed study, all the elements of the model have appeared in successive stages. Contact, closely maintained between the subject and the white page, allow the final formation of solid volumes, in which the blacks gain their luminous quality. Hence, when the result is satisfactory, a homogeneous work, an unbroken whole, of full and equal resonance.'

The daughter writes as well as her famous father, the unequalled commentary of a true artist, worthy of the great name she inherits.

'First of all, Matisse keeps in check all that might resist his control, allowing no play to his imagination. Yet, it is from those long-drawn-out studies that his plates spring spontaneously, entirely line, or reinforced with tone. . . .

'We owe certain of them to happy moments of relaxation, which happened while the painter was working on a canvas demanding extreme tension. Born of one of those moments of liberation, when the line seems to escape the consciousness of the artist and to trace itself, the plates have the liveliness of a snapshot in which each straight line curve or spiral takes on a significance; in which volumes, suggested in the arabesque, find force and light. The planes fall into place, space is created by balance established between the divers components of the subject. Sensibility is the conductor; light comes from emotion only, from the vibrations of life.'

Madame Marguerite Duthuit used to oversee the printing of those lithographs by three master printers.

'At the moment of printing the lithographs, it is essential that all the painter's intentions be respected, and the stone suffer no violence. All its subtleties must be considered: it has its peculiar reactions and wants to be treated with great regard. . . .

'They (the lithographs) after a few proofs have been taken, sometimes require a long period of rest to prevent the blacks from becoming solid. At other times, on the contrary, they require far more proofs taken than was intended for the whole issue—rarely more than fifty and sometimes less—before they are set in their full intensity. Each proof must be compared to the press proof, chosen from four different types of paper: Chinese, Japanese, and Arches of two colours. In such works, coming from the presses of M. M. Clot, Duchatel or Mourlot, are incorporated both the researches of Matisse and the qualities he has developed during a half-century of work.'[1]

Can one love colours without also loving white? A passion for white which, according to Bracquemond, is one of the essential elements of fine engraving, evident in Matisse's engravings and lithographs, as well as his culture and deep understanding of the rarest texts, early led Matisse into the great renewal of French books, dating from the beginning of the century, at its height during the years 1917–50.

Actually, the first book illustrated by Matisse appeared in 1900, *Les Jockeys camouflés* by Pierre Reverdy.[2]

From the beginning, and I am thinking of the splendid manuscripts illuminated in Islam—as in the library of the Evkaf at Istanbul—as well as in the

[1] *Henri Matisse, Lithographies rares, Notice de Marguerite Duthuit Matisse* (Berggruen et Cie, Paris, 1954).

[2] Here is the list of works decorated by Matisse, as he gave it to me: Pierre Reverdy, *Les Jockeys camouflés* (Circ. 1900); Mallarmé, *Poésies* (Skira, 1932); Joyce, *Ulysses* (Macy ed., 1935); Montherlant, *Pasiphaë* (Fabian ed., 1944); Tristan Tzara, *Le signe de la vie* (Bordas ed., 1946); *Visages* with poems by Reverdy (*Editions du Chêne*, 1946); *Lettres de la Religieuse Portugaise* (Tériade, ed., 1947); Charles d'Orléans, *Poésies* (Tériade ed.); Aragon, *l'Amour d'Elsa* (*Les XXX Bibliophiles de Lyon*); *Jazz* (Tériade ed.); Baudelaire, *Fleurs du Mal* (la Bibliothèque Française); Ronsard, *Florilège des Amours* (Skira ed.); André Rouveyre, *Envers* (le Bélier); René Char, *Artisse* (Zervos ed.); J. A. Nau, *Poésies antillaises.*

E. Odalisque à la culotte grise (1927)

Private Collection

West, in France, England, Spain and Italy, one may say that the decoration of books is as much pure ornament as inspiration from the text.

Thus, I asked Henri Matisse, 'was it as illustrator or decorator that you undertook to work on books?' I was little surprised by his reply, '*As decorator.*'

Henri Matisse was willing to enlarge on his ideas of book decoration.

'*I agree with your distinction between the illustrated and the decorated book. A book should not need completion by an imitative illustration. Painter and writer should work together, without confusion, on parallel lines. The drawing should be a plastic equivalent of the poem. I wouldn't say 1st violin and 2nd violin, but a concerted whole.*'[1]

Here Matisse is in complete agreement with his old friend, Aristide Maillol, also one of the great masters of the contemporary book.

Unlike Bonnard, who didn't care at all—in *Parallèlement* for instance—how Ambroise Vollard laid out his lithographs and arranged their typographical architecture, Matisse (who said he was a bibliophile before ever he owned a book) supervised every detail.

For instance, from the very cover of *Visages*, the artist is present. The brown-madder colour of the title, is signed Matisse, and the frontispiece and tail-piece lino-cuts, with a powerful accent reminiscent of Negro art.

The presence of the artist is felt on every page, not only in those moving *Visages*, in those loose-leaf lithographs, admirably printed in *sanguine* by the Mourlot brothers, but also in the sinuous, feline curves of the violet letters. This masterpiece was printed by Féquet and Baudier, but the *Editions du Chêne* felt obliged to acknowledge on the last page that it was executed after the design of Henri Matisse.

Another vexed question among book-lovers. 'Are you in favour of the coloured book, you who are the magician of colour?' '*Very much so.*' Matisse answered me, '*But . . . black is very beautiful and can be full of colour.*'

I pursued this important point:

'Did you know Bracquemond? You who make white so melodious, do you agree with the formula he evolved, do you feel as he did, that black and white is entirely adequate with a fine typography?'

And Henri Matisse replied,

'*I never knew Bracquemond, but I fully understand his statement.*'

The fact is that a colourist like Henri Matisse has some difficulty in giving up colour, even in a book. So one can believe that he found great satisfaction in *Les Seize Peintures* (1939–43) reproduced in colour by the *Editions du Chêne*, with

[1] Unpublished.

a brilliant introduction by André Lejard; also in the issue of *Verve* (Vol. IV, no. 13) entitled *De la Couleur*, for which he composed the cover and the frontispiece (the Fall of Icarus) and the title-page although these were rather documentary works than art books proper.

Matisse also summed up his ideas on book decoration in 1946. His notes entitled 'Comment j'ai fait mes livres', were published by Skira in his important *Anthologie du livre illustré par les peintres et sculpteurs de l'Ecole de Paris.* Alluding to his works decorated by lithographs, such as *Les Amours* by Ronsard, *Lettres de la Religieuse Portugaise*, *Les Fleurs du Mal* by Baudelaire and *Visages* by Reverdy, Matisse pointed out that in spite of their different aspects, those works were the result of two essential principles:

1. Relationship between the decoration and the literary character of the book.

2. The composition being dependent on the elements employed according to their decorative value: black, white, colour, style of engraving, typography; those elements themselves dependent on the harmony which develops as the work goes on. This never being decided before understanding the text, but developing in the course of inspiration.

Aragon has more than once described the effect of fine writing on the imagination of Henri Matisse.

First, in reference to *les Amours* by Ronsard, which Aragon, for extra-literary reasons perhaps, seems scarcely to appreciate:

'At the present time (it was 1942–43), Henri Matisse is making drawings for Ronsard. . . . I said to Matisse (before he had thought of decrying the Renaissance to me) "What have you to do with all that Renaissance? A taste for the antique . . . ?" He had no reply. He said, "*You think so?*" He showed me the first drawings—a woman—another woman—or the same one. And then faces drawn with a single line, masks, to open each poem. Of no more importance than a device for lettering, those faces, always the same face, so graphic, an ornament. . . . Treacherous word for what is the most bare, least adorned thing in the world. Matisse's approach to Ronsard is entirely his own. *Les Amours, Hélène.* Perhaps Ronsard will be read differently since Matisse, like "*Cette soie aux baumes de temps*".' Aragon quotes Mallarmé.

Another poet, Louis Gillet, biographer of Dante and Shakespeare, was unreserved in his praise of that *Ronsard*.

'Six months ago (the article appeared February 24th, 1943) he completed an illustration of Ronsard, such as he previously made for Mallarmé. He planned fifty drawings; he did three times as many. The sketches pinned up round the walls make a charming frieze; a cloud of smiles and graceful faces, bunches of flowers, doves, torsoes, kisses, embraces, idylls, Hélène, Marie, Cassandre, all *les Amours*. Youth is restored by the magician. The mistresses of the poet crowd about him, like goddesses the sun had drawn up from the sea. . . .'

There are no criticisms for Baudelaire. One of the first great compositions of Matisse took its title, *Luxe, calme et volupté*, from *L'Invitation au voyage*.

On this subject, Aragon speaks of 'Portrait of Baudelaire by Matisse, to illustrate Mallarmé's *Tombeau de Baudelaire*. The only portrait which holds its own with Nadar's photographs.'

Perhaps Aragon is right that 'Baudelaire would have adored Matisse'. 'I am astonished, at the end of *Phares*, not to find an extra verse, the verse on Matisse. Omission to be repaired. . . .'

And Aragon did repair that omission, in *Les Lettres Françaises*, September 25th, 1947.

Je défais, dans mes mains, toutes les chevelures.
Le jour a les couleurs que lui donnent mes mains.
Tout ce qu'enfle un soupir, dans ma chambre est voilure
Et le rêve durable est mon regard demain.

Toute fleur d'être nue est semblable aux captives
Qui font trembler les doigts par leur seule beauté.
J'attends, je vois, je songe et le ciel qui dérive
Est simple, devant moi, comme une robe ôtée.

J'explique, sans les mots, le pas qui fait la ronde,
J'explique le pied nu qu'a le vent effacé,
J'explique, sans mystère, un moment de ce monde,
J'explique le soleil sur l'épaule posé.

J'explique un dessin noir à la fenêtre ouverte,
J'explique les oiseaux, les arbres, les saisons,
J'explique le bonheur muet des plantes vertes,
J'explique le silence habité des maisons.

J'explique infiniment toutes les transparences,
J'explique le toucher des femmes, leur éclat,
J'explique un firmament d'objets par différence,
J'explique les rapports des choses que voilà.

J'explique le parfum des formes passagères,
J'explique ce qui fait chanter le papier blanc,
J'explique ce qui fait qu'une feuille est légère
Et les branches qui sont des bras un peu plus lents.

Je rends à la lumière un tribut de justice,
Immobile au milieu des malheurs de ce temps,
Je peins l'espoir des yeux, afin qu'Henri Matisse
Témoigne à l'avenir ce que l'homme en attend.

About Baudelaire, thanks to Charles Camoin who kindly lent me a letter written by Matisse from Vence on September 6th, 1944, we have the opinion of the master himself. As Camoin dearly loved Baudelaire (how many painters are cultivated and great readers) his old friend Matisse writes of his illustrations for *Les Fleurs du Mal*: '*I have illustrated your old pal, Baudelaire. I have done thirty-five heads of expressions corresponding to the pieces chosen. It is not the usual thing for illustrating this poet. One could easily imagine a series of more or less tormented pairs of up-turned legs. I hope the bourgeois will tolerate this, and give me credit for my unexpected work. You can tell that to Daragnès if you see him.*'[1]

Another poetic appreciation of Matisse would have come from Mallarmé, whom Matisse could not fail to illustrate.

And Aragon tells us how this great plastic artist could, on occasion, be the subtlest of literary critics.

'There is nothing to be said about Mallarmé since Matisse has commented on his poems with his illustrations. The other day he was troubled by:

Quelle soie aux baumes de temps
Où la chimère s'exténue
Vaut la torse et native nue
Que, hors de ton miroir, tu tends!

'About this quatrain, Matisse pointed out . . . that it strangely resembles one in *Emaux et Camées*:

A l'horizon monte une nue,
Sculptant sa forme dans l'azur:
On dirait une vierge nue
Emergeant d'un lac au flot pur.

[1] Unpublished. Daragnès, the great engraver, was commissioned to print that Baudelaire on his press in the Avenue Junot, where he was neighbour to Camoin and Galanis.

'Matisse,' adds Aragon, 'thinks Mallarmé must have known it: "*But*" he says, "*one is not such a dolt as to repeat what has been said by someone else, in a preceding epoch. . . .*" He means that one goes on from there: Mallarmé would have been a dolt had he put in his quatrain the "torso" which rises from the lake become a mirror, no, he was content with the *chevelure*. The cloud which became a torso for Gautier, *chevelure* for Mallarmé, strongly affected the painter's imagination. He showed me a series of drawings destined to portray the woman rising from a base of cloud and lifting her hair to join two poetic ideas, as it were.'[1]

La Religieuse Portugaise

The fruit of three years' quiet meditation, the lithographic illlustrations of the *Lettres de la Religieuse Portuguaise* finally prove the exceptional gift of Henri Matisse as commentator, decorator, one can say architect, of books.

Strange encounter, between Marianne Alcoforado, the passionate nun who cried to the man she loved 'I have felt you less dear to me than my passion itself', and Henri Matisse, hermit of Cimiez, who had reached the heights of fame and serenity, one of those masters of whom Barrès said to me that they are never so great as when they are old.

Result: a monument of unequalled quality.

In that masterpiece of a book, two great decorative themes accompany each love-letter. The pomegranate flower dominates with its red violence, and the face of the nun, always the same and always different, expressing ravishment, anguish, hope, pain, despair, anger, indulgence, resignation, all the tragedy of cloistered love.

The artist had known the countries of the Moghreb and the veiled women of Islam. He had contemplated the lovely face of the Dominican Sister Jacques-Marie during his illness. She had posed for him before taking the veil. Thus Matisse had all he needed for the study of the nun.

It is not only the series of simplified faces, fine floral decoration and large capital letters as flexible as wands, that the *Lettres d'une Religieuse Portugaise* owe to Matisse.[2] The presentation, lay-out, daringly narrow margins, the almost square size, the noble capitals very Iberian in taste, that calculated, dramatic energy, is all the work of the master of Cimiez, who would leave nothing to chance.

[1] *Henri Matisse, Dessins: thèmes et Variations* preceded by *Matisse-en-France*, by Aragon.
[2] Edition of the magazine *Verve*, Tériade, 1946.

Henri-Matisse
Tahiti

VI
THE SCULPTOR

Matisse and Rodin

'I could mention a very great sculptor who gives us admirable fragments; but composition to him is only a group of fragments, and the result is confusion in the expression.'

Those lines published by Henri Matisse in the *Grande Revue* of December, 1908, are certainly meant for Rodin, whom the young painter had met at the *père* Druet's. . . . According to André Gide's Journal, relations were not very warm between the thunderous old master at work on his portrait of Balzac, and lucid, passionate young Henri Matisse.

I wanted to know what Matisse himself had to say about his relations with Rodin, and he also defined the gap which separated their different conceptions of sculpture, and art itself. *'I was taken to Rodin's studio in the rue de l'Université, by one of his pupils who wanted to show my drawings to his master. Rodin, who received me kindly, was only moderately interested. He told me I had "facility of hand", which wasn't true. He advised me to do detailed drawings and show them to him. I never went back. Understanding my direction, I thought I had need of someone's help to arrive at the right kind of detailed drawings. Because, if I could get the simple things (which are so difficult) right, first, then I could go on to the complex details; I should have achieved what I was after; the realization of my own reactions.*

'My work-discipline was already the reverse of Rodin's. But I did not realize it then, for I was quite modest, and each day brought its revelation.

'I could not understand how Rodin could work on his St John by cutting off the hand and holding it on a peg; he worked on the details holding it in his left hand, it seems, anyhow keeping it detached from the whole, then replacing it on the end of the arm; then he tried to find its direction in accord with his general movement.

'Already I could only envisage the general architecture of a work of mine, replacing explanatory details by a living and suggestive synthesis.'[1]

This, indeed, is the antithesis of Rodin's doctrine. In reaction to the flabbiness of academic modelling, he was seeking the pathetic in an almost tetanic tension

[1] Unpublished.

Matisse 37

of muscle and nerve, a tempestuous movement of life under sensitive flesh, and he had come to be more interested in the part than the whole: even to this extent, that in accordance with a very debatable conception of the claims of his art he would not hesitate to present to the public works deliberately mutilated or deliberately left unfinished, justifying himself by referring to the sublime fragments of Selinonte, the Parthenon, of the Palermo and British Museums, all fully satisfying to lovers of great sculpture. How could it be forgotten that the sculptors of Sicily and Athens aspired above all things to orderly rhythmic composition, harmony and beauty of line endowing the whole created work with grace—and would never, superb artists that they were, have dreamed of confusing broken ruins with finished works. But completion according to such aspirations demands (to quote Eugène Delacroix) the heart of a lion.

What a destructive influence such examples must have had on young artists, the band of critics, art lovers generally, confronted with these 'notable fragments'.

Bourdelle was not mistaken, though, when he spoke of these museum collections of nameless sculptured heads, bodiless limbs and limbless bodies, as still capable of conveying some idea of splendour; 'For a true initiate', he said, 'for one whose soul has responded already to pure beauty, the masterpiece is still perceptible in the merest fragment.'

Unfortunately, as we know, this fanatical addiction to the fragmentary was to tempt Rodin to go beyond the limitations of his art and to forget that it is sculpture's first duty to be monumental.

Henri Matisse, who dreamed of monumental art, and for whom detail, however studied and exquisite as he always made it, only counted as subordinate to the whole, could not choose this artist of genius for his master. It was a technique leading in the opposite direction from his own.

Rather than of the master of the *Porte d'Enfer*, one is reminded of the great Daumier, whose admirable modelling is so little known, the portrait busts for *Caricature*, *Ratapoil* and *Emigrants*. This work of Henri Matisse is singularly refined, often as if it came from ancient times, much nearer the metopes of Selinonte temples or Archaic Greece than are the works of Gargallo, Laurens and Lipchitz for whom this resemblance is claimed.

Again, the great friendship of nearly fifty years between Maillol and Matisse, who witnessed the beginning of Maillol's career and lent him a hand, has led to some sort of legend on the relationship between them.

Matisse himself gives a definite answer to this:

'*I practised sculpture, or rather modelling, before knowing Maillol. I did it as a complementary study to put my ideas in order. Maillol's sculpture and my work in that line have nothing in common. We never speak on the subject. For we wouldn't understand one another. Maillol, like the Antique masters, proceeds by volume, I am concerned with arabesque like the Renaissance artists; Maillol did not like risks and I was drawn to them. He did not like adventure.*'[1]

One has only to look at Maillol's adorable terra-cottas, generously given to the Petit Palais by Zoubaloff, to examine those marvellous figurines of tender sensuality and delicious clumsiness, which make of him, as Maurice Denis said, a classic primitive, and it is immediately evident how far is such a plastic conception from that of Matisse, always in search of adventure and risk.

But Matisse's love of risk was supported by a vast erudition. As Aragon rightly says, far from despising anatomy, Matisse worked long at it.

We must not forget his studies at the modelling school of the Ville de Paris. 'Two years, he spent two years . . . copying a tiger by Barye, during evening classes in the *Ecole Municipale* of the *rue Etienne Marcel*, first with his eyes, with what he could see, then with his eyes shut by the feeling of volume obtained by touch alone.'

And, a detail which reminds one of Delacroix studying the tiger from a cat, 'To go further than the copy, he had asked an assistant at the *Ecole des Beaux-Arts* to procure him a dissected cat, the better to study the spine and the paws.'

Let there be no mistake, however, if Matisse himself said he worked 'with arabesque like the Renaissance men', it does not mean that analogous studies of anatomy ever lead him to a similar art. His taste was too sure for him to avoid seeing what we have lost with the art of the Renaissance, that 'decadence', that 'terrible decadence'. Aragon concludes, 'Whereas to men of the Renaissance, the elements of construction in their work were based on anatomy, Matisse, having once learned and understood anatomy, based his work on feeling.'

Let us examine his modelled and sculptured work, of such great interest and variety.

If the delicate modelling of Jeanette's face, (*Jeanne Valderin*, 1910) observed by Matisse with such subtlety, seems to foretell the nervous grace of Despiau, it is an accident due to the artist's age, in his early beginnings.

In most of the sculptures of Matisse we find the same adventurous spirit as in *Bonheur de Vivre*: the bust of a woman with heavy lids, reclining with the left arm raised; another standing figure with powerful hips; another standing with arms raised; another feminine figure leaning her elbows on a stela which does, in fact, foreshadow Laurens and Lipchitz.

[1] Unpublished.

But there are also calmer studies, seated woman or crouching man, in which one can see in his sculpture the artist's evolution toward a Mediterranean classic serenity, which did not come to him as to Maillol, a gift from the gods, but by the patient thoughtful effort of his own will.

Matisse must have put himself under severe discipline during those researches in sculpture to which, Aragon tells us, he devoted more than two thousand sessions, and which produced notably the statue of the *Serf*, with its pathetic expression. (Given by Matisse to the Cateau museum.)

Henri Matisse was one of the first to admire the power of expression in Negro Art, but certain feminine standing figures came nearer to Susan art, given the elliptic character of the Etruscans.

There is a young woman's head in a clown-like head-dress, which is related to the amazing terra-cottas Daumier made under Louis-Philippe for *le Ventre Legislatif*; and another face, on the contrary, of an almost virile femininity and classic calm, seems to have been treated, exceptionally for Matisse, in the mass, that is by Antique rule.

Several reclining figures remind one of Aegean art . . a crouching woman has the general line of the *Vénus pudique*; whereas a wonderfully elongated torso approaches, in Archaic style, the slender Apollo of Tenea, which Matisse must have seen in Munich.

The arabesque of *la Femme Assise aux bras levés* is so near the important painting *Figure décorative sur fond fleuri*, that the same model may have sat for both; and this is essentially classic, also in treatment, largely simplified, with daring planes, boldly synthetic.

Like certain paintings of the same epoch, the *Femme Assise* (1929) shows how his passion for taking risks was leading this emotional master from the North to a serene classic order. Maurice Denis' fine definition of Maillol's classic art applies as well to Matisse's *Femme Assise*. 'Classicism has the flavour of objective beauty. It demands reason and resemblance everywhere. It has great ideas, strong impressions, it liberates the ideal beauty of objects, but fortunately its feeling for the general is accompanied by a sense of the possible. In bending nature to the order of its spirit, it intends no violence, it creates no monsters: its inventions are robust and harmonious as natural objects.'[1]

[1] Maurice Denis, *Théories*.

VII

IN SEARCH OF THE ABSOLUTE

IT was during one of his three visits to America, all of which were short, that his decoration, *Le Concert* (about 3 m × 1 m 80) was placed in position. It was executed in 1938 for Nelson Rockefeller. About the same time, Mrs Rockefeller bought one of the best still lifes, *Torse antique et bouquet d'œillets blancs*, in which Matisse shows his life-long taste for Greek sculpture.

Although he went there three times, Matisse never stayed in America as long as he would have liked.

Before him, it was the fashion among official painters, come from France to the United States, and even among artists born in the U.S.A., to speak ill of the light of the New World, to declare it was not paintable. With the arrival of those faithful to pure colour—Henri Matisse, Raoul Dufy, Fernand Léger—suddenly 'the scene shifted'. The painter of *Bonheur de Vivre* had found such limpid atmosphere only in Nice.

'*Shall I tell you?*' he confided to Aragon. . . . '*Nice . . . why Nice? In my art, I have tried to create a crystalline state for the mind: I have found the limpid quality necessary in several places in the world, in New York, the South Sea Islands, and Nice. If I had painted in the North, as thirty years ago, my painting would have been different: there would have been mists, greys, gradations of colour in perspective. In New York painters say, "we can't paint here, with this sky made of zinc!" In reality, it is admirable. Everything becomes clear-cut, crystalline, precise, limpid. Nice was a help to me in that way. You must understand that what I paint are objects thought of plastically: if I shut my eyes, I see the objects better than with my eyes open, free of accidental detail; that is what I paint. . . .*'

And it was not only the crystal light which delighted Matisse in the United States. He was deeply interested in the museums of the New World, so rich in independent French painting. '*At the Barnes Foundation, in Merion,*' Matisse once said to me, '*I have seen the most beautiful museum of modern art. Our masters are represented by their most important works, of remarkable quality.*'

It is well known, also, what a large place is devoted there to the Ecole de Paris, glorious school which has spread the fame of French art all over the world. Its

real founders are, Henri Matisse, Picasso, and finally Raoul Dufy, Derain, Braque, Albert Gleizes, Fernand Léger, Chagall, Jacques Villon, Camoin, Jean Puy, André Lhote.

The portrait painter

Many will find it exaggerated praise, if I say that Matisse is one of the few masters of our time who has left beautiful portraits.

First of all, his self-portraits. One of 1900 (Henri Matisse coll.), painted with an energy exalted by the influence of Cézanne.

Le portrait de l'artiste en maillot rayé (Copenhagen museum), dates from 1906. It bears the stamp of the powerful Collioure period, when it was painted, the time of *Bonheur de Vivre*. Rough sailor's beard; broad bulbous forehead; large serious eyes; the nose a bit 'meandering' à la Greco. And indeed it would not be surprising to find this hardy fisherman seated with Peter in the *Supper in Simon's house* of the Chicago Art Institute. With its brutal ochre planes, outlined in ivory black, it could easily be placed among the Apostles of the *Pentecost* painted by Theotocopuli.

Eleven years later, another self-portrait (Henri Matisse coll.), painted during the early days of his stay in the marvellous town of Nice. There is austerity and even melancholy in that powerfully balanced canvas, in which black alone serves to heighten its pure, cold tones.

During the war: Jean Matisse had joined the army and the enemy was preparing the final offensive.

Twenty years later, the master himself said to Gaston Diehl: '*In those difficult days, I was always waiting for bulletins. I could no longer become absorbed in a work which would have demanded too much time to crystallize my feelings. . . .*'

His own image and the external world, such were his only models then. The time of the odalisques and nudes had not yet come, they needed too long a study.

That self-portrait which appeared in 1917, preceded but little the sober, vigorous effigy of the artist painting with the left hand (Matisse was ambidextrous), dressed with the elegance George Besson described in 1918, in an austere range of colour. (Henri Matisse coll.)

Then came a whole series of faces, drawn with a sometimes rough fidelity, like the one executed in 1937 for a book on himself[1] or a caricatural interpretation (1947) like the sketch reproduced in André Verdet's work *Prestiges de Matisse*.

[1] *Henri Matisse* by Raymond Escholier, Floury ed., 1937.

The series of eight portraits drawn in 1944 and published by *Verve* (Vol. IV, no. 13), on the contrary, aim at serenity rather than character.

And there are many portraits of the painter studying a female nude; beginning in 1903 with the artist revealed in the looking-glass which reflects the back view of *Carmelina*; and continuing in 1916 with the *Peintre et son Modèle* (Paris, *Musée National d'Art Moderne*). These two are in oils, whereas all the others—some of great psychological as well as aesthetic interest—are in charcoal or line drawing.

As well as a number of *Fauve* works, like the famous *Femme au chapeau*, *Portrait à la raie verte*, *la Guitariste*, *la Dame en vert* (the last named in the Moscow Museum of Modern Western Art), there exist admirable portraits of the artist's lovely, dignified wife, among the most notable *Madame Matisse au madras rouge*, 1908 (Barnes Foundation in Merion). She is like a beautiful fruit of Languedoc, prominent cheekbones, sensual mouth, sensitive nose, long almond eyes dreamy and enchanting under arched blue eyebrows, a vermilion kerchief on her head.

On his return from Morocco in 1913, Matisse was practising an art of simplification, and here again the beauty of the model is sacrificed to the artist's preconceived idea. Indeed, in the portrait of *Madame Matisse* (Moscow Museum of Modern Western Art) the little hat crowned with feathers among which is a small flower, is more striking than the expressionless face, already reduced to an oval; evidently, this *toque* of the hobble-skirt period was what attracted the painter's attention, so that he made it far less an abstraction than the portrait proper.

But one of the most beautiful portraits of Madame Henri Matisse will always be *Le Manteau écossais*, a very fine picture, with strong inner life, painted on a balcony in Nice.

Marguerite Matisse was her father's inspiration for an equally considerable number of works, among them, *Marguerite assise* (1904, Lionel Steinberg coll., Fresno), and the admirable *Liseuse* (1906), which Marcel Sembat and his wife Georgette Agutte left to the Grenoble Museum. It was undoubtedly *Fauve* painting, but there was as yet no synthesis in its realism. A forceful colour with nothing aggressive. Bent over her book, is the face of a tall dark girl, highly coloured, slightly sunburnt, heightened with black, lips like a sabre-cut, turned-up nose, long lashes, arched brows, the backs of the hands tinted viridian, a crimson lake dress with white spots and a large white collar, her brown hair tied up with a vermilion ribbon. A curious thing that no one seems to have remarked, the graded blues and pinks, lemon and orange of the background which lend a kind of magic to the *Fauve* figure, derive entirely from Turner, whom Matisse discovered in London and who is felt more surely in this canvas than is Velasquez, mentioned rather at random by Sembat. There is far more emotion and even tenderness here than in the *Femme au chapeau*, painted a year earlier, in quite a different, more aggressive spirit.

Really, at that time, Marguerite was the ideal model for her father. For more than fifteen years, his vital, intelligent daughter was the unfailing inspiration for remarkable canvases. For instance, in 1908, the full-face with the name, 'Marguerite' inscribed at the top of the canvas (Picasso coll.), of unusual technique for Matisse, reminiscent of both Chinese painting of the Ming period, and of Lautrec's coloured posters. Certainly here, the artist had particular reasons to say '*Le modèle, c'est moi*'. Reduced to essentials, after how many studies, that portrait shows a premeditated desire to go beyond appearances and discover what strange young being was hidden behind the Oriental gaze, pensive eyes, nose whose line proceeds strangely from the left eyebrow, expressive mouth about to speak, and long, domineering chin, like *père* Matisse, as Marquet said.

After that, no one can say Matisse is incapable of psychology. Never, not even at the time of Raphael's *Balthazar Castiglione* or of David's *Pius VII*, never did the art of portraiture achieve such penetration. Picasso must have recognized it at once.

In character and method, a great distance lies between those two pictures of Marguerite; one, the tall child, *La Liseuse*, of a rather conventional realism, the other a young girl full of life, in which one feels a deep and secret nature. One is amazed by the transformation of the model in two years, and by the difference in the technique.

A few years later, about 1913, with *Tête rose et bleue*, it is almost impossible to recognize the same model and the same artist. Admittedly, this is not a portrait, but variations on pink and blue, black and white (the background is solid black, as in so many Moroccan compositions).

Far more brutal and less flattering, was *Margot au Chapeau*, painted at Collioure, 1907 (Zurich, Kunsthaus).

There are many other pictures of Marguerite, *Portrait* (private coll. at Soleure), *Marguerite au chat noir*, 1910 (Henri Matisse coll.), seated full-face, the right-hand thumb strangely shaped, the head rounded under the brown hair like a turban. Work which still shows the *Fauve* influence.

Later came *Marguerite dans un interieur* (1915–16) (former Kann coll.); then *Mademoiselle Matisse à la jaquette rayée*, *Marguerite au chapeau de fourrure*, *Marguerite au boa* (Ohara Museum, Kurashiki, Japan), those last three dated

1917. Finally, in 1919, time of joy after the French victory, *Marguerite allongée dans l'herbe* (Barnes Foundation, Merion).

The portrait of *Pierre Matisse*, painted in 1909 shows intense life, ardent expression of the grace of childhood.

Indeed, the whole family gave numerous subjects to its head.

Such as the *Portrait de famille* (Moscow, Museum of Modern Western Art) which has been compared to a Persian miniature, showing Madame Matisse standing on the left, Jean and Pierre Matisse in the centre playing draughts, Marguerite with her sewing on a sofa on the left, against a richly ornamental background: in the foreground an Oriental carpet, a wall-paper flowered with tulips, a marble mantel-piece over a tiled fireplace, on which are bunches of flowers in vases.

Far more sober, almost bald in treatment, is *La Leçon de piano* (New York Museum of Modern Art) painted in 1916. Pure, austere tones predominate: pink, grey, Empire green, yellow ochre, black and cold blue. The only ornamental passages are in the wrought iron of the balcony and the open arabesque of the wooden music stand. The abstract quality is perhaps even more evident than in *Les Marocains* and *Les Demoiselles à la rivière*, in which for the first time appear faces reduced to a simple oval, as the decorator of Vence was to conceive the faces of the Virgin and Saint Dominique shortly before his death.

Agnès Humbert gives an excellent analysis of this composition: 'Although the large canvas is based on reality, we feel ourselves to be in an abstract world: through the open window, we see what is undoubtedly a garden, but to express this Matisse only required a large triangle of viridian, without modulation. The figure of a woman is listening to young Pierre Matisse practising his scales. She is perched on an artist's stool. . . . And to fill the large grey rectangle which serves as background, Matisse has elongated his model vertically. . . . In no other work has Matisse reached such geometric simplicity, such great austerity, thought-out and serene.'[1]

There is but one reservation to be made, but so important it is astonishing it has escaped the careful observation of Alfred H. Barr and Gaston Diehl. Obviously in this picture we are not seeing the Pierre Matisse of 1917, then in his eighteenth year. The child at the piano, although stylized, is more contemporary of the Pierre Matisse in *Portrait de famille*, which dates from 1912 or 1913, certainly before the 1914 war, since it is part of the Stchoukine collection, subsequently nationalized by the Soviet government. As for the Pierre Matisse of 1918, we find him again in *la Leçon de musique* of the Barnes Foundation, seated

[1] Notice by Agnès Humbert in *Henri Matisse* by Gaston Diehl, Editions Pierre Tisné.

at the same Pleyel, on which his father's violin reposes, but how changed: an adolescent with a long, thin nose and attentive eyes. He is at the age to fall in love, like his elder sister who is standing beside him in a long, pale dress with the black velvet ribbon round her neck mentioned by Gertrude Stein, waiting to turn the page, while in the garden Madame Matisse is working on an embroidery, and Jean Matisse, demobilized *poilu*, is squarely seated in an armchair reading with a cigarette. Indeed, *la Leçon de musique* could as well be called *La Famille heureuse*. . . .

There is a world of difference between these two canvases of the same dimensions (about 2 m 50 × 2 m 10), and to say nothing of the great difference in technique, the disparity in the ages of the young pianist poses a distinct problem as to the chronology, evidently faulty, of *la Leçon de musique* and *la Leçon de piano*. The same date cannot reasonably apply to the two pictures. In addition, it is enough to examine carefully the woman's figure listening to Pierre, to be convinced that she is dressed in the fashion of 1913 of hobble-skirts, and not in the full short skirts of 1916–17. That almost Gothic figure is truly the sister of *la Femme au tabouret* of 1913 (Stchoukine coll. and later Henri Matisse coll.). One cannot but feel in the large *Leçon de musique*, one of the most beautiful of French pictures, an atmosphere of relief and a promise of happiness. It is the time of exaltation after victory, when the artist, in his Odalisques, freed from anguish for his country and his son, let himself go to the enjoyment of the paradise of Nice and began to taste the sweetness of life. We find that same immeasurable joy and happiness which swept over France in those days, in another portrait, a contemporary of the *Leçon de musique*, the portrait of his violin by Henri Matisse.[1] A kind of bird's eye view, of very Mediterranean intimacy—one slatted shutter propped open, Italian fashion, giving on the intense light of Nice, the cerulean sky, the burning sand and aloe leaves; the other closed against the heat which slips, strident, between the dark slats. A great splash of light on the right, one window wide open. On the flat tone, almost black, of walls and carpet, a chair holds in its arms the violin case, where the red-brown of the violin sings out against the indigo lining.

Numberless other portraits by the painter of *la Danse* exist for our delight.

A bearded *Portrait d'homme*, with drooping moustache, head bent and the dreaming eyes of a Breton, probably painted before 1900 and which could be of Gustave Geffroy (the opinion of George Besson, who reproduces it in his excellent little book on Matisse).[2] The asymmetry of the eyes, peculiar to all human

[1] *Intérieur au violon*, Copenhagen State Museum, J. Rump coll.
[2] 'Les Maîtres' Collection, Editions Braun, 1954.

faces, is accentuated, as the individual character of the model, evidently an intellectual, is deeply studied.

There is the *Derain* of the Collioure period, brushed in with extreme violence, which the Tate Gallery acquired for over seven thousand pounds shortly after Matisse's death. When Derain sat for Matisse, he had just returned from three years' hard military service at Commercy. He was qualified as, 'Vigorous, fit for campaigning. . . .'

If, as is normal, Albert Marquet's vision and execution were modified by the years, he always remained faithful to the admirations of his youth. There was great constancy in the friendship he cherished for his old comrade in arms, '*Le père Matisse*', as he called him with his kind, slightly mocking smile.

Henri Matisse has left us two faithful portraits of his dear friend Marquet, simple and familiar, one of 1902, the other 1903, (Oslo Museum). Both give an impression of honesty, loyalty and modesty—fundamental virtues of Marquet's, in his art and his life. 'When I came into Marquet's life' said Madame Marquet, 'I knew at once that Matisse was his friend. . . . I am still touched when I think of his warm welcome, and his sudden concern when he asked me abruptly the first time I met him, "*Have you noticed that Marquet has a tender heart?*" '[1]

At the height of the *Fauve* period, Matisse became friends with the Steins and their relative Miss Etta Cone of Baltimore, of whom he painted a nervous, sensitive portrait, acutely lucid. And Miss Etta Cone, who also sat for Picasso, was to become, with her sister Doctor Claribel Cone, one of the first collectors of Matisse in the United States.

Portraits of *Greta Moll* (1908) and Olga Merson—*la Dame au corsage vert*—show great preoccupation with the characters of the young women. Particularly remarkable is the portrait of the Hungarian Greta Moll, who with her husband Oscar, was among the master's most faithful disciples. In that rather sheeplike face, with its heavy sensual mouth and pointed chin, Matisse naturally brought out an Asiatic character, which is heightened by the Oriental embroidery of the blouse and the background slashed with cinnabar and blue.

We find the Orient again in the drawing which is a masterpiece, *le Portrait de Serge Stchoukine* (Moscow Museum of Modern Western Art); an almost Mongolian mask, wonderfully modelled.

Far more synthetic, but just as expressive, is *Auguste Pellerin* (1915) in which one finds the same drawing and camaieu painting as in *Peintre et son modèle* (1916, Musée National d'Art Moderne, Paris).

[1] *Arts* No. 489, November 10–16th, 1954.

The same simplification in the *Portrait de Sarah Stein* (Palo Alto, California, Mrs Sarah Stein coll.). One may well prefer the study from life (1916, Henri Matisse coll.) shown at the *Exposition des Maîtres de l'Art Indépendant*, 1937, at the Petit Palais.[1] A marvellous painting, which El Greco might have signed, the beautiful face of one of those young Jewesses still to be seen in Toledo.

Matisse has felt all the influences of his time, and many others, as he says himself. Thus it is not surprising to find a sort of Cubist or Futurist picture of 1914, *Yvonne Landsberg* (Philadelphia Museum). Matisse's conversations with Gleizes, Metzinger and Severini, of which they have often told me, played a part in this unexpected picture. In these 'Great curved lines, which surround the woman like petals of which she is the pistil', he was using a procedure borrowed from Byzantium, and also much used by Gleizes at that time, for instance in his *Vierges à l'Enfant* entirely spherical compositions. Matisse himself called them '*Constructive lines*' thus returning to a phrase dear to the Cubists and Futurists.

How was this 'commissioned' portrait received? One has to smile in reading Agnès Humbert's witty and knowledgeable account. 'It is easy to imagine the confusion of the sitter's family confronted with such a new vision of the human form. In 1947 Henri Matisse said, "*Exactitude is not truth.*" He could have made that statement as early as 1914, in reply to the criticism of the sitter's mother. who declared the portrait could be called "*le chef d'œuvre inconnu*". The sitter's brother, however, was quite enthusiastic, and compares the portrait to a Byzantine ikon. He speaks of its superb colours; steel blue, black, white and orange. He adds that the painter repaints his picture entirely at each sitting,[2] and often draws with the handle of his brush long lines in the fresh paint leaving here and there pale tracks of bare canvas.'[3]

Painted two years later, the portrait of *Greta Prozor*, is again a work stripped down to essentials. The face under a large hat is like certain pictures of Marguerite; but the curve of the armchair and the body, which is felt under the dress, certainly date this great thoughtful canvas to the year of Verdun, 1916. Is it from the sitter that there is a sort of Lutheran austerity of feeling, an almost Ibsen-like quality?

Also much simplified was the *Michael Stein*, painted about the same time. But with the French victory in 1918, which so profoundly affected Matisse, everything changed.

[1] Reproduced in colour in *Henri Matisse* by Raymond Escholier, Floury 1937.
[2] According to Matisse's method, it must have been each time on a new canvas.
[3] Gaston Diehl, op. cit., Agnès Humbert's notice.

There was a return to nature, to the reality of life, what Gaston Diehl called 'the indispensable reference to sensation'. It was the reign of a new model, *Lorette: Lorette au fauteuil*, *Lorette à la tasse de café*, and many faces of Lorette. Henri Matisse coll., Bremen Museum, etc.

It is also the period of the lovely *Trois Sœurs*, formerly in the collection of Paul Guillaume, who began in 1917 trying to acquire the major part of Henri Matisse's production. One is inclined to prefer this large, fine composition in which each sister is acutely observed (in spite of the family resemblance) in the most joyful colours, to the same subject ordered by Dr Barnes for the Merion foundation as a decorative triptych, inevitably less concentrated by enlargement: *The Italian model Lorette and her sisters*.

Oriental influences still persist in the 1918 portrait of the antiquary *Demotte*, who practised 'Elginism' on a grand scale, to the detriment of France and our Gothic monuments, and went so far as to transport our cloisters of Gascony and Languedoc across the Atlantic—until with the Duke of Trévise I drew public attention to the matter. Matisse has immortalized him in a magnificent portrait, very close to an El Greco. Nailed to the mast by the penetrating, sometimes cruel, genius of Matisse, he is truly exposed for what he was. The skull narrowing to a point, eyebrows well arched, eyes on the look-out, ears large and faun-like, straight, strong nose above a long wavy moustache and grey beard, a somewhat apostolic countenance recalling more genuine ones of Toledo.

'Joie de vivre' entered the portraits with *Les Plumes blanches* of 1919 (Minneapolis Art Institute), triumph of the favourite model of the moment, dark Antoinette. Her canary-yellow coat is open, heart-shaped, showing her lovely *décolleté*, and the waves of her hair fall on bare shoulders. Dreaming face of a courtesan, rivalling the Venetian women of Aretino, Titian and Veronese, the cheekbones prominent, receding chin, mouth well drawn with lipstick, nose delicate and long, brilliant eyes flecked with gold and heightened by kohl, oblique Japanese eye-brows (plucking had not come into fashion) under a great 'Amazon' plume, a marvellous ostrich feather decorating her large straw hat.

This is Matisse, son of a Paris *modiste* and husband of another, always in love with feminine dress, the luxurious supple tissues of the East. He knew Poiret at that time, and followed his discoveries with intense interest.

Matisse told Alfred H. Barr how he became a milliner. Not finding what he wanted in the shops, the artist decided to make a hat himself. He bought a large hood, white ostrich feathers, and ribbon black on one side and white on the other, and proceeded to make a hat for Antoinette, after the style of Milady in the 'Three Musketeers', exaggerating the Baroque style, adding a lot of velvet curls to mingle with the real ones. One of the preliminary drawings is as fine as a Holbein.

Matisse more than once sacrificed his favourite baroque curves, in *Coin d'Atelier*, *La Leçon de Piano*, for example, and many others, But in general he avoids angles and triangles. His line, the essentially Matisse line, is principally curving and sinuous and sometimes almost rococo—witness his delight in Louis-Philippe and Second-Empire chairs.

The year 1924 is remarkable for three portraits. *La Baronne Gourgaud*, magnificent, tall American. I knew her well, and I never surprised that expression of melancholy, even profound sadness, given by this portrait. But Henri Matisse must have seen more deeply than a passing guest.

There is a curious premonition in this portrait, painted at a time when Lydia Delectorskaya was still unknown to Matisse. For this lovely face, whose likeness delighted the Baronne Gourgaud and her husband, most curiously foreshadows the splendid Lydia who was to be an incomparable model for the master during the last twenty years of his life, an accomplished secretary and unfailing source of inspiration.

In 1936 was a marvellous drawing of *Mrs Hutchinson* seated on a *Restauration* sofa, leaning on one elbow, slightly astigmatic, with the swan's neck dear to the middle ages and to Henri Matisse, the figure lengthened El Greco-wise, the nose long and delicate, the broad forehead heavy with thought.

About the same time, a new sitter, Princess Hélène Galitzine, posed for Matisse, in numerous compositions and for a portrait highly stylized, very Baroque in taste where she wears one of those gorgeous Venetian dresses launched by Fortuny.

It would certainly appear to be this beautiful dark young woman, in *la Femme à l'écharpe*, in *la Femme à la chaise rouge* (Baltimore Art Museum, Cone coll.) of 1936; in *le Collier d'ambre*, of 1937; in *la Liseuse sur fond noir*, of 1939 (Paris, *Musée d'Art Moderne*), in *L'Idole*, of 1942 (New York, Albert D. Lasker coll.); in *la Femme à la robe blanche*, of 1946.

It is Princess Hélène who reigns among the tricolour harmony of *l'Intérieur Tabac Royal*, 1942. (For Henri Matisse, who wanted to defend Verdun in 1916, everything was seen in red, white and blue in 1939, when he painted that intensely modern portrait, allied to the *Grand Siècle.*)

And often the master asked the dark Princess Galitzine and the fair Lydia to pose together. That is how the album of *Verve*, 1945, happens to be largely devoted to them.

Long before their time—as witness *les Plumes Blanches*—Matisse knew all about feminine elegance. Friend of Poiret, and follower of the Russian Ballet, where more often than not the show was in the audience: ambassadresses, Highnesses and princesses displaying the most magnificent *toilettes* in dress circle and boxes, with peerless diadems and jewels; received also by American magnates, and already familiar with the elegant royalties of Velasquez and Goya, Matisse was by no means discovering the splendours of great dress-making, as Agnès Humbert supposed, for the first time. But one must agree with her 'that the two young women delighting to wear "*de style*" dresses, with their ample skirts, and bright patterns, must have strangely stimulated the artist's genius'.

Of such are the three *Conversations* of 1940,[1] *la Robe jaune et la Robe écossaise*, princess Galitzine in a lemon yellow dress, seated in a cadmium yellow *bergère*, and the blonde Lydia displaying a romantic costume, a crimson bodice with short Charles X sleeves, and an ample tartan skirt of scarlet, ultramarine and viridian.

Most of the portraits painted between 1940 and 1945 are women's portraits, with the exception of two important ones, both in charcoal. One shows the proud image of an old pupil of Gustave Moreau, the Rumanian painter Pallady, whose delicated Iranian silhouette was long familiar to strollers on the *quai de l'Horloge*, painted in 1939. The other, of August, 1946, given by André Rouveyre to the Nîmes museum, *Paul Léautaud*, in which the thin, bitter lips, and eyes peering through glass, three sharp lines, give the whole character to this deeply studied, disquieting face.

Many other faces, often familiar ones. A sober, masterly drawing in silver point of the great composer, Serge Prokofiev, dating from 1921, a year after the Russian Ballet, *Chant du Rossignol*, for which costumes and sets were designed by Matisse. Again, the dreaming eyes and voluptuous mouth of *Madame D. Paley*, so Oriental in expression.

A vehement, imperious profile: *Montherlant*, a lino-cut; *Apollinaire*, idealized by memory; *Paul Matisse*, the master's grandson, a graceful youth whose narrow face reminds one of El Greco and Velasquez; *Ilya Ehrenbourg*, 1946, whose dreamy left eye is in contrast to the more observing right one; the adorable charcoals of *Jackie*, *Jacqueline Matisse*, the artist's granddaughter; and the vivid profiles of Madame Leriche.

As for *Professor René Leriche*, the charcoal portrait kept by this great practitioner has more depth and power than the drawing belonging to the *Musée des Arts décoratifs*.

[1] Thanks to the friendship of Henri Matisse, I received in 1947 a catalogue in manuscript of his production during the eight years of 1938–46. An original document of inestimable value in art history.

But for all that, the master's great inspiration, for her plastic splendour, beauty and expression of face, intelligence and wit, remains undoubtedly Lydia Delectorskaya.

He installed Lydia in Paris, at the Hotel Lutetia where I met her often, in 1935, and from that time on she was the source of masterpieces: *les Yeux bleus* (Baltimore Art Museum), extraordinary likeness, as I can testify; *le Rêve*, which advertised the *Exposition des Maîtres de l'Art Indépendant* in 1937, the facsimile for the poster having been made on my order by Fernand Mourlot; the *Nu au collier bleu*, 1936, P. Rosenberg coll., in which the barely indicated face is so recognizable.

Another admirable drawing of 1935; *Portrait de jeune femme*: Lydia, whose lovely face appears enlarged against the wall; Lydia dressed to go out, is seated in a large, Renaissance armchair, the straight lines of the chair contrasting with the curves of the face and the feminine body, enveloped in a large winter coat. (The charcoal drawing is dated November 20th, 1935.)

La Blouse verte, painting of 1936, is an equally good likeness of Madame Delectorskaya.

Much more stylized, but still in the character of the marvellous Slav model, *le Grand nu couché—fond à carreaux* (Baltimore Art Museum, Cone coll.) of 1935, which is also called *Nu rose*.

As well as the beauty of her figure, shown in so many drawings with minute precision, this is certainly, much simplified, the fine oval face of Lydia.

Again she, her plastic beauty heightened by such an ample costume as makes one think of Velasquez, in the glorious *Figure Décorative* painted in 1938 (MacIlhemy coll. Philadelphia).

Among so many pen-drawings dedicated to Lydia, like *le Peintre et son modéle*, 1935, like *la Blouse bulgare*, like the *Nu couché sur le dos* of magnificent foreshortening, among so many pictures, like *la Blouse brodée* (P. Rosenberg coll.) in the fresh tones of watercolours, one must place two above them all; two sublime drawings of 1936, the one in which Lydia is seen to the waist, the torso thrown back in an armchair, the bare arms raised and partly covering her voluptuous profile which surpasses Ingres for purity of line; and finally that lovely head, like Mélisande weeping for her long hair in the music of Debussy, the sensual mouth slightly twisted, each eye with a different expression, pathetic image of a dreamy race persecuted by men's cruelty.

That simple face in charcoal is enough to proclaim Matisse one of the greatest portrait painters of France.

I paint portraits

Yet many good judges, ignoring Vuillard and the Picasso of *Gertrude Stein*, have announced the decline and even the death of the portrait this last half century!

All the work of Henri Matisse protests. . . . But . . . quite obviously the photographic portrait in paint never meant anything to him.

And he said all there is to be said on the subject himself.

'*The chief interest of my work comes from an attentive and respectful observation of nature, as also the duality of feeling with which she inspires me, rather than a certain virtuosity which almost always follows honest and constant work.*

'*I can't speak too strongly of the necessity for an artist of perfect sincerity in his work, which alone can give him the great courage he needs to accept it in modesty and humility.*'

Which means that Matisse, faithful to his ideas, counted entirely on the shock which deep observation would give him—from his model.

Rembrandt, to whom Matisse from his youth had turned for help, Rembrandt would have helped him to overcome his hesitations and doubts before the model. '*We only know one saying of Rembrandt's*, "I paint portraits!" *I have often held on to that saying, in the struggle.*' he confided to Aragon.

Like his much-studied Rembrandt and Latour, like Raphael in *Balthazar Castiglione* which he had copied, Matisse continually broke through the barrier of appearance, in flight from the accidental to the eternal.

That is what Aragon meant when he said, 'There are portraits and portraits.'

But he is mistaken in thinking that all the great portrait painters, from Fouquet to Renoir, and Matisse, did not 'go beyond the portrait'. That is what makes their greatness. But to his honour be it said, he is hesitant.

'Beyond the portrait. . . .

'The portrait is a very singular acquisition of the human mind. A precious moment in art, but a moment. A prophecy of the photograph. It played a decisive part in French art, it is the essential characteristic of a certain time. But only until a later time. Have we reached it? I can't tell. . . . I don't say that the portrait has had its day, I say there are some men who have already gone far beyond the portrait. This is particularly felt with Matisse. . . . It is himself he understands in those women (his models), but one must believe he understands them also. There is the story of the American woman whose portrait he was painting. He made one drawing of her after another. She wanted to have them all, because she saw all her family in them, her mother, an uncle, a cousin . . .

and I suppose moments of herself she had never seen. One day she would be like this drawing, once she had been like that. Matisse had not seen her then, any more than he had known her mother left behind in Connecticut. He had done better—he had understood her. And through her, many things.

'Beyond the portrait. . . .'

Surely, the portrait itself, as it was understood by the old masters, and by Henri Matisse.

André Sauret published a whole series of *Portraits* in Monte Carlo (sixty in black and white and thirty-three in colour), from the portrait of *Nini Betron* (1896) to one of the last in 1953, *Georges Salles*.

Matisse told Professor Leriche, those swift likenesses '*were like revelations, coming after a careful analysis of the sitter which seemed at first to give no results: a sort of meditation*'. And the surgeon replied, 'That is exactly how I make a diagnosis. I am asked, "Why do you say that?" I reply, "I don't know, but I am sure." And I mean it.'

But Henri Matisse gave his clearest definition of the art of portraiture to a craftsman, the master-printer, Fernand Mourlot. In this text which will become as much a part of literature as Delacroix' writings, we must consider the essential.

'*The study of the portrait seems forgotten today. Yet it is an inexhaustible source of interest to one with that gift, or simply that curiosity. One might think that the photographic portrait is enough. For anthropometry, yes, but for an artist who seeks the true character of a face, this is not so: recording the model's features reveals feelings of the unknown even to the one who has brought them to light. If need be, the analysis of a physiognomist would be almost necessary to attempt an explanation of them in clear language, for they synthesize and contain many things that the painter himself does not at first suspect.*'

As with Daumier, memory played an essential part in this portrait painter.

'*Real portraits, I mean those in which elements as well as feeling seem to come from the model, are rather rare. When I was young, I often went to the* Musée Lécuyer *in Saint-Quentin. There were a hundred or so pastel drawings by Quentin-Latour, done before starting his great fashionable portraits. I was touched by those agreeable faces, and realized afterwards that each one was quite personal. I was surprised, as I left the museum, by the variety of individual smiles on those faces; although natural and charming on the whole, they had made such an impression on me that my own face was aching as if I had been smiling for hours.*'

When Matisse was eighty, in the prime of creative genius, he paid a moving tribute to his kind, sensitive mother. She had given him his first paint-box, and she showed him, after she had gone, the secret of portraiture.

'The revelation of my life in the study of portraits came to me in thinking of my mother. In a post office in Picardy, I was waiting for a telephone call. To pass the time, I picked up a telegraph form lying on a table, and made a pen drawing on it of a woman's head. I drew without thinking of what I was doing, my pen working on its own, and I was surprised to recognize my mother's face with all its subtleties.

'My mother had a face with generous features, which bore the deep distinction of French Flanders.'

That unconscious sketch opened a royal road to Matisse.

'I was still a pupil occupied with "traditional" drawing, anxious to believe in the rules of the School, remnants of the teaching of masters who came before us, in a word, the dead part of tradition in which all that was not actually observed in nature, all that derived from feeling or memory was despised and condemned as bogus. I was struck by the revelations of my pen, and I saw that the mind which composes should keep a sort of virginity towards the chosen elements and reject all that is offered by reasoning.'

Truly, '*the portrait is one of the strangest of arts. It demands especial gifts of the artist, and an almost total relationship between the painter and his model. The painter should come to his model with no preconceived ideas.*

'It should all reach his mind like the smell of the earth in a landscape, and of the flowers in harmony with the play of clouds, the movement of trees and the different sounds of the countryside.'

The first sitting, which is hardly ever decisive:

'After half an hour or an hour, I am surprised to see gradually appearing on my paper an image more or less precise and resembling the person with whom I am in contact.

'That image is revealed to me as if each line of charcoal erased some of the mist from a mirror which until then had prevented me from seeing it.'

Such is, ordinarily, '*the meagre result of a first sitting.*' Between the first and second sittings, a rest is obligatory, which gives time for meditation.

Then, from one sitting to another, '*the record made at the first impact*' will fade, '*to allow a vision of the most important features, the living substance of the work.*'

At last, '*something is born*' between the painter and his model: '*an interpenetration of feeling which makes each feel the warmth of the other's heart, and which will give rise to the completion of the painted portrait or else the possibility* (for the artist) *of expressing in "rapid drawings" what has come* (to him) *from the model.*

'I gain a deep knowledge of my subject' concludes Matisse, *'After long work in charcoal, made up of studies corresponding more or less to each other, visions arise which may appear summary, but which are the expression of the intimate exchange between the artist and his model. Drawings containing all the subtle observations during work arise from a fermentation within, like bubbles in a pond.'*[1]

'He "lifts" his watch . . .'

The year 1940, or rather its opening, brought some marvellous work: *la Nature morte à l'ananas, la Nature morte au coquillage, la Nature morte aux roses de Noël et aux huîtres, la Jeune fille à la blouse roumaine, la Dormeuse à la table violette.* And from Ciboure, where Matisse took refuge that year from 'too noisy neighbours', came one painting (Albi Museum) and a whole series of drawings inspired by one of those Voltaire armchairs, now only found in the provinces, whose scrolls and curves evoke the comfortable days of Louis-Philippe, the Citizen King.

It was because of that red armchair, left by chance in a yellow room, that Matisse stayed in the house in Ciboure. And that takes one back to Balzac and the *Curé de Tours.* Aragon felt this. 'He drew this chair endlessly, patiently, in a secret flirtation with the room, until he should have absorbed enough to discover its mystery.'

And this was not the only armchair which counted in the life of the artist, to whom things, as much as women, were objects of delight. 'Compare that armchair' writes Aragon, 'to another in the life of Matisse: that Baroque rocking-chair in his room in Tahiti, which he would draw placed alone in front of the incredible landscape and sky . . . Matisse would say of that curious diversion, that flirtation, it is like the conversation of a pick-pocket with his victim: *"during that time, he 'lifts' his watch."* '

And Henri Matisse wrote to Aragon, on April 20th, 1942, to tell him of a find. *'I have at last found what I've wanted for a year. It is a Venetian Baroque chair, it's silver toned with varnish, like enamel. You have probably seen such a thing. When I met it in an antique shop, a few weeks ago, I was quite overcome by it. It is splendid. . . . I think of nothing else. I shall jump slowly back with it on my summer return-journey.'*

It was in such an armchair, in the month of May, 1940, that Matisse learned the dreadful news. Battles lost on the frontiers, the battle of France lost, Paris trampled by barbarians, the Pyrenees threatened.

[1] The whole context, written at the request of Fernand Mourlot, is found in *Portraits* by Henri Matisse (André Sauret, *Editions du Livre,* Monte Carlo, 1954).

He told me his own sad story on July 12th, 1940, at the Hotel Ferrière, where he was staying, in Saint-Gaudens:

'*I escaped from Saint-Jean-de-Luz, where I thought I should be quiet. I had brought a lot of things for a long stay, and on the declaration of war with Italy, I had sent from Nice a Greek torso of fine quality.*'

When the enemy occupied the Basque coast, the artist had luckily been able to take away all he possessed. But he was held up in Saint-Gaudens, until the trains should run again to Nice. Knowing I had managed to bring a large part of the Petit Palais and Carnavalet collections to Ariège, Henri Matisse asked me to add a very beautiful marble statue to them, belonging to him, which I did readily.

But that was only a beginning. Three days later, July 15th, 1940, Henri Matisse sent me such an important letter from Saint-Gaudens that I had to give warning to my friend and colleague J. G. Lemoine, curator of the Bordeaux Museum, who already knew, and another friend, Goulinat, director of restorations in the National Museums—and expert. Thus the situation was saved.

The cause of concern was the Paul Rosenberg collection of pictures, most of which had been deposited in Bordeaux on its way to the United States. Of course there were many paintings by Henri Matisse, already robbed by the Germans in 1914. But one can never forget, when there was so much cowardice, the passionate determination he showed to preserve those masterpieces for France.

'*I am sending you . . . a letter from M. Lemoine, curator of the Bordeaux Museum. Will you do me the service, the great service, to tell me what you think of it. I give you my word of honour to destroy your answer, and no one shall hear of it.*

'*It seems that because the pictures belong to a dealer, no official interest can be taken in them. But the works of very important artists are at stake. There are not only my pictures, I saw them when I was in Bordeaux: there are two very important Corots: a figure and a landscape; Courbets, two beautiful drawings and two pictures by Renoir; Cézannes; fine Bonnards, pictures by Braque, a very beautiful Picasso.*

'*You see those pictures lying about, abandoned, will be lost or confiscated by the Germans. What will be said, when the story is known, of those who could save them? It seems to me a matter of interest to the Beaux-Arts directors. I mean to write there, but to whom and how?*

'*You could help in advising me on this.*

'*I cannot see whether and in which capacity the director of the Mont-de-Piété might store those pictures. What do you say?*

F. La robe blanche (1946)

Paris, Private Collection

40. La serpentine (bronze)

New York, Museum of Modern Art

41. Nu (vu de dos) (i) (bronze)
London, Tate Gallery

42. Nu (vu de dos) (ii) (bronze)
London, Tate Gallery

43. Nu (vu de dos) (iii) (bronze)
London, Tate Gallery

44. Nu (vu de dos) (iv) (bronze)
London, Tate Gallery

45. Vénus assise. Femme aux bras levés (Nu assis) (bronze). Vénus

Baltimore, Museum of Art (Cone)

46. Grosse tête (bronze)

San Francisco, Museum of Art

47. Nu couché (bronze)

London, Tate Gallery

48. Nu rose

Baltimore, Museum of Art (Cone)

49. Grande robe bleue

Philadelphia, Private Collection

50. Lydia aux anémones

Private Collection

51. Le manteau écarlate

Private Collection

52. Le manteau rayé aux anémones

Private Collection

53. Portrait de jeune femme (Elena)

Private Collection

54. Le grand intérieur rouge

Paris, Musée d'Art Moderne

55. Les coloquintes
New York, Museum of Modern Art

56. Nature morte aux citrons et mimosas
Private Collection

57. Le chapeau bleu

Private Collection

58. Intérieur au rideau égyptien

Washington, Phillips Memorial Gallery

'I also want to write to the Société des Indépendants *in Bordeaux. M. Lemoine, who seems very much concerned by this frightful neglect, could make an inventory which would lessen the responsibility of whoever puts them in safety. What about putting them in storage? We could have crates made, which I will pay for. What do you say?'*

When everyone else was losing his head, Matisse remained cool and responsible. But the complaint of his youth broke out again at one of the worst moments of his life.

'I received your letter yesterday' he continued *'I thank you for agreeing to rid me of my statue, with no responsibility whatever, of course. I am suffering from enteritis as a result of present conditions; as you know, I am supposed to be on a strict diet. I even have to stay in my room. I'm better, and I think in a week I shall be able to bring you the thing. I shall take a taxi . . . I hope I can get there, and shall go straight to Mirepoix. I will let you know, of course. Henri Matisse.'*[1]

Finally, all those pictures were saved, but only just; and that, as Kipling says, is another story, which I hope to tell one day.

On July 26th, Matisse gave up trying to join me in Ariège. The truth was, that in spite of his state of health, he thought only of his work.

'I despair of being able to go to Mirepoix, because of the complete lack of petrol, and I see no other means of getting my Greek torso to you, except by sending it to Mirepoix station.

'I expect to go back to Nice in a few days. I am sorry not to be able to spend a moment with you, and perhaps with your son if he is demobilized. (Our son, Claude, encouraged by Matisse in the early days of his painting.) *But I am too tired by the indisposition from which I have barely recovered.*

'I can't wait to be back in my studio. I have done nothing since the end of April —and I miss the work which lightens these depressing days. For three weeks now I have been dragging about the streets of Saint-Gaudens, occupied with trifles. There is the mountain, indeed fine, but again idleness. . . .

'Thanking you again for the great service you are doing me, I beg you to accept the cordial feelings of your devoted.

Henri Matisse'[2]

A letter of August 1st, 1940, shows how he prized his Greek sculpture.

'Yesterday went the crate containing the Greek statue (torso) to the following address: Monsieur R. Escholier, chez Monsieur le Dr Roques, en gare de Mirepoix. . . .

[1] Unpublished. [2] Unpublished.

'If the need arose to open the crate, one side is screwed down. After having stood it up or laid it down, it is only necessary to lift the lid. The torso is held in the crate by two wooden braces which prevent it from moving.

'It remains for me to thank you for taking this charming person as a lodger, regretting that I can't send what is lacking of her!'[1]

From Cimiez, Matisse was good enough to continue his story! *'Regina, Cimiez, Nice, August 31st, 1940.*

I have been in Nice for two days, where I found your card of August 10th. My return was quite difficult. I am happy to know you had your two sons with you. Like everyone else, they will take up life again with courage. Of course it is not easy, I know what it is, one is tempted all the time to listen to a voice saying "What's the good?" We haven't yet digested the catastrophe.'

Expecting to find himself in the right frame of mind for work in Nice, he was much disappointed: *'It was easier for me to keep my mind on work in Saint-Gaudens, even in Saint-Jean-de-Luz, than here in this house, between walls where I knew outward peace.'*

It was largely the fault of the Fascists. *'The fact is, I am very near to turbulent neighbours who could occupy Nice at the slightest provocation. I have the Armistice Commission almost next door, and they are unpleasant customers, it seems.*

'It was very kind of you to ask me to stop at Mirepoix instead of Carcassonne (Hôtel Terminus). But I went there because a car was willing to take me on its way to Narbonne. The trains were impossible, arriving at Saint-Gaudens already full. I went to the station twice, and had to go back to the poor hotel at Saint-Gaudens where I had had enteritis a few days before. I was stuck in Carcassonne, not knowing when I could leave. Finally I was able to get a sleeper, and reached Marseilles, where I spent a week with my grandson of eight (Paul, son of Pierre Matisse) *leaving for New York with an American boarding-house keeper. (Departure from Lisbon after endless negotiations in Marseilles.)'*

The attack of enteritis from which Henri Matisse had suffered cruelly when our disasters were at their worst, had an almost fatal sequel. In the first fortnight of January, 1941, in great pain, the artist was hastily taken to the Clinique du Parc, Lyons, where he was operated upon by the remarkable surgeon and philosopher, René Leriche. (His *Philosophie de la Chirurgie* is a masterpiece.)

Matisse sent me a courageous and friendly reassurance. He was seventy.

'For the time being,' he wrote on January 15th, 1941—*'I am in the Clinique du Parc, Bld des Belges, for a slight operation without danger. It is to take place tomorrow. . . .'*

[1] Unpublished.

But the patient had no illusions. On April 20th, 1941, convalescent, he wrote me from Lyons: '*Two weeks ago, I left the clinic which I entered at the beginning of the year: three months! I got it in the neck, not a slight operation, as I wrote you, not wanting to fuss. I was operated on for a stoppage in the intestines. I suffered a lot, but now I am stronger than I was before. I might have died like a rat in a trap at Saint-Gaudens, where the good, sympathetic old doctor, related to Foch, didn't see what was wrong. Well, all is for the best.*

'*I have stayed a few weeks at the hotel before returning to Nice, but I shall be back at the end of the week.*

'*Things seem to be moving fast, now. I don't let myself think more than two days ahead, not to worry about the respite accorded me—by Providence. The sisters at the convent called me the "Resurrected one"! I am in good shape. I eat enough for four, anything I like, and digest it perfectly. My strength has returned. We shall see what sort of work I can do when I am quite well again. . . .*'[1]

He added a humorous postscript, '*I hope my little girl is up to no mischief and gives you no trouble. If not, let me know.*'

A few days later, Matisse announced his return to the Regina. Although very thin, he seemed full of hope.

'*At last, here I am in Nice, and I have to find my balance again. I thank you for the welcome you gave my fragment of a young Greek. When you are tired of her, let me know. I shall send her to another school. I hope I shall not be without news of you. It is good, just now, not to feel too lonely. Also I shall write to you when I feel like it.*

'*With my good wishes to you and yours, I send you my friendly greetings.*[2]

Henri Matisse'

His good humour was not feigned. The courage and serenity he had shown at the approach of death was to enrich his art.

That fine writer of deep understanding, André Rouveyre, had seen the value of this turning-point in the life of the artist.

'It is well known that the approach of death gives the spirit a sort of condensation and fundamental vision of the whole life. That is certainly what Matisse felt and realized, what he reached in the course of these last years and after such a trial. It was first of all a period of cruel, bitter suffering, a terrible voyage on the Styx, from which he returned, and from which he brought back a renewed will and power to concentrate and gather all that was best in him.'

He wrote me this himself, with moving simplicity, '*I derived great moral*

[1] Unpublished. [2] Unpublished.

benefit from that operation. Clarity of ideas, a clear vision of my career and of its continuity.'

Professor Leriche has since admitted to me what concern and even anguish he had felt for the state of the man on whom he was to operate.

A Dominican sister, native of Montauban, belonging to the Mother House of Gramond in Aveyron, devoted her days and nights to him. The little nun, who had seen so much suffering, was well named Sister Marie-Ange.

Fourteen years later, almost blind, Sister Marie-Ange received me, with the Prioress in the Dominican House of Gramond, and talked to me for a long time about Henri Matisse.

'I have never seen' she confided to me, 'a braver patient, more heroic even, nor more considerate. He was evidently very strict and orderly, and if we forgot something prescribed by the doctor, M. Matisse never failed to remind us of the order, but always with great patience and perfect courtesy. When at last, after so much suffering valiantly borne, he seemed out of danger, M. Matisse fell into the habit of talking a lot with me, whenever possible. That is how he came to tell me much about his journeys to Spain, England, Russia, to Africa, the South Sea Islands, America, and he also told me about his home in Nice, his island birds and exotic plants. And then one day he said to me: "*I am thinking of something. I would like to build a chapel as an expression of gratitude for all you have done for me, Sister Marie-Ange, you and the other sisters.* (The Gramond Dominican nurses are attached to the *Clinique du Parc* in Lyons.) *Does the idea seem possible to you? It seems that it might do some good. Do you think your Order would welcome such an undertaking? I should so love to do it.*"

'The idea of Matisse then, was that the chapel should be built here, in the Aveyron, at Gramond, Languedoc, and not in Provence.

'I discussed the scheme with the Mother Superior, and she gave her consent.

'From then on, we spoke of little else with the "Man raised from the Dead". And, in spite of the pain he was still feeling, how he worked in his bed for that chapel! His large sketch-books became covered in drawings, plans for architecture, sculpture, paintings, stained glass windows, holy ornaments. . . .

'Imagine, every day he showed me five or six pages of new drawings.

'Gradually, the chapel was growing on paper, and its progress was a visible support for our patient, carrying him far from his unhappy bed, miraculously restoring his inclination for life.

'And he never tired of saying, "*It seems to me that it might do some good.*"

'Back in Nice, M. Matisse kept me informed of his great project, in letters which I unfortunately had burned, in 1945, when he sent me the plans of the chapel; but I was blind then; I was about to have an operation, and was preparing to leave this world. That's why I asked to have all my papers burned. And that was our misfortune. For, at that time, it was at Gramond that Matisse's chapel was to be built.'

'What impression have you kept of him?'

'I have never known a man as sensitive, sensitive like a child or a woman,' went on Sister Marie-Ange, smiling.

'Every night, before he went to sleep, I had fallen into the habit of going to say "Good night" to him. But once, a very serious and urgent operation kept me in the theatre long after the usual time. It was nearly midnight before we left the patient. Much too late to go and say "Goodnight, M. Matisse. . . ." I told the master's night-nurse.

'But there. I had not been in my cell a quarter of an hour, when a bell rang. The Mother Superior wanted to see me. I went to her bidding.

' "Sister Marie-Ange," she said "what are you thinking of? Why haven't you said 'Goodnight' to M. Matisse?"

'I replied that I had thought it impossible at such a late hour, and besides I had told the young nurse and asked her to make my excuses to the great artist. I think however she had forgotten to do it.

'But the Mother Superior would hear none of this.

' "M. Matisse is asking for you most insistently" she said to me, "and he won't sleep until you have been to see him. You must go when he calls you, Sister Marie-Ange."

'It was an order. Impossible to argue about it. I found our great patient in tears. He was in a dreadful state.

' "*Sister Marie-Ange*," he said to me, "*I must have hurt your feelings. Sometimes I speak roughly . . . I really didn't mean to hurt you. If I have, forgive me. Because you didn't come this evening, like every evening, I've spent some dreadful hours. Forgive me!*"

'Poor dear, great man! I had nothing to forgive him. On the contrary, I repeat, he was as gentle as a woman with us. I told him this, and at last I saw his eyes were drier. He became calm again. He was going to be able to sleep.'

Henri Matisse seemed to be cured when Francis Carco met him, a few months later in that same year, 1941.

'Matisse . . . was as good-looking as ever. He had never appeared more at ease with his conscience than on that day. He gave the impression of complete balance and honesty. The neatness of his person, the brightness of his eyes, an indefinable air of youth and serenity, struck me at once. "*Come and see me.*" he said "*I've done a lot of work.*" '[1]

The author of *L'Homme Traqué* took advantage of the invitation.

History will retain his vivid description of the wonderful surroundings of Henri Matisse at the Regina-Cimiez, overlooking the *baie des Anges* which curves from Mont Boron to the wooded hills of the Estérel.

Beyond the antechamber, where stood the archaic Apollo of Delphi surrounded by Oriental carpets, Indian shawls, cashmeres and moucharabies—climate of the Odalisques—Matisse welcomed his visitor in the large room on the left which he used as a studio. The artist's drawings were hanging on the walls. He was making a whole series of variations in ink, developing two or three feminine or floral themes indefinitely.

'*The fact is, everything amuses me, I am never bored. Come,*' he added, '*You will see how I have arranged things.*'

Birds have always been a passion with Matisse. 'Paradise at home,' said Louis Gillet. And Pierre Marois aimed a pretty arrow at this foible. 'Matisse has a famous aviary and consoles himself by living among birds—but all his birds are caged.'

Had this artist with the serene blue gaze really need of consolation? It does not seem so, from the words he used to Carco.

'A second room, also on the left, contained two aviaries. Bengalis, cardinals, Japanese nightingales displayed their bright colours enhanced by contrast with the long black plumes of the widow-bird. Fetishes and negro masks lent an exotic atmosphere to the room; but it was only an antechamber into a conservatory where Tahitian philodendrons spread their enormous leaves, we passed through it rapidly, to find ourselves in a sort of jungle, maintained by an ingenious irrigation system in all its green and tropical splendour. On a marble tray, calabashes and great pumpkins made an extraordinary contrast with Chinese statuettes, wherein the disproportion of the various elements allowed full rein to the artist's fancy.

'*Here we are in what I call my farm,*' said Matisse. '*I potter about here for several hours every day, because these plants require a tremendous lot of care. But while I look after them I get the feeling of their species, their weight and flexibility, and that helps me in my drawings. Do you see, now, why I am never bored? For more than fifty years, I haven't stopped working an instant. From nine to twelve, first session. I lunch. Then I have a short rest and go back to my brushes at two until nightfall. You wouldn't believe me. Every Sunday, I am obliged to tell*

[1] Francis Carco op. cit.

all sorts of fibs to my models. I promise them I will never ask them again to pose that day. Of course, I pay them double. Finally, when I feel they are not convinced, I swear I'll give them a day off in the week. "But, Monsieur Matisse," one of them answered me, "this has been going on for months and I have never had an afternoon free." Poor things. They can't understand it. . . . But I can't sacrifice my Sundays to those children, on the pretext that they have a lover. Put yourself in my place. When I lived at the Hotel de la Mediterranée, the Battle of Flowers was almost torture to me. All that music and cars and laughter on the Promenade. The girls couldn't sit still. So I installed them at the window, and painted their back view.'

These are his memories of the good old hotel, since demolished, with its pretty Italian ceilings, its tiles, its rococo salon where Matisse painted so many nudes and odalisques, in the almost artificial light filtering through the blinds; and the apartment in the Place Charles-Félix has been charmingly described by Michel-Georges Michel in *De Renoir à Picasso* (A. Fayard, 1955).

The great humanist, René Leriche, also kept a warm memory of his illustrious patient. 'That grand man' the author of *Philosophie de la Chirurgie* wrote me, was the most grateful person on whom I ever operated. . . . Every year, for fourteen years, he sent me either one of his precious drawings or one of his books. Gratitude is the privilege of great souls. And this was addressed to surgery. We had long talks about life and art when he was at Montparnasse. I used to spend hours with him. . . . How lovable he was! I made a great mistake in not taking notes. They would be precious now. But one never thinks the day will come to part. What a brain! One of the three or four great ones I have met in my life.'

And Matisse never tired of expressing his gratitude to René Leriche: *'I owe you these few years, since they are a bonus . . .'* he wrote to the famous professor.

'He had read in medical books' Leriche explained 'that a case like his could only live on for fourteen months, but it turned out to be fourteen years!'

We spoke of the marvellous draughtsman Matisse was.

'What struck me most,' said René Leriche, 'was that Matisse drew without ever looking at his paper. He kept his gaze on the model. And his line was never broken, except to place the eye.'

A letter from Matisse is pasted behind a charcoal drawing of the Professor hanging in his drawing-room. The artist had evidently intended to paint the surgeon in oils.

'Dear Professor and friend,

'What do you think of this preliminary drawing for your portrait? If you don't care for it as a likeness of Leriche, perhaps you would keep it as one of my

best drawings. If not, je me le garderai (*I'll keep it myself*), *as we say in Cassis and Nice.* (It was in Cassis that René Leriche had his villa.)

H. Matisse

16.11. 50 (51)'

Finding himself back in Nice early in 1943, can only have increased for Henri Matisse his serene frame of mind. Sometimes, to relax from his labours, he would go down into the garden. He smiled at the crystal-clear light.

'*Everything is new,*' he said, '*everything is fresh, as if the world had just been born. A flower, a leaf, a pebble, they all shine, they all glisten, lustrous, varnished, you can't imagine how beautiful it is! I sometimes think we desecrate life; from seeing things so much, we don't look at them any more. Our senses are woolly. We feel nothing. We are spoiled. I think that to really enjoy things, it would be wise to deprive ourselves of them. It is good to begin by renouncing, force oneself from time to time to take a cure of abstention. Turner lived in a cellar. Once a week he had the shutters flung open, and then what dazzling incandescence!*'[1]

The thought of Renoir, still working in spite of his paralysis, haunted the painter.

'*I was very struck*' he said to me, '*by the example of old Renoir. I used to go and see him at Cagnes. The last years of his life, he was a bundle of pain. He was carried about in his armchair. He fell into it like a corpse. His hands were bandaged, his fingers twisted like roots by gout, so he could no longer hold a brush. They used to pass the handle of the brush through his bandages. The first movements were so painful, it made him wince. After half an hour, when he got going, he rose from the dead: I have never seen a man happier. I swore that I would not be a coward, either, when the time came.*'

And indeed, he was quite the reverse. The energy which Matisse had in his early youth, only increased with the years.

'I am suddenly struck by a physical resemblance between Hugo and Matisse,' says Aragon, 'a resemblance between the Matisse of today and the Hugo of after 71.'

And in the midst of the enemy occupation, he wrote,

'I do not know what is coming to us. But I am indeed proud to have spoken here at such length on Matisse. In those days, they will say later on, at least they had "Matisse-en-France".

'Matisse-en-France, it has the ring of Puy-en-Velay, Marcq-en-Barœul . . . Matisse-en-France.

[1] Louis Gillet, 'Une Visite à Henri Matisse', in *Candide*, February 24th, 1943.

'At the darkest hour, they will say, he was making his drawings full of light.'

'At seventy,' said André Lejard, 'Matisse invented painting all over again.'

And as if to justify those words, came a flowering of paintings by Matisse: *Nature morte sur la table de marbre vert*, (1941)—the malachite table—clear harmony of white, green, lemon yellow, blue and pink; *Conversation* (1941) fair woman in blue against black; *Femme à la Violette* (1942), a pink make-up under the yachmak's embroidered tulle; *Danseuse à la robe bleue* (1942), with flesh like clay; *Danseuse assise dans un fauteuil* (1942) in which lemon yellow and almond green predominate.

The precious number of *Verve* (Vol. IV, no. 13), reproduces in colour a whole series of important pictures painted in 1942–43; *La Jeune Fille devant la fenêtre* dressed in white seated in a red and yellow chair; *Robe violette; Jeune fille à la robe rose*, the window open and the shutters closed; *Porte noire*, with its rich range of burnt sienna, cadmium and scarlet lake; *Le Luth*, and its powerful melody of ultramarine and cadmium reds; *L'Intérieur au tabac royal*, where the blue armchair, with a lute is balanced by the throne-chair where a girl in white with bare arms is seated; *Michaëlla*; and that admirable picture, *La Robe jaune et la Robe écossaise* brilliant in colour, with its silky cadmiums, reds, blues and viridian green, in opposition to the lemon yellows of the carpet and of the dress of the dark young woman; *Danseuse sur fond noir au fauteuil rocaille; l'Idole*, one of the purest, most significant works of this great period, the beautiful black hair, large black eyes, carmine mouth, rosy flesh-tones, white dress, and background of red and blue; finally, the still lifes: *Nature morte rouge au magnolia; Citrons et saxifrages* (the saxifrages are really primroses), and particularly *Citrons sur fond rose fleursdelysé*, which inspired André Rouveyre to write the delicate lines:

'Lemons, a Chinese vase shaded with a singing blue, and such a tender mystery of feeling it seems a rare woman might readily weep before it. In the vase, a bunch of hyacinths, also softened with shadows, from which rise strange little vegetable horns. A peaceful background of crimson, imperceptibly tinted with violet, heraldic fleurs-de-lys drawn in with a sable brush in half-tones, come there perhaps from a neighbouring Charles d'Orléans which Matisse was drawing at the time. This is undoubtedly one of the painter's most accomplished works, of one of his happiest moments.'

What increases the interest of this number of *Verve*, is that Henri Matisse gives all the elements of his palette, parallel with the reproductions of his paintings.

Youth

Like all great men at the end of their lives, who have reached a mastery in art or poetry, Matisse never ceased to think about youth. It is a fine thing, in the evening of life, to look to the future, and say with Vigny, 'Young posterity of one living now who loves you!'

On April 30th, 1945, Matisse addressed himself directly to youth:

'*The young painter who can't detach himself from the preceding generation is going to be sucked under.*

'*To preserve himself from the spell of his immediate elders, whom he esteems, he can seek new sources of inspiration in the works of various civilizations, according to his affinities. Cézanne was inspired by Poussin.* ("Faire du Poussin vivant.")

'*A painter, if he is sensitive, cannot lose the discoveries of the preceding generation, for those discoveries are in him, in spite of himself. Yet it is necessary he become detached from them, in order to bring something new in his turn, and a fresh inspiration.*'

And a warning to those who paint 'like Matisse'.

' "*Steer clear of the ruling master*", *said Cézanne.*'

And words of wisdom from a long, rich experience, which the young may well consider:

'*A young painter, who surely doesn't suppose he has to invent everything himself, should put his ideas in order, particularly by reconciling the different points of view in the fine works which impress him and, at the same time, by questions put to nature.*

'*After making himself familiar with his means of expression, the painter should ask himself: What do I want? and proceed, in his search, from the simple to the composite, to try and find out.*

'*If he knows how to keep his sincerity towards his deepest feelings, without cheating or self-complacence, his curiosity will not leave him; neither, until the last, will his ardour for hard work and the need to learn. What could be more wonderful!*'[1]

'*I have worked for years*' he said to Aragon, '*in order that people might say,* "*It seems so simple to do.*" ' And he would recite over and over again, those verses of Mallarmé, which express the return to youth and purity which he was seeking:

Imiter le Chinois au cœur limpide et fin
De qui l'extase pure est de peindre la fin

[1] Henri Matisse, 'De la Couleur', *Verve*, Vol. IV, no. 13.

Sur des tasses de neige à la lune ravie
D'une bizarre fleur qui parfume sa vie
Transparente, la fleur qu'il a sentie enfant,
Au filigrane bleu de l'âme se greffant. . .[1]

That was exactly what Matisse was seeking, when he asked Aragon, '*Is not a drawing the synthesis, the result of a series of sensations which the brain has retained, assembled, and which a last sensation sets in motion, so that I execute the drawing almost with the irresponsibility of a medium?*'

And that led him to speak of that 'love at first sight', which André Lhote was to expound with such subtlety. Lhote also wrote of Henri Matisse in 1939, 'We have watched during twenty-five years, one of the most gifted painters of our time, progressively renouncing most of his early conquests—*those which instinct arrives at spontaneously when reined in by no discipline*—and to fulfil himself and give his message its most perfect form, voluntarily giving up the most brilliant acquisitions.'

The mechanics of that patient effort toward purification have been analysed also by André Lejard:

'The whole work of Matisse "that fruit of brilliant light" of which Apollinaire speaks . . . shows a continuous aspiration toward an ever-increasing simplification, an almost absolute renouncement. That will to purification is not the sign of asceticism, a drying-up of sensitivity, it is on the contrary the expression of a power sure of itself, of a creative force which neglects accident, sacrifices the useless, retains only the essential. Tériade quite rightly said, "A work of Matisse is what is left after the dynamic play of research and freely made sacrifice. It is only what is left, that is what is lasting. It is all we need. . . . True riches are not profusion, but election, choice, possession of what matters, what really matters, only what matters." '

Love of birds

In 1942, N. G. Vedrès had the good fortune to find Matisse still 'among his pictures and birds'. Of the birds, he had just spoken to the public of Nice. He had agreed to give a lecture in Nice, with an alacrity which surprised everyone.

[1] *Translator's note:*

Like the Chinese of clear subtle heart
Whose pure ecstasy is to paint the last
On snowy cups ravished from the moon
Of one strange flower perfuming his life
Transparent, flower he smelled as a child,
Grafted on the blue filigree of his soul.

'The hermit of Cimiez' came down from his hill one evening, and talked of birds, nothing but birds.

The day came when there were no more birds, alas, on the third floor of the Regina, and Matisse deplored it himself to André Verdet: '*A few years ago, here in this big room, there were over three hundred birds. Parakeets, blackbirds, pigeons, rare species. They flew about in their aviaries. The pigeons were free in the room. One might have been in a forest.*'

Since living in Issy, in 1907, Matisse had never been able to do without a garden, a garden of Paradise—When he could no longer go out in the sun, when he had to stay in his large room, in the big bed facing the *baie des Anges,* that tireless traveller made a little garden on the wall in which he could still wander. His 'garden', a vast composition made of cut-out paper, blue, orange, violet, almond green and moss green, took up half the room. '*There is foliage, fruit, a bird . . . a moderate, soothing movement. I took away that* motif *you see down there, by itself on the right; I took it away because it had a violent movement. . . . That movement falsified the general score. An andante and a scherzo which disagreed.*'

About gardens, Fernand Léger quoted Delaunay: 'The Matisses are in flower. A great gardener, that man.' He agreed.

His garden never flowered better than between 1944 and 1946. In 1944, *la Jeune fille en blouse brodée rouge sur fond violet; La Liseuse aux tulipes et aux anémones; la Nature morte aux saxifrages et aux roses de Noël; le Chapeau bleu; la Jeune fille à la pelisse*; in 1945, that great decorative panel in triptych (1 m 80 × 1 m 80), which renews the voluptuous theme of 'Leda'; finally in 1946, *l'Intérieur rouge et jaune citron; l'Intérieur jaune et bleu; le Fauteuil rocaille vénitien; la Dame à la robe blanche; Asie*, a strange figure in sumptuous dress.

'One must stay a child all one's life'

After two visits to Paris and quite a long stay in Vence, at the villa 'Le Rêve', Matisse returned to settle on the third floor of the *Palais Regina*. The birds had been silenced forever. But youth was still there.

They were mostly young artists who admired him and came to ask his advice.

Yet since the days of his school in the one-time *Sacré-Cœur* convent, Matisse seemed to have renounced the teaching which had done so much for French art and for his reputation abroad. . . . Here is his conclusion, half a century later:

'*There is no such thing as teaching painting. At the Ecole des Beaux-Arts, one learns what not to do. It is the perfect example of what to avoid. That and nothing*

G La robe jaune et la robe écossaise (Les deux amies) (1941)

Paris, Musée d'Art Moderne

else. L'Ecole des Beaux-Arts? A machine for making Prix de Rome scholars. No one believes in it any more. It only exists in its own surroundings. It will die a lonely death.'

'The time spent at the School should be replaced[1] *by a free stay in the Zoological Gardens. The pupils would gain knowledge there in constant observation of embryonic life and its vibrations. They would gradually acquire that "fluid" which great artists come to possess. You understand: break with habit, the conformist routine. Toulouse-Lautrec exclaimed one day, "At last I have forgotten how to draw." Which meant he had found his true line, his authentic drawing, his own language as a draughtsman. It also meant he had left behind the means used for learning to draw.'*

Finally, as the aged Louis XIV wished to see 'children everywhere' at Versailles, Henri Matisse said that an artist worthy of the name, like a woman who knows how to make herself loved, should always keep 'the grace of childhood'.

'One must be able to keep the freshness of childhood still at the contact of objects, preserve that naïveté. One must stay a child all one's life, yet be a man, drawing strength from the existence of objects.'

Swan Song

Following that continued progress toward the greatest simplicity of expression, one remembers the last phases, usually the finest, of other great sculptors and painters.

Maillol, life-long friend of Matisse, at eighty reducing to a few lines the charming feminine arabesques suggested by the little Catalan girls bathing at Banyuls.

Cézanne, in 1906, writing to Emile Bernard, 'I still study from nature and I think I am slowly making progress.'

Delacroix, engaged on his last great work of the *Chapelle des Saints-Anges*, in 1861: 'Painting leaves me no rest . . . how is it that this endless struggle gives me new life instead of casting me down; brings me consolation rather than discouragement, and fills my thoughts when I am away from it?'

Goya in Bordeaux, well on in years, writing simply, '*Aun aprendo.*' ('I am still learning.')

Poussin, whose only ease from suffering came from painting; 'They say the swan sings most sweetly when he is near to death. I shall try also to do better than ever.'

[1] The word is 'abolished' in André Verdet's version, but this makes the rest pointless.

It is the privilege of the masters to revive, by their example, the memory of those who went before. Matisse never denied what a great artist owes to those who precede him. '*One doesn't put one's things in order*' he wrote, '*by throwing out of the window whatever is in the way. That would be an impoverishment, a void, and a void is neither order nor purity.*'

It was not 'deformation' that was so new in the work of Henri Matisse. That was practised in the Golden Age of painting by both Ingres and Delacroix.

It was by rediscovering pure colour at last, for it exists in the primitives, that Matisse opened a new road to painting.

All the acquisitions of the Renaissance were rejected by him. First, the suggestion of real space, fanatical religion of perspective, those effects of modelling obtained in surrounding atmosphere, chiaroscuro which drowned colour for the sake of values.

In fact, Matisse followed and enlarged the way opened by Cézanne and Gauguin. For him, the sole means of expression is colour.

It took him years to reach that perfect detachment. André Lhote defines the stages of that long progress with three examples: *Ma Chambre à Ajaccio*, 1889; *la Nature morte aux oranges*, 1913; *la Robe bleue dans un fauteuil ocre*, 1937, showing 'that inner alchemy of which the mature artist is the product.'

La Chambre of 1889, with its splendid rich texture, presents wonderful modulations, 'there are none more beautiful in the pictures of the best Impressionists. . . . Beautiful texture, complicated play of shades, depth, the expression of intimate life—these were the startling discoveries of the beginning. . . . Fourteen years later, in *la Nature morte aux oranges*, the intimate atmosphere, half-tones, "passages", the sumptuous texture of the painted forms, have given way to a precise distribution, to an already merciless plastic expression.

'Finally, no more atmospheric envelope, no more depth. One is confronted with a final purge, in the noblest sense, in which traces of hesitation have practically disappeared, in which the research (which was laborious) is not admitted: a dazzling result which makes one wonder in amazement how it was achieved.'

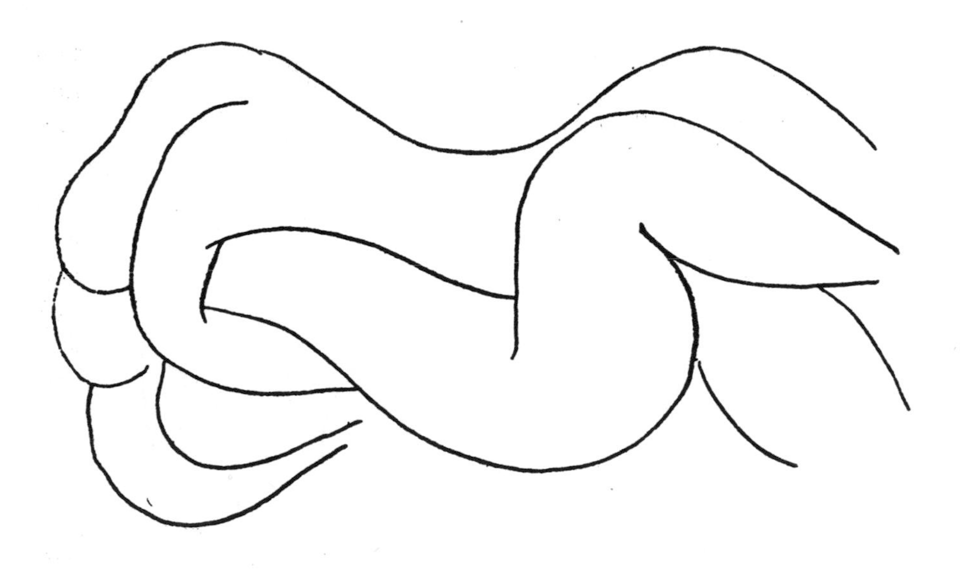

Haut

Bas

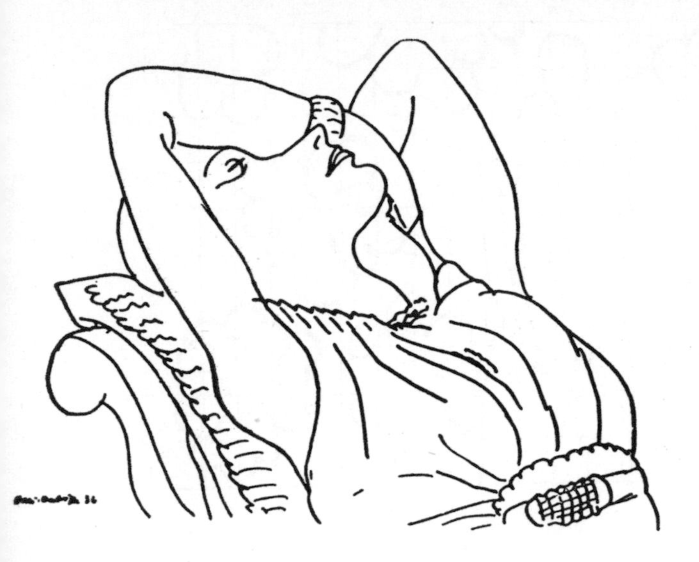

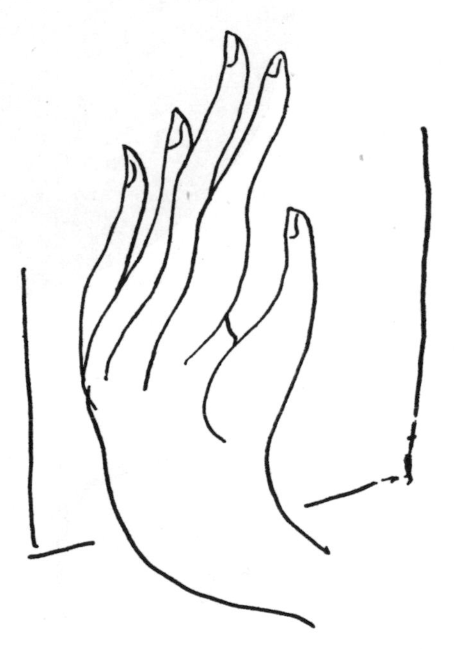

M

E.M.L.

AVE

VIII

THE ROAD TO PARADISE

Expression and decoration

Such an austere approach and his fundamental nature, were bound to lead Matisse toward decoration on a grand scale. His son-in-law, Georges Duthuit, remembers his saying, '*Expression and decoration are one and the same thing, the second term being understood in the first.*'

In 1935 the master of *Joie de Vivre* composed the magnificent hanging, *Tahiti*, for the looms of Mme Cuttoli (whose Rouaults are so rich in texture and spirit), and he has left a whole series of tapestries like *la Nymphe et le Satyre* in 1942. Later, between 1946 and 1948, using paper cut-outs, he produced sober and elegant effects for two hangings: *Polynésie: le Ciel* and *Polynésie: la Mer* woven in low-warp by Beauvais; also for two linen hangings executed by Ascher, of seaweeds, corals, ornamental birds, in a simple style on coloured grounds.

But these were only by-products imposed by circumstances on Matisse. He never really ceased to think of the great decorations he had the power in him to create. That is why, in a despondent mood, he said, '*Our civilization has no need of painters, or so little.*'

Matisse never forgave the State that he was condemned to do all his big decorations abroad; and he showed his displeasure by his gift of a Cézanne to the City of Paris for the Petit Palais.

Delacroix, ignored by the Third Republic as Matisse was by the Fourth, was commissioned by Adolphe Thiers to decorate the Chambre des Députés and the Palais du Sénat perhaps because he was the suspected son of Talleyrand. Matisse had not this good fortune.

At the beginning of 1944, in view of a possible enemy landing, the inhabitants of the coast were planning to leave. I was expecting Bonnard to come to me, in Ariège, and Maillol thought of renting the house of the former bishops of Mirepoix, which would have saved his life. But Matisse took it all as a joke.

'*Dear old Camoin,*' he wrote from Vence, February 2nd, 1944, '*are you going to lend me a hand with the evacuation?*

'*What will tomorrow bring?*

'*Where will my remains lie? The right hand in a mimosa bush, the left foot*

in the pretty garden pond, and the rest, who knows? On the peartree, perhaps, and my heart in the flowers.

'If I had time, I should go to the lake of Annecy. It is more convenient.

'But I don't believe a word of it, and I am your faithful,

H. Matisse'[1]

He was working ceaselessly, while so many threats hung over *la douce France*. He amused himself with memories of a certain Veronese ball given by Van Dongen, rue Juliette Lamber, where he and Camoin and Marquet expected to find a bohemian party and not a fashionable gathering! With the help of Madame Matisse, who told me about it, Matisse dressed up as a Renaissance pope; and he was horrified when he found himself faced with the nobility of the *Faubourg* Saint Germain, and stars from the Comédie Française. . . .

'*My dear Camoin*' wrote Matisse, April 4th, 1944, '*your letter gave me great pleasure. An old formula which says everything. Memories, and of happier days, luckily.*

'So Besson George has just brought out an issue of the review "Le Point" *on Marquet. I should like to find a second copy to send you, if you can't find it in Paris. Among the photographs, our Van Dongen Carnaval. I laughed aloud remembering our escapade.'*

For Matisse, like all Northerners worthy of the name, loved humour and fantasy. Artists' festivities attracted him even in his eightieth year, and reminded him of his hard-working, sometimes wild, youth. In July 1948, four years after the Liberation, he happened to be in Paris, at 132 Bld Montparnasse, and attended a very successful ball for young artists, organized by the photographer, Marc Vaux and his wife. Afterwards, he wrote to congratulate them:

'Dear Monsieur Marc Vaux, dear friend,

'What a good evening I spent at the Fête du Foyer des Artistes de Montparnasse! I laughed heartily, which no one does often nowadays. I watched people of all ages enjoying all sorts of hilarious and harmless nonsense. It took me back to my first 4(z)Arts Ball, the only one of my life, when I had nothing to bless myself with but a sheet off my bed as burnous, a strip of red calico for turban, and my eyes full of burnt cork. This sort of physical relaxation is the best antidote for our worries. But, as with all good things, such occasions are rare. Few parties have the quality of yours at the Foyer, where youth is stronger than poverty, and enthusiasm is the main part of the feast. I hope I shall not miss the Montparnasse night next Spring.

'Dear Marc Vaux, I congratulate you and your wife on the intelligent devotion

[1] Unpublished.

you give to this work, great though modest, which you imagined, founded, and which remains your great preoccupation. I need not bid you have courage, but I must say to you both that you have found the secret of happiness, in helping others to find theirs.

'*Your devoted*

Henri Matisse'[1]

The Great Trials of Matisse

In the spring of 1944, a few weeks before the Allied landing in Normandy, Matisse was far more preoccupied with others than with himself. The April raid on the Gare du Nord goods depot, inspired the un-warlike Raoul Dufy with horror. He had just returned to his studio in the Impasse Guelma (he wrote me a frantic letter), and the hermit of Vence was filled with gloomy forebodings.

He was afraid some old comrade of the Butte had been hit by the bombardment, and on the 28th of April, wrote to ask his 'dear Camoin'.

'*Le père Puy wrote me he was worried about your fate—living in the shadow of the Sacré Cœur as you do—and what of Daragnès and Galanis who are not far off?*

'*Send me a post-card quickly to say you and your family are all right.*

'*Here, in an atmosphere of anxiety, I am awaiting the outcome and working. What drama are we living through?*

'*My love to you all. Quick, a reassuring line, I hope.*

Your Henri Matisse.'

The following letter justifies his anxiety. Matisse was struck to the heart in his most lasting and truest affections.

Two heroic women affiliated to the Resistance and secretly working for the country's liberation, had been arrested by the Gestapo. One . . . Margot, Marguerite Matisse (Madame Duthuit), and the other Madame Henri Matisse, the daughter and the wife of the great artist.

'*My dear Camoin*' wrote Henri Matisse on May 5th, 1944, '*I am glad of the news you give me of the good health of yourself and your family. But change your perch, for Heaven's sake. No matter where, out of danger. Your collectors will follow wherever you go.*

'*I expect you have reassured old Puy, who has a rare good heart.*

'*As for me, I have just had the worst shock of my life, and I suppose I shall bear it by working.*

'*My wife and my daughter have been arrested separately, in different places.*

[1] Montparnasse, *Carrefour des Arts*, No. 3, summer 1948.

'I heard it two days later, with no further details and since, nothing.

'I don't know if anyone is looking after them. It is very tricky just now, and highly compromising.

'Yet I have someone who is trying to help. He wrote me about it, but nothing since.

'I don't know how they are, if they are lacking everything, and I can do nothing from here.

'I have been told not to speak of it. I have told no one.

'Keep this to yourself and tear up my letter when you have read it, without even telling your wife. If she reads this letter, I hope she will understand and not be offended with me.

'If I were in Paris, I should go to no matter whom, but I am the only one who could do it.

'Life is hard!

'Affectionately,

H. Matisse.'

Six weeks later, fifteen days after the landing, worried by the silence of his son, Jean, the sculptor, he again turned to his 'kind Camoin', and wrote to him on June 26th.

'Again, for the sake of our old friendship, I ask you to send me news of my son Jean, 21 Av. de Clamart, at Vanves, from whom I haven't heard for a long time. His letter is dated June 2nd and I received it on the 13th. He promised in that letter to write me every day.

'He lives in the suburb so badly bombed, and he gives me no news of his mother and Marguerite.

'Perhaps he has none, but he could reassure me about his health and family.'

Matisse had to admit, then, that so many trials had come between him and his work.

'My dear friend, life is hard. Are you perhaps, no longer in Paris? You have found a corner to shelter you. I hope you are still working. Myself, I am too worried to be able to work seriously.

'If Jean is not at home, route de Clamart in Vanves, he is probably in my old studio, higher up in the same avenue which has been divided and renamed.

'You will know how to manage.

'Do forgive me all this trouble.

'Thank you a thousand times.

'Yours,

H. Matisse'

The post was in a precarious state in those days, and he added a prudent postscript.

'If you see Jean, send me a line all the same. Two letters are less easily lost than one . . . thank you.'

Again, *having a chance to get a letter posted in Paris*, Matisse explains his great anxiety to Camoin:

'About Madame Matisse and Marguerite, you can imagine how I have suffered, especially without news. I force myself to hope the situation has improved, without giving way to my imagination. I have worked a lot so as to keep calm. I refuse to think of it, so my life can be bearable.

'I count on you, if the steps you have so generously taken with your relatives, happily for me, should bring anything to light, you will write me at once.

'Thank you, old man.

'I have written to Galanis, but I'm afraid my letter will be late in reaching him; yet I think I marked it, AIR MAIL, first flight.

'Write to us; old and tried friends are precious.

'My compliments to your family.

'Affectionately,

H. Matisse.'[1]

For philatelists

One fine day, it was decided to ask Matisse to design—a postage stamp! The French government never commissioned our greatest artist to decorate a single wall! It is thanks to the *Ville de Paris* that the French can see a decoration by Matisse at the Petit Palais.

However, his friend Camoin needed a definite answer about the postage stamp, and Matisse would not disappoint him.

'For the stamp project, I leave it to you.

'I had your letter last night, and must reply this morning. So it has scarcely sunk in. If it weren't for you, I should not accept.'

At that time, Marquet was naturally anxious about Matisse. *'I have just had a line from Marquet, written by his wife, asking for my news. . . .'*

In the end, Matisse seemed interested in the postage stamp scheme, and asked for details with his usual methodical care:

'I agree, gentil *Camoin,* mon gentil *Camoin, to make a stamp . . . at least I am willing to try; but I must know:*

'(A) the size of my drawing to be reduced, (*the usual size*).

[1] Unpublished.

'(B) What sort of drawing? My line-drawings are complete in themselves, and if the drawing is a good one, it can stand reduction, without loss.

'(C) The colour. Is it left to me? What suggestions can one make? I think a certain yellow, or salmon, or orange tone, a major colour would go. I shall try an unusual colour.

'Can the stamp be in two colours? I mean one colour and the white, like this? (here three heads in blue and red).

'Or two nude figures wrestling style of Hercules and Antæus.

'I can try.

'Should I make a drawing to be engraved?

'What does the stamp carry in the way of typography?

'Can one use two tones?

'The designs of stamps enclosed are only indications. The style has to be evolved.'[1]

Matisse took everything seriously, The details as well as the whole, like an artist of the Middle Ages or the Renaissance.

South Sea philosophy

Matisse wrote to Camoin on July 23rd, 1944, recalling the happy days of Morocco and the South Sea Isles. At last he knew something of Madame Matisse and Marguerite; but the silence of his son, Jean, and the mystery surrounding Marquet, continued to distress him.

Forced to keep his bed at last, and unable to work, he returned to '*ce vice impuni*'—reading (his literary, philosophic and scientific erudition was vast) and he derived some solace from it.

Hearing that '*gentil* Camoin' had just been knocked down by a bicycle, Matisse teased his old friend, who had a well-known weakness for the girls.

'Very dear Camoin,

'I am most touched by what you did for me, with such unfortunate results for yourself. I hope your knee is quite healed. And that the bruise has not led to rheumatism or water on the knee. (Doctor Matisse!)

'Was the cyclist pretty? If she had nursed you, I dare say you would have forgotten the pain without much medical science.

'I have received the information I wanted from Galanis, who wrote to me, thanks to your telling Madame Galanis.

'You probably know that poor Madame Matisse was condemned to six months. I am hoping the three months of arrest will count in her sentence. Madame

[1] Unpublished.

Matisse, that sweet petulant partner at dominoes, in Tangiers. . . . Do you remember those days as good days?

'We have worries all our lives. Luckily we forget them, thanks to new ones.

'But we must realize we can't live without them.

'That is the great lesson I learned in the South Sea Islands, where the natives detest worries, and are willing to plead guilty to anything rather than defend themselves.

'On the other hand, the Europeans who live there find life drags because they lack worries.

'They have had them since childhood, doses of medicine, school, lessons to remember, restraining parents, etc., and all the rest until they die.

'In Tahiti, no worry, but boredom, which makes the European long for five o'clock so he can get drunk or inject himself with morphia. Forgetting himself with women isn't enough, his conscience won't let him.

'For my part, I thought I had experienced everything, sufferings physical and moral.

'But no! There was still this last trial. I dare not think of Marguerite, we know nothing of her. Not even where she is. . . .'

At the beginning of 1944, Marguerite had been sent to Brittany by the Resistance to prepare the patriots for the Allied landing. Denounced by people serving the enemy, Madame Matisse Duthuit was captured by the Gestapo, tortured and sent to Germany in one of those trains packed with prisoners which only stopped at Ravensbruck. Madame Henri Matisse, for having typed some clandestine news-sheets, was condemned to six months' imprisonment, and served her sentence in Troyes prison. Henri Matisse wrote to Camoin:

'As for me, I am exhausted. For the last three months, in order to bear my anxiety, I have worked without stopping. I have worn myself out, and now I must recharge my batteries. I have been in bed for nearly a week, the liver out of order, fearing a complicated return of the gall-bladder trouble which, a year ago, brought me within a hair's breadth of an operation I certainly would not have survived.

'And in that state, my dear old friend, or in spite of it, one must draw and paint with serenity.

'In David Copperfield *or* Oliver Twist, *Dickens makes his hero say, it is nothing to laugh when you feel like it, it is laughing when you don't that counts.*

'For you, I think if you were not determined to make a recovery, life would not be too easy, with the complications of war—the lack of fresh air—for it must be

hot under your roof. If one can't laugh at all, which is hard, one must at least be able to bear it.

'In a new book on the life of Charles-Louis-Philippe, I read: "Beside a rack containing ten pipes, one, the favourite, a trumpet-pipe, a notice bearing this idea from Dostoïevsky:

'If a man is asked to suffer even more, it is because he is worthy of more suffering.'"

'Our old friend Moreau also gave us a consoling thought: The more we have to bear in life, the more strength God gives us to bear it.

'Enough.

'Well, my dear Camoin, thank you again for having responded so readily. An old friendship is one of the best things in life.

'Affectionately yours,

Henri Matisse'

'Dear friend, may I ask you to write me when you have some news? My Jean does not surprise me, for I was like him when young (*though not a great philosopher*)*. I loved my parents, but was very slack in writing.*

' "When will the negligent Henri Matisse deign to write to his parents?" My father wrote me.

'I was not at all surprised by his letter, and calmly stuffed it in my pocket. I was sure of my feelings.

'I must write to dear Puy, a letter owing for months, and a long affectionate one. . . .'[1]

On reading Bergson

The long-awaited hour of liberation had at last come to the coast—not without some damage.

But the artist had a fighting spirit, and he found his sense of humour again, telling his old friend how, thanks to a bombardment, he had been able to read in peace—Bergson:

Vence, September 6th, 44

'My dear Camoin,

'Here we are, liberated since the 27th (August). *All went off for the best. Vence was spared, nothing was touched—luckily. If a bomb had fallen among this pile of old houses, pressed together like the cells in a honey-comb, nothing would have been left but a handful of dust.*

'One funny thing, three stray shells fell close to my house. The last burst

[1] Unpublished.

twenty metres from my windows, only scratching the garage door and the shutters.'

And this charming omen of peace.

'I still have by my bed, an olive twig, torn from the tree by the exploding shell, which arrived at midnight, when we were fast asleep. I went down into a comfortable shelter-trench in the garden, in which I remained thirty-six hours—quite undisturbed.

'I spend the day reading Bergson, which I had only skimmed at home, distracted by the drawings and paintings on the walls round me.

'We have had some white bread to eat, and we still hope to see many promises fulfilled. But no post yet, not even from Nice, where the political status of the town is still in question.

'So I don't know what has become of my wife, who was just about completing her sentence, and of my daughter awaiting trial in Rennes prison.'[1]

In the exuberance of liberation, Matisse illustrated his letter with funny drawings. He found no one to take the letter to Paris until September 19th, when he added:

'Dear old friend, I add this to my letter of the 6th, which hasn't gone for obvious reasons.

'All is well here, but one sees things terrible and strange. I can't say more.

'If you want to give me your news, will you send your letter to 132 Bld Montparnasse, within five days from now.

'It seems that travellers have a lot of trouble. They have to know how to swim.

'A handshake,

H. Matisse'

'The person who posts this letter will take any letters for me at 132, and bring them.

'What of our Marquet of the Route du Beau Fraisier?'

Victory gave back her freedom to Madame Henri Matisse and, thanks to an allied air-raid, Marguerite escaped from dire peril. She did not perish, as did so many Frenchwomen, in the camp at Ravensbruck.

It was Camoin again who announced the unhoped for news, and his old friend replied in great joy:

'Vence, October 4th, 1944

'Dear Camoin,

'Thank you for your card, which brought me such amazing good news. I hope when you have seen her, and have more details, you will tell me more.

[1] Unpublished.

'After this, all is well.

'Affectionately,

H. Matisse.'

On 16th November, Camoin had not yet been able to see the escaped daughter, and her father, who already knew all about the tortures inflicted upon her by the Gestapo, could not hide his anxiety from his 'dear old Camoin':

'You must have seen Marguerite. What can you tell me of her? You know the feelings of a father, since you are one.

'I know already what those brutes made her suffer, perhaps more than she told me'.

Everyone at that time urged him to go to Paris, but his state of health made it impossible.

'I simply cannot go to Paris, I am sorry.

'The Marquets are trying to get back to Paris. I have had a post-card from them.'

The Picasso room caused a great stir, or scandal—at the Salon d'Automne. But the generous-hearted Matisse remembered his good qualities, and was ready to plead for him, and for others.

'Have you seen the Picasso room? Everyone is talking about it, and there were demonstrations in the street against it. What a success!

'If they applaud, you will hiss.

'Those who don't like it, say the moment is ill-chosen. . . .

'Well, what do you think of our "fellow travellers"? They are lying low.

'Only Vlaminck has been arrested. It must suit him very well. He will be freed, or has been, and will make a new book of his "prisons".

'The man of Saint-Tropez (when I say man, I should say "Seigneur") seems to want to be forgotten.

'Really, I don't know why we should torment people because their ideas differ om ours. But that is what we call Liberty today.' (It will be observed that tisse's fundamental patriotism had no relation to what is now called 'involvement' in art and literature.)

He had always indeed had a poor opinion of Othon Friesz, who made good use during the occupation of his Germanic name; For he had written to Camoin from Nice, as long ago as April, 1935.

'I have seen the magnificent Goya exhibition, and the shabby Friesz exhibition, with his league of Nations tapestry cartoon. He won't create harmony with that, if the representatives have sensitive eyes.'

A letter of November 16th, 1944, ends on a comic note.

'Au revoir, you lucky dog, running about Paris from North to South.

'I hope you are all three in good health and temper. Men are always wrong. Ask women, sensible, well-balanced creatures, misunderstood until now. However, they are eligible for the highest posts in the new organization of society. (*See America and Russia.*) *Let us hope they will have a pal who will do their job when they are ill or not up to the mark!*

'I must stop. Burn this letter. I am afraid of feminine terrorists.

'I embrace you,

(*I dare not sign*)'[1]

Many other letters to Camoin, show how much he liked to relax. This was perhaps not understood by his other faithful friend, Jean Puy, who wrote to me:

'He had made himself a high cloud, from which he looked down like God Almighty on us, poor humans, in another sphere. He was a famous inventor of magic formulas—the key to one period of his researches. And all his life he was after new formulas. He was a true prototype of Balzac's painter, "*Le Chef d'Œuvre Inconnu*", carried away and ruled by his painter's passion.'

His natural simplicity appears in the charming letter asking me to hand over the graceful Greek statue, which had lodged with me for eight years, to his son Pierre.

'132 Bld Montparnasse, July 11th, 1948.

'Dear Friend,

'I would have liked to go myself and fetch the girl's torso you have been so kind as to harbour these past years.

'But I cannot, unfortunately make such a journey.

'My son Pierre is going to Toulouse and is willing to undertake the transport of the girl in question. He expects to be in Mirepoix on Thursday morning and will go to see you at Malachite. He brings you all my gratitude, my appreciative friendship, and a copy of "La Religieuse Portugaise", which I beg you to accept and hope will be to your liking.

'I regret that the present troubles have prevented you from completing the second volume devoted to my work. Perhaps someone will take up the idea. I hope so.

'I hope my son will find you in good health in your gentleman farmer's life which does not keep you entirely from Paris and the Côte d'Azur, where I hope to see you soon.

'Awaiting that pleasure. I shake you cordially by both hands,

H. Matisse'[2]

[1] Unpublished. [2] Unpublished.

Indeed, we met again, in Paris and in Nice.

I found him, one day of January, 1952, so magnificently handsome (without a wrinkle) and eternally young (not at all an old man at eighty-two), I noted my impressions that very evening. I felt I must send them to René Leriche who had saved his life, and who had undoubtedly the deepest knowledge of the secret soul of Henri Matisse. The great practitioner hastened to express his delight in the news.

'Your letter gave me the greatest pleasure. I am happy that you found Matisse as you describe him so well and so vividly in your note. Olympian! It is the word which describes him. It's exactly what he is.

'I adore talking to him: he dominates from a high level whatever he touches.

'I mean to write to him soon, for I have just seen an amazing collection of Matisses in Baltimore. (The Cone Coll.)'

René Leriche quite rightly called Matisse the most grateful of patients.

Eight months before, on March 16th, 1954, Matisse dictated this note to his faithful secretary.

'*Dear Professor Leriche and dear friend,*

'*What has become of you? I am at Cimiez, my sight troubled by insufficient eye-fluid, and unable to work just now. I much regret being unable to see you in Paris. But it is now two summers since I have been there.*

'*The first of those summers I spent in Nice, in terrible heat, and last summer I spent three months in the country near Nice where I regained much strength, which enabled me to work this autumn.*

'*I don't think I shall be able to go to Paris next summer, for I rather fear the fatigue of the journey.* (He was then in his eighty-fifth year.)

'*So I can only hope that you will have reason to come here and we shall have the pleasure of being together.*

'*I have news of you sometimes, either from professor Wertheimer, or his sister Doctor Schiff, who comes from Paris sometimes to look after my eyes.*

'*I hope we shall see each other again soon.*

'*Yours affectionately,*

Henri Matisse.'[1]

Even the signature was dictated, but Matisse made the effort of affixing his initials at the foot of the page: H.M.

In spite of his failing eyesight, he continued to be interested in the health of his friends. And having no news of Madame Marc Vaux, he wrote to her a month later, April 15th, 1954, and even suggested remedies for her insomnia.

[1] Unpublished.

'Dear Madame Marc Vaux,

'It is a long time since I had news of you, and I hope all is well, and you have no more insomnia.

'I often think of you, as they have at last found a way to give me peaceful nights. For a year now, I have been able to sleep six good hours a night, which has greatly improved my health.

'After your experience with acupuncture, I dare not advise you again. But, for what it may be worth, I tell you of the medicines which have worked so well with me.

'Before dinner I take both Eunoctal 0,10 and Largactil. The first is meant to put you into deep sleep and the second to prolong it at will.

'At first the doctor prescribes the proportions, and later one modifies them oneself, according to the preceding night's sleep. . . .'

To put life in the new buildings

As we were speaking of the future of painting one day, I said to Matisse:

'Since the great disaster, we are living among ruins. So many spiritual values have been destroyed. Humanity will try to rise again, as best it can, as after the great Barbarian invasions. And then art can play a vital part. Is it not as closely allied to the soul as to the body? What part, do you think, will painting play in the rebuilding of our shattered world?'

And Matisse told me what he hoped.

'Painting should be used to put life into the new buildings. But it must have a sane and modest beginning. I believe it is possible after a number of blunders.

'When I visited the Tapestry Museum, the old part, I understood that this is possible, with patience and with modesty.'[1]

Clearly, Matisse could only see tomorrow's painting as a setting for life.

And this great artist who, like Delacroix, had few chances to cover a large surface, really thought in terms of decoration.

Pierre Marois understood the disappointment underlying obvious contradictions.

'It is time' he said, 'that painting should return to the cool spring of decorative art; but this cannot be improvised; it must find its enduring reason in a collective soul and a certain faith. A decorator should not be solitary, and yet the last great decorator, Delacroix, was so; his subjects and myths were never adopted by the crowd, who no longer understood them. The singularity of Delacroix's subjects is significant. They should have been imposed on him, whereas they

[1] Unpublished.

H. Jazz (Cut paper design from book) (1947)

Editions Verve

only sprang from his personal taste. Freedom is not always a good thing for an artist, and he can be the first to suffer from it.

'We must not reproach Delacroix and Matisse with an isolation for which we are responsible. . . . In an epoch when life becomes more difficult and loses a little of its savour every day, he only wished to celebrate the joy of life, but he had to reduce his naturally monumental art to a personal experience, almost a confidence.'[1]

Cut-out paper

Since those lines were written, in 1947, the art of Henri Matisse has abandoned its confidential note to become, in fact, monumental.

And this is primarily due to cut-out paper.

It was for the Russian ballet, so greatly admired by Matisse when it first came to Paris, that he first resorted to cut-out paper.

He had, indeed, always used this technique from the time of his decoration for the Barnes Foundation, *La Danse*, in 1933, but in a more confidential manner.

Gaston Diehl had an interview with him on the subject:

'*I had conceived* La Danse' he admitted, '*long before, and had put it in* la Joie de Vivre, *then in my first big* La Danse *composition. But, this time, when I wanted to make sketches on 3 canvases of one metre, I couldn't get it. Finally, I took three canvases of 5 metres, the very dimensions of the panels, and one day, armed with charcoal on the end of a bamboo stick,*[2] *I set out to draw the whole thing at one go. It was already there, in me, like a rhythm which carried me along. I had the surface in mind. But once the drawing finished, when I came to colour it, I had to change all the pre-arranged forms. I had to fill the whole thing, and give a whole that would remain architectural. On the other hand, I had to be closely allied to the masonry, so that the lines should hold their own against the enormous, projecting blocks of the down-curving arches, and even more important, that the lines should follow across them with sufficient vitality to accord with each other. To compare all that and obtain something alive and singing, I could only proceed by groping my way, continually modifying my panels in colours and in black.*'[3]

Gaston Diehl goes on to explain;

'It was then, with a stroke of genius, that Matisse thought of using cut-out

[1] Pierre Marois, *Des Goûts et des Couleurs*, pp. 151–2, Editions A. Michel, 1947.

[2] This shows that Matisse used charcoal fixed on a long bamboo cane in 1932–3 (he was just sixty), long before his serious operation.

[3] Conversation between Matisse and Gaston Diehl, Paris, *Les Arts et les Lettres*, April 19th, 1946.

papers—a process which he later raised to the dignity of an amazing personal technique. With that he could alter his coloured surfaces at will, and his secretary undertook to pin up papers on the wall according to his directions.'

But when it came to substituting paint for paper, the effect alters and betrays the artist.

'*I had placed the darkest tones*' goes on to explain the painter of *La Danse*, '*which were my blacks, against the arcades themselves, but when I replaced paper with colour, I had again to make certain modifications because of a brilliance peculiar to the pictorial texture, which upset the previously established balance.*'

The wiser for that experiment. Matisse kept to coloured paper after that, and did not dream of substituting paint for it.

That was how, in 1938, he made the settings for *l'Etrange Farandole*, which René Blum commissioned for the Monte Carlo ballet.

But it was not until *Jazz*, the album of coloured cuts published by Skira in 1947, that Matisse mastered the technique, far more difficult than one would suppose. He explained to André Verdet:

'*Sometimes the difficulty appeared: Lines, volumes, colours were put together, and then the whole thing collapsed, one part destroying another. It all had to be done again, the music the dance, and the balance, had to be found and conventionality avoided. A new departure, new trials and errors, new discoveries. . . . It is not enough to put colours one against another, however beautiful; the colours also have to react on one another. Otherwise, cacophony results. . . .*'[1]

Sculpture had haunted him from his youth, and in this instance, in his presentation of *Jazz*, Matisse did not hesitate to use 'direct carving', dear to the Egyptians and the image-makers of the thirteenth century:

'*Cutting straight into paper, reminds me of the sculptor's "direct carving".*'

Four years later, when he had quite mastered the art, he spoke of its advantages to André Lejard: '*Just now I am inclined to duller, more direct surfaces, which leads me in search of a new means of expression. Cut-out paper allows me to draw in colour. For me it is a matter of simplification. Instead of drawing the contour and then filling in with colour—one modifying the other—I draw directly in colour. . . . That simplification guarantees precision in the union of the two modes of expression, which are then one. . . . The result is there from the beginning.*'[2]

The magician and the black dancer

Matisse was a man of great culture and, as we know, always recognized how

[1] André Verdet, op. cit. [2] *Amis de l'Art*, new series, No. 2, October, 1951.

deeply he was affected by external influences. Even after eighty, his dynamic power was continually renewed. And with his cut-out papers he seems to make a bridge between the paleolithic art he admired (he has often described to me what a marvellous revelation to him were the cave drawings of Altamira and Lascaux) and abstract art from which he had long been kept aloof by his passion for nature.

Anyone who has seen *Le Sorcier dansant* in the cave *des Trois Frères* in Saint-Gironnais, or merely turned the pages of Abbé Breuil's fine book on cave drawings, will immediately recognize the far-distant origin of *La Danseuse nègre* composed by Matisse in 1950.

It is known that on his way to Pittsburg, his ship putting in at Fort-de-France, Matisse saw a black girl dancing, and was so fascinated by her choreography from the dark ages, that he wanted to stop in Martinique to make drawings from that magnificent model; and it is possible that he was still haunted by that obsessing '*biguine*', and that the encounter of 1932 was still present in the execution of *La Danseuse nègre* in 1950.

André Verdet's description makes it clear that there is a stronger influence. He writes:

'*La Danseuse nègre* is an apparition. She takes the whole height of the wall at the end of the room and her feet even seem to touch the floor; they dance on the floor. Yes, the sumptuous negress comes toward one with all the rhythmic power of her dance, the whole vibration of her body, at once disjointed and harmonious, and birds fly round her like a nimbus.

'Here, as elsewhere, one sees that Matisse had all the notes of the dancing body at his fingertips, and kept only a chord. The joints are sensitive, concentrated and simplified in the extreme. There are sudden spaces between certain parts of the body. Air glides through these spaces, increasing the feeling of the whole movement. Space between the breasts and the belly, space between the belly and the hips. And the former, isolated, seems to vibrate at the centre of the dance.'[1]

These eloquent spaces have their counterpart in the *Sorcier* of the *Trois Frères* cave, and many other figures of the Reindeer age. And Matisse did not hesitate to adopt the technique used by his ancestors twenty thousand years ago.

More than that. A large panel of cut-out paper (about 2 m 50 × 2 m 50), *Zulma*, dates from the same year 1950, and there, most strangely, a sort of weird fluid ectoplasm emanates from the centre of the massive dark figure . . . recalling again so many figures in Paleolithic art, and strange apparitions of the

[1] André Verdet, op. cit.

romantic gothic age, even of ages most Baroque, of El Greco's *Opening of the Fifth Seal* and Goya's *La Quinta del Sordo*.

Anxious as he was to keep contact with nature until the end, Matisse seemed loath for a long time to give in to abstract art; but I know how highly he esteemed Kandinsky for instance, whose gift of Asiatic colour enchanted him. When I came back fascinated from a large comprehensive exhibition of Kandinsky in the Kunsthaus, Zurich, in 1946, I remember with what interest Matisse questioned me about it one October day of the same year, when he seemed to me in great pain. It was in Paris, Boulevard Montparnasse.

Matisse spent some time on Divisionism, under the influence of Signac, then in Cubism, which he didn't trust, and until the end of his days, he was avid to know everything. He was always young and seemed incapable of growing old. So it is not surprising that he left at least two important works in cut-out paper, coloured in gouache, inspired by non-representative art.

The first was entitled by the master himself, *Panneau abstrait sur racine de réalité*.[1]

'As is natural with Matisse, colour here is not a simple accident, nor a simple anecdote, but the fundamental note in a chord. In that chord, lines, volumes and colours each play their part, and it is the quality of the whole which gives its virtue to the work, of a new space in a new reality.'[2]

In 1952, at the *Salon de mai*, the Musée National d'Art Moderne acquired another abstract work, *Tristesse du Roi*, also in cut-out paper, where one finds those hands discovered in profusion in the prehistoric caves of Ariège and the Haute-Garonne.[3]

Cut-out paper was to allow him to realize the dream of his life.

A celestial sign

At the age he reached in 1943, age of maturity for Titian, at the time of the publication of *Thèmes et Variations*, Henri Matisse had confided to Aragon his great secret.

'*Everything seems to indicate that I am about to start working on large compositions.*'

But Aragon couldn't understand, he was unable to read the future.

'You were saying, everything seems to indicate. . . .'

'*That I am about to paint large compositions. Funny, isn't it? As if I had my whole life before me, or the whole of another life. . . .*'

[1] Translator's note: 'Abstract panel grafted on reality.'
[2] *Thèmes et Variations*, Aragon, *Matisse-en-France*, Fabiani 1943. [3] André Verdet, op. cit.

And then, the supreme avowal, which Aragon was incapable of grasping, for all his critical talent, and which seems luminous today:

'PERHAPS, AFTER ALL, I BELIEVE WITHOUT KNOWING IT, IN ANOTHER LIFE . . . IN SOME PARADISE WHERE I SHALL PAINT FRESCOES.'[1]

'In Some Paradise where I shall paint frescoes . . .'

In spite of his illness, perhaps to make up for the trials awaiting him at the turn of his seventieth year, Matisse did find himself, in his lifetime, in 'some Paradise', where he could decorate on a large scale.

The Paradise was the golden land of Nice by the sea.

Everyone knows what religious art owes to Maurice Denis and George Desvallières, who founded the *Atelier d'art Sacré* at the beginning of the century. But it can never be overstressed how fruitful was the activity of Father Couturier, young Dominican of frail health, noble spirit and great heart, who had the wisdom to trust the renovators of religious art.

We owe it to him that Luxembourg Cathedral is enriched by stained glass of enchanting colours; that the grey lancet windows of Notre-Dame choir were replaced, by red blue and violet panes; and that we have the church of Assy: *Notre-Dame de Toute-Grâce*, at the foot of Mont Blanc. Its courageous chaplain Abbé Devemy, took me to visit it in 1948 before it was finished. I saw there the work by Léger on the outside walls, the bronze doors by Braque, sculptures by Lipchitz and Germaine Richier, Lurçat's tapestries, Rouault's stained glass, and paintings by Matisse, Bonnard and Derain.

How Henri Matisse was led, in his turn, to build a Catholic sanctuary, he told me himself when I stopped to see him in Nice on my way back from his beloved Corsica.

I found him in his room at the Regina, seeming in splendid health although in bed. At his head was some beautiful Coromandel lacquer work, on either side two cabinets containing Far Eastern treasures, Korean pottery and Chinese dancing figures—like Tanagras—of the Ancient Han dynasty.

His secretary, Madame Lydia Delectorskaya, led us to a large model of a building, brilliantly coloured.

[1] '*There is no break*' Matisse declared, '*between my old pictures and my cut-outs; only with more formality, more abstraction, I arrive at a form decanted to the essential, and of the object I used to present in the complexity of space, I keep the sign necessary to make it exist in its proper form, and in the whole for which I have conceived it.*' (Maria Luz twentieth century, No. 2, January, 1952.)

I have turned into an architect

'*That is my work from now on,*' said Matisse. '*You see that, I have turned into an architect.*'

Architect of the chapel Notre-Dame-du-Rosaire, in Vence.

A year later we were to visit that chapel, faithful to the first model, with its large peaceful windows, its nearly flat roof surmounted by an immense wrought-iron cross, and the adjoining convent covered in blue and white Roman tiles, the colours of Our Lady.

With its clipped lawn, which the builder had indicated, it made a true Matisse colour-harmony: pearl grey, ivory, emerald-green and orange.

Paper reigned supreme . . . Paper flowers, as Cézanne used them, paper garlands, plans for windows made with cut-out paper. . . . With this passion for paper, Henri Matisse went back to the masters of his youth, Chinese and Japanese.

All along the light wall, designs for the Stations of the Cross, in numberless variations. By means of charcoal fixed on a bamboo-cane, the master had been able to make the drawings from his bed or his armchair.

When Matisse showed me his model, I little thought that religious decoration, a few weeks later, would give rise to such fantastic interpretations.

A certain 'sensational' journalist claimed that Matisse had sacrificed eight hundred million francs for the sake of the Dominican Sister Jacques—a palpable absurdity—and that when Aragon and the painter's friends protested, Matisse replied in exasperation:

'*Yes, I am going to decorate a chapel. A chapel, a banqueting room,* a maison de rendez-vous (a coarser word was generously substituted) *it's all the same to me . . . I am going to put flowers everywhere.*'

When, on January 15th, 1952, two years later, I mentioned this to Matisse, he just shrugged and said, scornfully; '*You who know me, can you imagine I should express myself in that way?*' And I answered 'I am quite sure of the contrary. I remember as far back as 1908, you spoke of "the almost religious feeling" you had for life.'

When I visited him on April 24th, 1950, there was nothing in Matisse's room and vast studio but *prie-Dieu*, candelabras, tiles, designs for chasubles, miniature embroideries and particularly a delicious garden, very medieval in feeling, which would have enchanted children.

'*Ah!*' Matisse confided, '*I've had some trouble with the architect who is working under me. Brother Rayssiguier couldn't get over that immense iron cross placed on an Italian roof. . . . So I appealed to our friend Perret: Perret came and, luckily, said I was right.'*

Auguste Perret was the bold architect of the church of Raincy.

La Chapelle du Rosaire

Mgr Rémond, Bishop of Nice, laid the first stone, on December 12th, 1949, of that sanctuary in Vence, so much visited and discussed since 1951. Most people have some difficulty in understanding the idea which Matisse put into its architecture, paintings, stained-glass, iron-work and ceramics.

Father Couturier understood at once, but he is a man of vision. He it was whom Matisse asked to pose for his Saint Dominic.

For the almond-shaped oval of the Virgin with the Child, Matisse used the face of a girl barely twelve years old, Claude Plent, whose mother, Henriette Darricarrère, had sat for him in 1921. He found the long faces of El Greco's madonnas again in that pure oval.

He draped Saint Dominic superbly, but like the great artists of twenty thousand years ago, he found it superfluous to indicate eyes, nose and mouth even with a few lines. The same for the Virgin and the Child. Father Couturier defended this ancient but disquieting effect, in *Art Sacré*.

'When Matisse said, *I want those who come into my chapel to feel purified and relieved of their burdens,*' no doubt he was thinking of the character he meant to give to that chapel: not a place where complex things would be described and taught people by windows and paintings, which they already know; but a place which would change their hearts by its beauty, where souls would be purified by beauty of form.

'But similarly, the true aim of the work and of life are clear: those of whom Matisse thought ceaselessly in building his chapel, are those very anonymous people . . . the old woman who said one day, on the route de Saint-Jeannet. "Its much better for the Holy Virgin to have no face; everyone can see her as he likes." When people no longer come here to admire or criticize, but only to pray, to find peace of heart in the silence! when many sorrows have been consoled here and many hopes revived, then the chapel will take on its full meaning, and Matisse will have found his reward and crowned his work.'[1]

The Act of Faith

The great Catholic writer, Daniel-Rops, author of *Jésus en Son Temps*, with his feeling for beauty and the deep needs of Christian art, has said the last word on the Chapel of Vence, in 'l'Acte de Foi de Matisse'.

[1] *L'Art Sacré*, July–August 1951.

'A white cube, fastened on the hillside as if suspended over the valley. Beyond the terrace where oleanders flower, there is a long view on to the hill of Vence, covered in houses like bunches of grapes, on to the undulating hills and the horizon of the sea. The place lends itself to meditation and to silence.

'This is a moving thing, of which one must speak with respect. A great artist, one of the leaders of contemporary painting, has given all the care and love of his last days to the building of an oratory where a tiny community of Dominican Sisters may pray, a gift of gratitude—simply because one of them, during his illness, had lavished on him the treasures of her Christian charity.

'Undoubtedly an act of faith. No visitor to the *Chapelle du Rosaire de Vence* can escape it, however he may be surprised and disconcerted at first by the work as a whole. Ultimately he must feel the impact of this truth.'

An act of faith. But what faith? The one which drives an artist on his quest and gives him the will to achieve? No doubt. But is that enough when raising a house of God, decorating it so that souls will be disposed to pray? This little chapel puts that question, like so many religious works of our time. 'To paint Christ, one must live in Christ.' Fra Angelico used to say with some anguish. Can an artist create a deeply religious work without adhering heart and soul to the faith he proposes to glorify? Did Matisse feel himself a Christian when he devoted his zeal and genius to the little Dominican chapel? We climb the hill seeking the answer from his work.

'The first impact is a happy one. The exterior of the chapel is simple, denuded to the purest grace. The high, narrow bays of the small nave, the larger ones of what will be the choir, the delicate invention of Roman tiles varnished blue and white, and particularly the suggestion of a steeple in the wrought iron cross against the sky, give at once an impression of inner concentration and esthetic achievement. Whereas so many contemporary religious realizations suffer an inner discord from heterogeneous elements—the church of Assy, for instance—the slightest detail of the chapel of Vence—even the exquisite little cactus garden designed like a Persian carpet—has been conceived in a single artist's vision. The peace emanating from its sober forms bears witness to this.

'Has one this same feeling as clearly when one goes inside? Perhaps not entirely, in any case, not in the same way. The Chapel appears as a sort of hall, on which is grafted a small wing serving as choir for the nuns. At the angle of these two architectural elements, on a platform, the altar is placed obliquely, facing both the nuns and the faithful; an admirable altar of powerful sobriety, in which candlesticks and crucifix are careful not to break the line. That is an authentically religious part of the whole—and it is good that it should be so.

In the noble light of three colours, pure blue, shining yellow and vivid green passing through simple windows, there is an impression of spiritual plenitude; it is a place devoted to prayer, and the Christian (even if he does not feel that sensitive impregnation by the spiritual as in the poor nave of Saint Damien of Assisi) finds here nothing between himself and God.

'Can one say as much for the big compositions which decorate two of the walls, and which, to Matisse, surely were the essential? Here there is no colour, search for harmony or values. The black lines on white tiles—Dominican colours—are sufficient in themselves. Complete intentional simplicity; ultimate point where full style is attained, as in Japanese art, by bare tracery of a deliberate line.

'So these three great compositions are a simple play of line; the immense Saint Dominic, larger than life, is reduced to the oval of a head and the folds of his mantle; the Virgin with the Child is merely indicated by a double silhouette surrounded by the suggestion of a floral garden; and the Stations of the Cross, which at first glance look like the pages of a sketch book, gradually reveal a perfection in their studied disorder. It must be admitted, such simplification hardly lends itself to sensibility. Before a Virgin by Raphael, or the great Crucifixion by Mathias Grünewald, something stirs in the depths of the heart which is untouched by the art of Matisse in Vence. To recapture the emotion, the spectator must use his imagination, or, better, his spiritual life, in an effort to take part.

'It is the same with this art as with that of the first Christians in the catacombs, where very simple lines suffice to suggest the inner spirit of a prayer or the messianic symbols of bread and fishes.

'The Vence chapel is a sanctuary of monastic prayer—and not a church for all comers. Those who pray here, in the peace of morning and evening's silent abandon, do not need prompting by figurative works of art. Their spiritual meditation only needs these pure lines as an opening. (And the final result was exactly what was required of the artist.) Would this technique be adequate in a large church designed for the crowd? It is most unlikely. But here, where ten nuns pray in solitude, it is perfectly fitting.

'Thus a kind of certainty grows in us. Was the artist who gave his time and love to this masterpiece a Christian? Those stones, walls, lines, are evidence enough in the eyes of Heaven. This even beyond the limits of obedience and formal appurtenance.

'For there is a point of absolute sincerity and disinterested love where Christ always knows his own.'[1]

[1] Daniel-Rops 'l'Acte de Foi de Matisse', *Journal de Genève*, September 22nd, 1951. We thank M.D.R. for permission to reprint this beautiful extract.

Later, in January, 1952, I asked Matisse which was the best time and season to visit his chapel. He answered without hesitation,

'*The most favourable season is winter—And then the best hour is eleven o'clock in the morning.*'

'Because?'

'*Because of the windows which, as you know, are designed to transfigure the black and white which reigns in that Dominican sanctuary, and make it luminous with all the colours of the rainbow.*'

And indeed opinion is unanimous about the glass. Picasso may prefer the Stations of the Cross, another the altar, another the delicate workmanship of the chasubles or the admirable door of the confessional, like Irish lace, but all are entranced by the luminous magic of yellows and greens transforming the whiteness of the walls.

What deep thought he gave to the work, Henri Matisse explains in his pamphlet on *la Chapelle du Rosaire*: in it appear the words, '*my revelations*'.

Testimonies

A serious question, to be put to people worthy of trust. The first I consulted on the subject was Mrs Dorothy Bussy, author of the masterpiece *Olivia*, widow of Simon Bussy, painter of delicate talent and great friend of André Gide—and of Matisse. She gave her opinion willingly.

'In my opinion, Matisse was, and always remained, completely unbelieving. We have no authority to suppose that the building of Vence chapel, which to me was nothing but a supreme "artistic divertimento", led to the least inclination in him, properly speaking, towards religion.

'It was certainly with gravity and respect that he conceived and elaborated it, but with no other than artistic fervour. There had never been room for God in his soul, which was entirely occupied by art. He never concealed this, but the Church obviously, and it is not surprising, does its best to make people believe Matisse worked in faith.' (The attitude of Mgr Rémond, Bishop of Nice, and the Dominicans, so prudent and so reserved, is entirely contradictory to such a supposition.)

'For my part, I cannot believe it, as I cannot believe he would have approved a religious burial, but as I was not in Nice when he died, I don't know who was responsible. . . .'

A reply to the author of *Olivia*, I have from Madame Henri Matisse and Madame Marguerite Duthuit: those responsible were the widow, the daughter and the sons of the great man, who were all agreed to ask for a religious ceremony, and that without the slightest pressure from the Church.

'Because,' said Madame Matisse, 'my husband wanted our marriage blessed by a priest. He wished, as I did, that our children be baptized. Henri never had two opinions about that. "*Why not*" he said to me, "*do as my parents and grandparents have done before us down the centuries?*"

'And indeed, through his family, particularly his mother whom he adored, and his aunts, Henri had received a Catholic upbringing. He was baptized and also confirmed. And, despite the pressure of extreme left-wing friends, notably Signac and Marcel Sembat, my husband always refused to take part in manifestations against the Catholic Church.'

But we have something quite different to the testimony, precious as it is, of the wife and daughter of Henri Matisse, the simple and decisive words of Sister Marie-Ange, already given.

Almost every day, when he showed her the plans and details of the sanctuary he was then proposing to build in Gramond, Matisse would repeat, '*Do you think it would be a good thing? I so much want it to be useful?*'

And another figure appears, in white, black-veiled—Sister Jacques-Marie. She came from *la Vendée*, and had taken refuge in Nice with her father, a retired army officer. She had a nurse's diploma, and was looking for work. She was told of Henri Matisse and the great care demanded by his state of health. The young girl, who was very beautiful, called on Matisse and was immediately engaged as nurse.

During the summer of 1942, her presence was to prove very necessary. At that time the doctors of Nice insisted that Matisse should have an operation. But Professor Wertheimer and Professor Gutman proved to them 'what folly it would be for this vascular patient to be again placed on the operating table'.

If one is to believe Alfred H. Barr, usually well informed, Matisse made a number of paintings from the young *Vendéenne*, and notably *l'Idole* of 1942. (Lasker coll., New York.)

Questioned by Madame Juliette Bompard at my request, Sister Jacques-Marie replied,

'It is true Henri Matisse made a series of drawings of me, but I never sat for any of his paintings.'

It is certain, however, that later when the lovely *Vendéenne* had taken the veil, she was the inspiration of Matisse for the marvellous profile of *La Religieuse Portugaise*.

It is also true that the young refugee had decided then to enter a nursing order, and if she postponed her decision for a time, it was to look after Henri Matisse.

He was much better when she became a novice of the Dominican order in 1947. She was sent to the Foyer Lacordaire in Vence, a nursing home for girls threatened with tuberculosis.

The convalescent and his nurse were hardly parted, since the villa of Matisse, *le Rêve*, and the Foyer Lacordaire were almost opposite each other on the *route de Saint-Jeannet*. It was only necessary to cross the road.

At that time, Mother Gilles, Superior of the Foyer Lacordaire, was thinking of repairing the old oratory, gutted by fire.

One day Sister Jacques-Marie spoke of it to Matisse, and showed him a small design for stained-glass windows. The water-colours interested the master, and even more, the idea of a chapel to restore, or perhaps—build.

It was two years since Matisse had lost sight of Sister Marie-Ange, and suddenly here was another Dominican talking of a chapel to be raised toward heaven. . . .

It was he who designed those windows. And Sister Jacques-Marie guessed that this reminded him of a long-cherished plan.

'Without being absolutely pious,' she said, 'Henri Matisse was not at all hostile to religion. . . . In fact, I felt I was watching a long-ripening project come into flower. To me, *la Chapelle du Rosaire* is the logical outcome of a spiritual development unknown to most.'

Positive minds may object to such testimony as prejudiced, formed under the veil. But that objection cannot be raised about the great scholar, philosopher and surgeon, René Leriche.

'*I saw*' Matisse told him often, '*in the fact that I was wonderfully nursed in Lyon by one Dominican sister, and then by another in Vence, who told me about the* Chapelle du Rosaire, *I saw in that a true celestial sign, a sort of divine indication. . . .*'

How Aragon reacted at that time was amusingly told by Matisse to a friend of Alfred H. Barr. He called, and as usual the conversation took a friendly turn. After an hour, Matisse pointed to a corner where the model stood on a table.

'*You haven't said a word about my chapel*,' said Matisse mischievously, '*Do you like it?*'

Actually, Aragon had taken in the chapel at a glance as soon as he arrived, but he had decided to ignore the offensive object. Even then, he didn't want to turn his head to look at it. At last, pretending to be furious, Matisse seized an ink-bottle from his writing table and threatened Aragon with it. *'Go on! Look at that model, or I'll break this over your head!'* he said, half-serious.

The poet was forced to give in. After looking in silence for some time, he said what he felt.

'Very pretty, very gay. When we come into power, we'll turn it into a dance hall!'

Matisse exploded instantly.

'Oh, no! That will never happen. I have a formal agreement from the Municipality of Vence that if ever the nuns be dispossessed, the chapel will become a museum, an historical monument.'

Matisse told Professor Leriche what followed.

'Aragon came back to the subject, and held forth with all kinds of reproaches, until I had to answer him, "I do what I please. And what's more, I have wanted to do this for a long time. . . ." As he went on and on, I had to send him away, shouting after him again, "I do what I please. You couldn't understand!"'

Already in 1948, Joseph A. Barry attributed to Matisse, in the *New York Times Magazine*, these words, *'I have always praised the glory of God and his creation. I have not changed. . . .'*

The master said he wanted to give his work *'the lightness and joy of spring, whatever it may cost'*. And that is what rejoiced the heart of Father Couturier, who exclaimed 'At last, we shall have a gay church!'

The editor of the *Vie Catholique Illustrée*, July 15th, 1951, published a saying which was certainly written by Matisse, although not in connection with the *Chapelle du Rosaire*. It appeared originally in *Jazz*, 1947.

'Do I believe in God? Yes, when I am working. When I am submissive and humble, I feel as though I were being helped by someone who makes me do things beyond my power.'

'My revelations'

The fine pages in which Matisse presents the *Chapelle du Rosaire*, are written by the same man who regretted the golden age of Angelico, and said to his friend, Jean Puy, *'I should like to live in a cell like a monk, provided that I had the means to paint without interruption or worry.'*

'I have been affected all my life by the opinion current in my youth, when only observations made from nature were acceptable, when anything from imagination or memory was sneered at and considered valueless in building a work of art. Masters at the Beaux-Arts said to their pupils, "Copy nature stupidly."

'I have reacted from that opinion, which I could not accept, during my whole

career, and that struggle has caused different transformations on my way, during which I have sought possibilities of expression beyond the literal copy, as in Divisionism and Fauvism.

'This rebellious spirit has lead me to study each element of construction separately: drawing, colour, values, composition; how those elements can be brought into a synthesis without the eloquence of one being diminished by the presence of the others; and how to construct with those elements undiminished in their intrinsic quality by their union, that is to say, by respecting the integrity of the means employed.

'Each generation of artists sees the production of the preceding generation differently. The pictures of the Impressionists, constructed with pure colours, showed the following generation that those colours, while they can serve the description of things or natural phenomena, have in themselves, independently of the objects they serve to express, an important action on the feelings of the observer.

'Thus, simple colours can act upon the intimate feelings with all the greater force for their simplicity. A blue, for instance, accompanied by the radiance of its complementaries, acts on the feelings like a loud stroke on a gong. The same is true of yellow and red, and the artist should be able to make use of them accordingly.

'In the chapel my aim was to balance a surface of light and colours with black designs on a flat white wall.

'This chapel is to me the outcome of a whole life's work and the flower of a great effort, sincere and difficult.

'IT IS NOT A WORK CHOSEN BY ME BUT TRULY A WORK FOR WHICH I HAVE BEEN CHOSEN BY DESTINY AT THE END OF MY ROAD, *which I continue according to my findings, the chapel giving me the opportunity to fix them by bringing them together.*

'I foresee that this work will not be USELESS *and that it could remain the expression of a period in the history of art, perhaps past, but I do not think so. It is impossible to tell yet, before the new movements are realized.*

'The errors that may be contained in this expression of human feeling will fall of themselves, but a living part will remain which may perhaps link the past with the future of plastic tradition.

'I hope that part, which I call MY REVELATIONS, *may be expressed with sufficient force to be fruitful and return to its source.'*[1]

'Vence?' wrote René Gaffé to James Thrall Soby in a letter dated October

[1] *Chapelle du Rosaire des Dominicaines de Vence* by Henri Matisse (*Mourlot frères et les fils de Victor Michel*, 1941).

15th, 1951, 'Vence? I think it is to modern religious art what the year 1789 was to France, a revolution. A perfectly successful revolution, of absolute purity. And what resplendent light through those green and yellow windows. Never has Matisse seemed to me so young!'

At eighty years old, life had captured him again. In spite of the sufferings of his illness, Matisse declared that—thanks to incessant work and the marvellous Nice climate which was always favourable to him—he knew at last how to enjoy living.

I had visited the chapel of Vence six months before, when I rang his doorbell on the third floor of the Regina, the 15th of January 1952.

The doctor was leaving Matisse as I went in. He was in a fine humour. All was well.

One of the master's grandsons, Paul Matisse, a tall dark, distinguished youth, showed me into the room entirely hung with immense drawings.

Henri Matisse, in ample, pale fawn, angora pyjamas, was seated in an armchair near his lively granddaughter, Jacqueline-Jackie.

At eighty-two, he seemed hardly sixty, so vigorous and handsome, with his tall, straight figure and smooth Jupiterian face.

'*This morning*,' he said, '*I took a long walk in the sun.*'

Lydia had just appeared, lovely as twenty years before when I first met her. Once again, rather than of the lady of the house, she gave the impression of a slave, a very beautiful slave.

Then Matisse stood up, radiant with life, as I wrote to Professor Leriche a few days later.

As we were speaking of *la Chapelle du Rosaire*, and what such a magnificent gift entails, something which had shocked me returned to my mind.

I had always been frank with him, and I repeated it, without giving the name of the libeller.

'Matisse never gives anything to anyone'—one of his supposed friends had said to me. It was the common opinion in Nice. I mentioned his gift of the *Trois Baigneuses*.

The Olympian blue eyes twinkled through thick glasses, obviously delighted by the recollection.

'*Yes, I like to give . . . I have given canvases to Albert André for his museum in Bagnols; I shall give a lot to Le Cateau. . . . But I like it to be worth-while.*'

He showed me then, '*A new plan for stained glass . . .*' more cut-out paper. Two cold colours predominated, green and blue, which would be warmed by sunlight.

There were also charcoal sketches of tree-trunks with leaves, recalling the Renaissance tapestries of Ferrara, decorated with hamadryads.

'What beautiful trees!' I said deliberately. I had been at the Royal Academy banquet, when Sir Alfred Munnings had said, 'Matisse and Picasso are incapable of painting a tree that looks like a tree.'

'*Actually*,' remarked Matisse, '*Sir Alfred is right . . . and Matisse is not wrong. . . . If one wants a tree that looks like a tree, it is best to go to a photographer. The artist's objective is quite different. For me, it is a matter of expressing the feeling inspired by the contemplation of a tree. . . .*'

It is sad that Sir Alfred has never seen the marvellous sketches by Matisse of 'leaves and branches', nor read his sayings recorded by Aragon on, precisely, trees.

Also in the studio, was a large panel drawn in charcoal—a woman's body overthrown, the belly fore-shortened, thighs opulent and round. A splendid study done from Lydia, preparatory to a Leda, which the Master was to stylize endlessly. . . .

'*The chief interest of my work comes from attentive and respectful observation of nature, and from the quality of feeling it stirs in me, rather than a certain virtuosity which nearly always follows honest, constant work.*'

Matisse never ceased to work. 1954 found him often fighting asthma or angina, but as soon as he had a moment's respite, he returned to his task. This was the stained glass windows for Crépieux-le-Pape, humble village near Lyon; and the tiles for a villa now belonging to Pierre Matisse in Saint-Jean-Cap-Ferrat.

Henri Matisse had always been intensely interested in ceramics, as in sculpture, and he devoted great effort to this in his eighty-fifth year. For that large decoration of four metres by three, an Apollo surrounded by flower motifs, in which a warm Naples yellow balances blue, white and green, the master had drawn and painted each of the sixteen panels between two of his torturing attacks. The tiles once fired must have weighed over two thousand five hundred kilos.

It was his last heroic undertaking.

Like Titian, Voltaire, M. Ingres and Hugo, once Matisse had passed his eightieth year, he was able to participate in his own fame. He watched his own apotheosis.

Homage of all kinds was paid to him on his eightieth birthday, his eighty-second, and on the day after his noble heart had ceased to beat on the height of Cimiez where, by his own avowal, Henri Matisse had known full happiness.

One of our best young artists, André Marchand, expressed how the painter of *Bonheur de Vivre* had been the painter of happiness. 'Henri Matisse, in whom happiness lived, during his whole lifetime pursued tirelessly, with attention both amorous and enchanted, the thousand aspects and inner echoes of the earthly hour. He had the deep gaze of a child examining veins of a leaf. What a gaze! What a Paradise regained for men!'[1]

Also François Desnoyer, himself a master of colour, wrote in his praise, 'We have still with us a very living Matisse, and we would give him even greater life. Spiritual son of Delacroix and Cézanne, he has *shouted* colour to our great *Joie*; he has enabled us to see life more than rose-coloured, true and beautiful; humanity is more beautiful thanks to him, flesh, women naked or dressed in vivid colours. . . . Slowly and surely he has forged his century. We are grateful to him.'

Lurçat, to whom surrealism owes so much, who gave new life to French tapestry, also praises the inexhaustible vitality of the Cimiez master. 'We can never thank Henri Matisse enough for the confidence in life expressed in all his art, and for the freshness and invention he gave us all through his career.'

And Jean Puy, richly talented and faithful comrade of the *cage aux Fauves*, says, 'No longer human, too human, but superhuman, his plastic art far above our poor earth-bound efforts.'

Fernand Léger, from his youth, had seen what Matisse owed to Delacroix, as he told Henri Rousseau.

'About 1908–10, with Apollinaire, Delaunay, Max Jacob, we discovered the *douanier* Rousseau. One day, in the rue Vercingétorix, Rousseau took me aside and asked in an undertone,

'Why doesn't Matisse finish his pictures?'

'I think because he is rather a romantic, and you are a classical painter (you like David's portraits, don't you?) You don't get it.'[2]

Fernand Léger was right, as Charles Camoin bore witness: 'I remember Matisse wrote me "*There is in me a scientific half and a romantic half*".'[3]

But no finer homage is paid to Matisse than the unwitting one in his own words, an appeal to the young, during an interview with André Verdet.

'Tell the young artists that the painter's work has nothing to do with dilettantism and is absolutely incompatible with the business of fashion, bluff or speculation. An artist's consciousness is a pure and faithful mirror in which he should be

[1] *Arts*, no. 489, November 10–16th, 1954.

[2] These tributes of Desnoyer, Lurçat, Jean Puy and Léger, appeared in *Les Lettres Françaises*, December 26th, 1952.

[3] Letter from Charles Camoin to R.E., January 14th, 1955.

able to see his work reflected, each day, on rising, without a blush. The creator's permanent responsibility toward himself and toward the world is not a hollow phrase: in helping to shape the Universe, the artist maintains his own dignity.'

Until his last breath, Matisse felt responsible for his own dignity, not only toward youth, but toward childhood. What could be more moving than this remembered incident which Mlle Ulrich, of Saint-Germain, sent to *Paris-Match* in December, 1954?

'The death of the painter, Henri Matisse, has profoundly moved me, and I pay a last tribute to the whole work of one of the greatest representatives of contemporary painting. Having lived for many years in Nice, at one time close to the immense Regina palace which dominates the town from the hill of Cimiez, I was twice able to visit important exhibitions of the master.

'At the time of the first visit, I was thirteen and in the fourth class at school. One of our teachers took us in a group to a gallery which was showing some of Matisse's finest pictures. At one moment we all stopped dead in front of a picture we couldn't understand, judging it with one of those terrible spontaneous criticisms of childhood, "that's good" or "I don't like that". And to our eyes, conditioned to perfect classical art, that work appeared as just "bad". Judgement I considered irrefutable at the time.

'Matisse, who was walking incognito among the visitors, passed behind our little group at that moment, and we recognized him because we had seen his photograph in the papers the day before. One of us asked him, very politely too, if he were not "Monsieur Matisse"?

'The old man he was even then, retired behind his white beard and spectacles and said he had nothing to do with the painter. Excuses, regrets, doubts. . . .

'As we were preparing to leave the gallery, the same old gentleman discreetly took our teacher aside: "*Madame, I am indeed the painter, Henri Matisse, but I should never have dared admit it to children who judged my painting so severely. The ruthless criticism of children, although without thought, has the power to intimidate me so much that I believe they are the only ones who see rightly, and for the moment I hate that picture in my heart for having shocked the eyes of a child, even if the critics should later call it a masterpiece. Forgive me my fib, Madame.*"

'And the old man disappeared in the crowd.'[1]

The reserve and proud bearing of this master ill-concealed his modesty. He had a great love of children, whom he always wished to please.

[1] *Paris-Match*, No. 297, December 4–11th, 1954.

Sometimes in those days he returned to his copy-books, and made strokes in them to keep the firmness of his line. Aragon says, 'I have known him to spend his nights drawing letters, relearning the alphabet, at seventy-six.'

And speaking of his drawing to the author of *Matisse-en-France*:

'*Instantaneous drawing is not my final word; it is simply the filming of a sequence of visions which come to me incessantly during a preliminary inner process: for a picture resulting only from a series of precise reconceptions which, in the stillness of my mind, have affected and exalted one another. I suddenly think of the soaring lark. . . . However, beginning with a trill, I should like to end on an organ-note.*'

For Henri Matisse, at dusk on November 3rd, 1954, a new life began, perhaps the one he had glimpsed twelve years before, during an interview with Aragon. That evening, the Angel of Death cast his mortal form away. It was the last great renunciation.

The blow fell suddenly. He died quietly, in the arms of his daughter, Marguerite.

The two nuns dressed in black and white had understood that Matisse was on the way to the last sacrifice when he built the chapel of Vence and dedicated it to *Notre Dame du Rosaire*, its walled garden, the windows letting in the crystal light through the colours of his magic palette, and his Stations of the Cross. That is how he did end on an organ note.

The Archbishop of Nice, Mgr Rémond, officiated at the funeral of the great artist in the church high up in Cimiez, where Raoul Dufy had been similarly buried two years before.

'*When the spirit has gone*,' said Henri Matisse, '*little matter where the body is laid, so long as it is a decent place.*'

But no one could forget that Nice had been his most favoured dwelling. And so his faithful friend, M. Jean Médecin, deputy-mayor and moving spirit of that enchanted town, had suggested, with the consent of the family, the purchase of a small plot of ground adjoining the cemetery of Cimiez, as he had done for Raoul Dufy, there being no room in the cemetery itself.

Some were surprised that Mgr Rémond should accord a magnificent religious ceremony to this painter reputed agnostic, but the prelate had in mind the terms in which Henri Matisse had offered him the chapel of Vence, four years before.

'*Your Excellency*,

'*In all humility, I present you with* la Chapelle du Rosaire des Sœurs Dominicaines de Vence.

'I devoted four arduous years exclusively to this work, and it is the result of my whole active life. I consider it my masterpiece.[1]

'I hope that the future will confirm my judgement, by a growing interest, apart from the higher meaning of the building.

'I leave it to your long experience of men and your deep wisdom, to judge this attempt, the result of a life devoted entirely to the search for truth.

H. Matisse.'

The mass was celebrated by Father Léon, in the presence of the Matisse family, the Dominicans of the Convent of Nice, the General-Prioress of the Dominicans from Monteils in Aveyron, the Mother-Superior and Dominicans of the Foyer Lacordaire of Vence and the Mayor of Nice, who later pronounced a fine appreciation of the master who had worshipped light. The music was the finale of Bach's Passion of Saint John, and *In Paradisum* by Gabriel Fauré, another lover of the Mediterranean.

That *Notre-Dame-du-Rosaire* was a religious work, crowning a life entirely devoted to the search for truth and light, the Bishop of Nice did not hesitate to affirm, and he prayed that God would give His own light and eternal peace to the artist who had expressed it with so much grace, in the creation of his own 'monstrance of gold'.

Then, in the porch of the Convent, it was the turn of the laymen to speak, M. Jean Médecin, Mayor of Nice, and Jean Cassou, representing the Minister of Education who had not found it necessary to come. And we may note that the Government of the Republic never thought of conferring the Grand Cross of the Legion of Honour on Henri Matisse, who, like Delacroix, had no more than the Commander's ribbon.

But for him, it only matters that his body lies in peace, close to his garden, in the earth of Nice.

One remembers the words of Hugo, 'Art is a form of courage.' And this, by Romains, which as well applies to Matisse as to Delacroix:

'The supreme greatness is to conquer the angel, to wrest his secret from him. The angel would open the door of the invisible to us, it is his mission, but he does not open it without a struggle; he does not open it to the indolent and half-hearted, but only to those who are not afraid to wrestle with him in order to pass. . . .'

'God is in us,' said Victor Hugo. 'It is that inner presence which makes us

[1] When Henri Matisse, modest as he was proud, used this word he must have been thinking of his distant ancestors, master artisans, who had all necessarily to achieve their 'master pieces' before they could rank as 'masters' in the Guild.

admire the beautiful, which delights us when we have done well and consoles us for the triumphs of evil. It is He, no doubt, Who is the inspiration in men of genius and enchants them at the sight of their own works. There are men of virtue as there are men of genius; and both are favoured by God. . . . Their inner satisfaction in obedience to divine inspiration is sufficient reward.'

We know from Louis Gillet how much Matisse appreciated the idea of the agnostic, Shelley, 'Art is the spirit of God come into the work of man.'

But the best expression of the deep thought of Matisse comes from his oldest master, Leonardo, who spoke the words as a decree from Heaven:

'THE SCIENCE OF PAINTING IS SO DIVINE THAT IT TRANSFORMS THE PAINTER'S SPIRIT INTO A KIND OF SPIRIT OF GOD.'

Malachite
Mirepoix, Ariège
May, 1945 to
November, 1955.

INDEX

M. stands for Matisse, Henri

(*a*) GENERAL

INDEX

(*b*) MATISSE, HENRI-EMILE-BENOIT, WORKS BY: (S) INDICATES SCULPTURE:

(for arrangement and classification *see* pages 12–16)

(*c*) LITERARY WORKS MENTIONED, INCLUDING PERIODICALS, (ASTERISK INDICATES BY, OR DECORATED BY, MATISSE).

Themes:

standing nude in interior
seated "
flowers
reclining nude outdoors
reclining nude flowers & fish
nude dancers
boy + butterfly net
window
interior - table with bouquet + chair
fruit -
shutters -